IT English
Reading and Writing
初级IT英语读写教程

Preliminary

2

总 主 编 **司炳月**
分 册 主 编 **曹 麟**
分册副主编 **吴美萱　刘菁菁　陶博通**

清華大學出版社
北 京

内 容 简 介

本书为顺应经济全球化和信息技术的发展趋势，培养兼具 IT 专业技能和外语能力的人才以适应 IT 行业发展需要编写而成。全书共有 8 个单元，内容涉及 IT 专业、IT 课程、云科技、信息泄露、IT 生活、网络社交、IT 行业的女性、3D 打印八个方面。每个单元分为 Section A 和 Section B 两大部分，每部分包含一篇主课文和与主课文相关的生词和短语，并设计了大量形式多样、内容丰富的练习，同时还配有科技文写作和学术写作技能方面的指导，以全面提高学生的阅读、写作和翻译能力。本书部分课后习题的参考答案请读者访问 ftp://ftp.tup.tsinghua.edu.cn/ 下载使用。

本书适合作为 IT 及其相关专业本科高年级学生和科技英语专业学生的英语教材，也可作为从事 IT 相关工作人士自我提升的参考资料。

图书在版编目（CIP）数据

初级 IT 英语读写教程. 2 / 司炳月总主编；曹麟分册主编 . —北京：清华大学出版社，2017
ISBN 978-7-302-48995-5

Ⅰ.①初…　Ⅱ.①司…　②曹…　Ⅲ.① IT 产业 – 英语 – 阅读教学 – 高等学校 – 教材　②IT 产业 – 英语 – 写作 – 高等学校 – 教材　Ⅳ.① F49

中国版本图书馆 CIP 数据核字（2017）第 295983 号

责任编辑：徐博文
封面设计：平　原
责任校对：王凤芝
责任印制：杨　艳

出版发行：清华大学出版社
　　　网　　址：http://www.tup.com.cn, http://www.wqbook.com
　　　地　　址：北京清华大学学研大厦 A 座　　邮　编：100084
　　　社 总 机：010-62770175　　　　　　　邮　购：010-62786544
　　　投稿与读者服务：010-62776969, c-service@tup.tsinghua.edu.cn
　　　质 量 反 馈：010-62772015, zhiliang@tup.tsinghua.edu.cn
印 刷 者：北京富博印刷有限公司
装 订 者：北京市密云县京文制本装订厂
经　　销：全国新华书店
开　　本：185mm×260mm　　印　张：15.25　　字　数：322 千字
版　　次：2017 年 11 月第 1 版　　　　印　次：2017 年 11 月第 1 次印刷
印　　数：1 ~ 3000
定　　价：48.00 元

产品编号：073637-01

初级 IT 英语读写教程 2
Preliminary IT English Reading and Writing 2

编 写 组

总 主 编　**司炳月**

分 册 主 编　**曹 麟**

分册副主编　**吴美萱　刘菁菁　陶博通**

编　　　者　**陈丽凤　胡晓玉　王 健　王珞珈　王晓华　张晓博
张雅欣　邵 林　刘晓静　刘 欣　于 芳　张婉婷
宋 辉　曹 放　郝利群**

本教材是 2016 年辽宁省社会科学规划基金项目"专门用途英语理论在大学英语教学中的实践与应用——基于辽宁省 IT 英语人才培养模式的研究"（项目编号：L16DYY005）的阶段性成果；是辽宁省教育科学"十三五"规划 2017 年度立项课题"IT 专门用途英语教材体系建设研究"（项目编号：JG17DB103）的阶段性成果；也是 2016 年国家社科基金项目"信息技术背景下中国外语学习环境'生态给养'转化有效性研究"（项目编号：16BYY093）的阶段性成果。

前言

一、编写背景

1.《国家中长期教育改革和发展规划纲要（2010—2020年）》

信息时代的悄然而至，使得我国教育在面临难得的改革与发展机遇的同时，也面临着全新的挑战。传统的教育教学理念、教育模式、教学内容、教学方式、教学手段、教育结构乃至整个教育体制都将随之发生变革。2010年，教育部颁发了《国家中长期教育改革和发展规划纲要（2010—2020年）》（以下简称《纲要》），《纲要》中提出要"优化学科专业、类型、层次结构，促进多学科交叉和融合。扩大应用型、复合型、技能型人才培养规模"。在对创新人才培养模式的论述中提出，要"加强教材建设，确定不同教育阶段学生必须掌握的核心内容，形成教学内容更新机制"。

2.《全民科学素质行动计划纲要实施方案（2016—2020年）》

2016年3月，国务院办公厅印发了《全民科学素质行动计划纲要实施方案（2016—2020年）》（以下简称《方案》）。《方案》中对高等教育中的教材要求有清楚的阐述："加强各类人群科技教育培训的教材建设。结合不同人群特点和需求，不断更新丰富科技教育培训的教材内容，注重培养具有创意、创新、创业能力的高层次创造性人才。将相关学科内容纳入各级各类科技教育培训教材和教学计划。"

3.《大学英语教学指南》

《大学英语教学指南》（以下简称《指南》）是新时期普通高等学校制定大学英语教学大纲、进行大学英语课程建设、开展大学英语课程评价的依据。《指南》在对教材建设和教学资源的论述中明确阐述了："鼓励各高校建设符合本校定位与特点的大学英语校本数字化课程资源；鼓励本区域内同类高校跨校开发大学英语数字化课程资源。"

二、编写原则

本套教材是与IT及其相关专业密切相关的知识课程，符合新形势下国家对复合型人才培养提出的要求，符合语言学习规律和新时代大学生的认知水平，也满足大学生专业学习和未来职业发展的实际需要，有利于促进复合型人才培养目标的实现。本套教材在设计与编写过程中遵循以下原则：

1. 满足社会对于复合型人才培养的需求

当代大学生正面临多元化社会带来的冲突和挑战，复合型人才的培养成为国家、社会发展的需求。因此，为社会提供既具有专业知识又具备跨语言交际能力、能够直接参与国际交流与竞争的国际化通用型人才是高校人才培养的重点和难点，也是全球化对人才提出的更高、更新的要求。

2. 满足学生对于专业与外语知识相结合的需求

高校开设大学英语课程，一方面满足了国家、社会发展的需求，为国家改革开放和经济社会发展服务；另一方面，也满足了学生专业学习、国际交流、继续深造、工作就业等方面的需要。本套教材旨在满足 IT 及其相关专业学生的需求，帮助他们在掌握专业知识的同时提高英语水平。此外，教材亦体现了专门用途英语理论对大学英语教学课程设置的具体要求。

3. 满足大学英语教学大纲和教学目标的要求

大学英语的教学目标是培养学生的英语应用能力，增强学生的跨文化交际意识和交际能力；同时发展其自主学习能力，提高综合文化素养，使他们在学习、生活、社会交往和未来工作中能够有效地使用英语，满足国家、社会、学校和个人发展的需要。本套教材编写的目的就是使学生能够在 IT 专业领域中使用英语进行有效的交流；能够有效地运用有关篇章、语用等知识；能够较好地理解有一定语言难度、内容较为熟悉或与本人所学专业相关的口头或书面材料；能够对不同来源的信息进行综合、对比、分析，并得出自己的结论或形成自己的认识。

三、编写依据

1. "专业知识" + "外语能力" 的 "复合型" 人才培养目标

大学英语课程作为高等学校人文教育的一部分，兼具工具性和人文性。在进一步提高学生英语听、说、读、写、译基本能力的基础上，学生可以通过学习与专业或未来工作有关的学术英语或职业英语获得在学术或职业领域进行交流的相关能力。本套教材是根据大学英语教学大纲和教学目标的要求，采用系统、科学的教材编写原则和方法编写而成。从教材的前期策划和准备、单元设计、教学资源开发、编写团队、内容设置和编排到教学效果的评价和评估都有整体的体系构建，以满足教学大纲和课程目标的要求。本套教材不但注重培养学生听、说、读、写、译这些语言基本技能，而且强化学生思辨、创新能力的培养。

2. "学生为主体" + "教师为主导"的"双主"教学理念

《指南》中提出大学英语教学应贯彻分类指导、因材施教的原则，以适应个性化教学的实际需要。新一轮的大学英语教学改革中也明确提出了"以教师为主导，以学生为主体"的"双主"教学理念。在教学过程中，教师的主导作用主要体现在课堂教学设计、教学组织、教学策略使用、教学管理和协调、课堂教学评价和评估等方面，而教师对课堂的主导方向要以满足学生的个性需求、促进学生的个性发展和自主学习为目的，只有两者相互结合，方能相得益彰，顺利实现大学英语教学改革目标。

3. "语言输入" + "语言输出"的"双向"驱动教学体系

本套教材在课堂教学活动和课后练习中设计了很多"语言输入"和"语言输出"的互动环节，教材采用任务式、合作式、项目式、探究式等教学方法，体现以教师为主导、以学生为主体的教学理念，使教学活动满足从"语言输入"到"语言输出"的需求。课后练习的设计关注学生自主学习能力的培养，引导和帮助他们掌握学习策略，学会学习；促使学生从"被动学习"向"主动学习"转变，真正让学生成为学习过程中的主体，实现课内和课外学习"不断线"。

4. "平面教材" + "立体化教材"的"双辅"交互优势

本套教材将大力推进最新信息技术与课程教学的融合，凸显现代学习方式的自主性、移动性、随时性等特点，发挥现代教育技术的推介作用。积极创建多元的教学与学习环境，利用互联网等信息基础设施和网络交流平台，使"平面教材"呈现出信息化教育的特征，形成"立体化教材"。

此外，本套教材鼓励教师建设和使用微课、慕课，拓展教学内容，实施基于"教材平面内容"和"网上立体课件"的混合式教学模式，使学生朝着主动学习、自主学习和个性化学习方向发展，实现教学资源网络化、教学环境虚拟化、教学个性化、学习评估过程化等。

5. 以教材为引导，推动教师的自主专业发展，实现"教""学"相长

《纲要》明确指出，要"建设高素质教师队伍。提升教师素养，努力造就一支师德高尚，业务精湛，结构合理，充满活力的高素质专业化教师队伍"。教师的专业发展能力受多种主客观因素的影响，需要外在环境和管理机制的保障。教师专业发展的规律性特点可归纳为

长期性、动态性、实践性和环境依托性。本套教材的编写和使用正是根据实践性和环境依托性的特点，编写和使用新教材的过程也是教师更新教学理念、提高教学技能的专业发展必经过程。

四、教材结构

本套教材共包含"读写"和"听说"两大系列。其中，"读写"系列分为初级、中级、高级三个级别，共六个分册。"听说"系列分为初级和中级两个级别，共四个分册。

在"读写"系列中，每册书有 8 个单元。每个单元分为 Section A 和 Section B 两部分。Section A 根据大学英语教学大纲的要求编制，包含一篇精读课文，课文后有生词表、短语和表达、缩略词、术语和课后练习。Section B 按照专业英语学生的培养目标和要求编写，包含一篇与 Section A 同主题的阅读文章，旨在补充和强化专业阅读内容。两篇文章一易一难，每个单元都可以满足分级教学的需要和不同程度学生水平的需求，两个部分的练习形式多样，具有丰富性和系统性的特点。练习设计遵循语言学习的规律，针对不同层次、不同年级的学生，选材的难易程度、知识侧重点等方面均有所不同。

在"听说"系列中，每册书有 16 个单元，每个单元分为 Section A、Section B 及 Section C 三部分。其中，Section A 为听力技能训练，听力内容围绕 IT 相关主题展开。该部分由 Text A 和 Text B 两部分组成，前者针对 IT 及相关专业（非英语专业）学生，题目设计相对简单；后者针对英语专业（如科技英语）学生，题目设计难度有所增加。Section B 为口语技能训练，旨在培养学生的口头交际能力。Section C 为听力考试强化训练，该部分侧重应试，根据当下国内外几大英语考试（如大学英语四六级、托福、雅思等），全方位、多角度满足学生对英语学习的需求。希望通过题型多样、题量丰富的强化训练，让学生一方面熟悉并适应听力考试的多样题型，另一方面检测自己的英语听力水平，提高自主学习能力。

五、教材特色

1. 素材原汁原味

本套教材的所有阅读和听力文本均选自英美国家真实的 IT 专业文本，包括 IT 相关专业的学术网站、期刊及英语原版教材。编者在选择文本时尽量选择新颖、有趣的分支话题，文章的语言也尽量避免过于严肃和刻板，使学生在理解和分析课文的过程中既能利用专业知识进行思考和判断，又不觉枯燥。

2. 内容注重实用性

本套教材的"读写"系列避免了国内同类教材培养目标单一、片面的缺陷，注重提高学生的多种技能。每个单元不仅包括阅读板块、翻译板块和写作板块，还针对 IT 及其相关专业的英语阅读、翻译、学术写作等技能进行系统的学习和训练。而在"听说"系列中，编者在选择听说文本的话题时，一方面迎合当今 IT 产业就业的发展趋势，另一方面也考虑与高校 IT 专业课程紧密相关，并参考国内各大重点高校 IT 专业设置，挑选出 IT 领域相关的热门话题，这些话题广泛涉及 IT 相关专业学生所关心的 IT 就业方面的问题、IT 专业知识的学习方法、全国重点高校 IT 相关专业课程中开设的典型编程语言、当今的网络环境、时下 IT 领域前沿技术等内容，以便在提升学生英语语言能力的同时了解和学习与 IT 相关的专业知识，突出语言运用，通过文本传递 IT 知识，重现真实 IT 场景。

3. 练习内容和形式丰富多样

本套教材在阅读和听力理解、语言知识学习及技能训练方面都设计了大量的练习，而且练习形式富于变化，如简答、判断、填空、选择、配对、翻译、图表、口语交际等，学生不仅可以学习词汇、短语等语言点，还可以提高阅读和听力理解能力、分析语言的能力及表达能力。

六、适用对象

本套教材特别适合计算机科学与技术、信息管理与信息系统、软件工程和网络工程等与 IT 相关专业的学生学习和使用，可以分阶段或分学期选用；也特别适合从事软件系统需求分析、设计、开发、测试、运行及维护工作的工程师和管理人员查阅和参考。编者在选材上保证与 IT 信息技术密切相关的同时，努力确保文章内容贴近生活，所选材料涵盖了当前教育、工作和社会领域的诸多热点，文字形象生动、可读性强。因此，本套教材也比较适合那些有一定英语基础，同时也喜爱计算机应用技术和互联网文化的人士阅读，以扩展知识，开拓视野。

七、编写团队

本套教材由大连外国语大学软件学院教师担任主编团队。参与编写的编者有来自全国各高校的大学英语教师、专业英语教师、计算机专业的教师、IT 职场的企业专家以及定居海外的专家和学者。

本套教材在编写过程中得到了校企合作教材编写组的大力支持，是校企合作的成果之一。该编写组在教材编写过程中充分考虑 IT 职场的整个工作流程和环境，将职场所需要的语言技能、专业知识、职业素养有机地整合在一起，真正做到了学习需求与社会需求相结合，教学理论与社会实践相结合。

本套教材在编写过程中也得到了大连外国语大学软件学院的领导与英语教研室所有老

师的鼎力支持，尤其是祁瑞华教授在编写过程中提出了许多宝贵的意见，在此致以诚挚的谢意！

　　本套教材还是"2016 年辽宁省转型发展试点专业建设"项目的成果之一。我校专业共建合作伙伴——国际商业机器全球服务（大连）有限公司、埃森哲信息技术（大连）有限公司、大连华信计算机技术股份有限公司为该套教材的编写提出了许多参考意见，在此一并谢过！

　　由于编者水平有限，错误与缺点在所难免，恳请读者批评指正。

司炳月

2017 年 6 月

Contents

Unit 1
IT at School

Dancing in all its forms cannot be excluded from the curriculum of all noble education; dancing with the feet, with ideas, with words, and, need I add that one must also be able to dance with the pen?

— *Friedrich W. Nietzsche (German philosopher)*

Education does not mean teaching people to know what they do not know; it means teaching them to behave as they do not behave.

— *John Ruskin (British art critic)*

Both education and learning are life processes, and they have no limit on when to start and stop. In our daily lives we learn new things and this helps us in changing the way we live. Education provides us with information, and then we have to learn and process this information for our own use. It is very important to make education accessible at any time to every one; this will help in reducing illiteracy. Information technology has the ability of speeding up information delivery, so this ability can be used in improving our education environment. With the implementation of information technology, costs of accessing educational material are cut down and it makes it easy for students to learn from anywhere.

Section

Pre-reading Activities

I. Read the procedures of creating a microlecture listed below. Sequence the numbers in front of each item in the way you think is the most reasonable.

1. Write a 15 to 30-second introduction and conclusion. They will provide the context for your key concepts.

2. Upload the video and assignment to your course-management software.

3. Record the main elements using a microphone and web camera. The finished product should be 60 seconds to 3 minutes long.

4. List the key concepts you are trying to convey in the 60-minute lecture. That series of concepts will form the core of your microlecture.

5. Design an assignment to follow the lecture that will direct students to readings or activities that allow them to explore the key concepts.

II. Work in pairs and discuss the following questions.

1. In your opinion, what is the most important part during the process of creating a microlecture?

2. If you were a teacher, what teaching materials would you like to show to your students through a microlecture?

3. Do you think it's a good idea to realize your academic development through the use of microlectures? Why or why not?

4. What are the advantages and disadvantages of using microlectures in classroom teaching?

 Text A

Microlecture—Knowledge Burst

1. Haven't heard about the microlecture? The term is becoming quite popular among educators, especially those in large lecture classes. A microlecture is a short recorded audio or video presentation on a single, **precisely** defined topic. Used as a component of online, blended, or face-to-face teaching, these brief lectures can be **interspersed** with learning activities that **reinforce** lecture topics. Microlectures fall in line with the concept of "flipping" the classroom—changing the format of the classroom so that students complete their homework in class with instructors' support after watching the lecture at home. The **abbreviated** format of these lectures can be highly effective by attracting students' attention to a single topic for a short time, limiting the **opportunities** for not being **absorbed**. Because students control the playback, they can refer to the instructor's presentation as often as needed.

2. Now, most college students would likely **concur**—90-minute lectures can be a bit **tedious**, and many of them **confess** they suffer self-control **deficit** to be **competent** for a lecture with a traditional time **span**. With current research indicating that attention spans (measured in minutes) **roughly** mirror a student's age (measured in years), it begs the question as to the **rationale** behind lectures of such length.

3. Given that it is tough to prove the traditional lecture time frames, it is no surprise to see online educational programs seeking to offer presentations that distinguish between the traditional ways and shorter **podcasts**. But in an astonishing switch, David Shieh of the Chronicle of Higher Education recently took a look at a community college program that **features** a microlecture format, presentations varying from one to three minutes in length.

4. While one minute lectures might be beyond the **scope** of imagination for any **veteran** teacher, Shieh reported on the piloting of the concept at San Juan College in Farmington, N.M. The concept was introduced as part of a new online degree program in **occupational** safety last fall. According to Shieh, school administrators were so pleased with the results that they were spreading the micro-lecture concept to courses in reading.

5. The designer of the format, David Penrose, **proclaimed** that in online education "everybody involved is serious about the lecture and tiny bursts can teach just as well as traditional lectures when paired with **assignments** and discussions." The microlecture format begins

with a podcast that introduces a few key terms or a critical concept, then immediately turns the learning environment over to the students. "We didn't thrust it upon students. It's a framework for knowledge **excavation**. We're going to show you where to dig, we're going to tell you what you need to be looking for, and we're going to watch over that process." Penrose said.

6. Public microlecture site such as Khan Academy has made the microlecture format a familiar **staple** of informal learning, and colleges and universities are also equipping formal coursework with the microlecture coursework.

7. In 2009, an early example emerged at San Juan College, where brief recorded lectures, each with an introduction, a few key points, and a conclusion, were developed for a new online degree program. While the microlecture is still seen **primarily** as a tool for online learning, it is also seeing usage in hands-on activities in the classroom and lab.

8. At the University of Illinois at Urbana-Champaign, students in Animal Science learn the **adequate** technique for milking cows. Previously, the professor taught this skill by lecturing as he demonstrated the **exposure** procedure, but as class size grew, some students had to stand on tiptoe to see over the heads of their classmates. A microlecture and demo, delivered via iPad, provided **novices** at the dairy barn with effective one-on-one, on-location, just-in-time training. Surveys have indicated that particularly in large-enrollment courses, students appreciate the **flexibility** of microlectures, which allow them to revisit material as needed to reinforce learning.

9. Microlectures are easy to integrate into the courses because they can be used in a variety of ways and are short enough to fit almost anywhere. They can be posted as a trailer in a course site to be viewed by students before the course begins. Prior to class, they might introduce a topic, raise awareness, or **pique** curiosity. Afterward, they might cover points only touched on in the session lecture, going beyond the facts to explore the implied meaning. Activities or written follow-up assignments can be easily **condensed** in a microlecture to ensure that students understand the material presented. The briefness of the form gives instructors the ability to make quick fixes, adjusting or updating course content as needed. In some instances, particularly where they cover basic concepts, these brief lectures can be a reusable resource, available in more than one course or to more than one instructor. Where the content covers difficult concepts, students can view these lectures multiple times in a course, wherever repetition is useful to learning. For institutions or individual faculty members looking to move beyond traditional lecture format, microlectures offer a **beneficial** instructional approach.

10. Instead of the framework being defined by seat time, the microlecture format exceeds the traditional notion that all students are obliged to spend the same amount of time in class to receive credit. The concept focuses on what is to be learned and it allows, in the online environment, students of various skills and abilities as much time as they need to **digest** the learning objectives related to the microlecture.

11. Given such assets and positives, one would think the format would soon become a critical component of every online course.

(908 words)

Notes

Khan Academy: a non-profit educational organization created in 2006 by educator Salman Khan with the aim of providing a free, world-class education for anyone, anywhere. The organization produces short lectures in the form of YouTube videos.

Podcast: an audio file similar to a radio broadcast, that can be downloaded and listened to on a computer or MP3 player.

The Chronicle of Higher Education: a newspaper and website that presents news, information, and jobs for college and university faculty and Student Affairs professionals (staff members and administrators).

Community college: primarily two-year public institutions of higher education. Many community colleges also offer remedial education, GEDs, high school degrees, technical degrees and certificates, and a limited number of 4-year degrees. After graduating from a community college, some students transfer to a university or liberal arts college for two to three years to complete a bachelor's degree, while others enter the workforce.

San Juan College: a community college located in Farmington, New Mexico. Founded in 1956 as a branch of the New Mexico College of Agriculture and Mechanical Arts, San Juan College became an independent community college following a county election in 1981.

The University of Illinois at Urbana-Champaign: an institution which was founded in 1867 as a state-supported, land-grant with a threefold mission of teaching, research, and public service.

❸ New Words

precisely	/prɪˈsaɪsli/	*a.*	exactly; just 精确地；恰好
intersperse	/ˌɪntəˈspɜːs/	*vt.*	to vary sth. by placing other things at irregular intervals among it 点缀；散布
reinforce	/ˌriːɪnˈfɔːs/	*vt.*	to give more support to (sth.); to emphasize 给……更多的支持；加强
abbreviated	/əˈbriːvieɪt/	*a.*	shortened 缩短的，缩写的
opportunity	/ˌɔpəˈtjuːnəti/	*n.*	[C, U] favorable time, occasion or set of circumstances 良机；机会
absorb	/əbˈsɔːb/	*v.*	to take (sth.) in; to suck up 吸收（某事物）；吸进
absorbed	/əbˈsɔːbd/	*a.*	with one's attention fully held 精神集中的

concur	/kən'kə:(r)/	*vi.*	to agree; to express agreement 同意；意见一致
tedious	/'ti:diəs/	*a.*	tiresome because of being too long, slow or dull; boring 令人厌倦的；烦人的
confess	/kən'fes/	*v.*	to say or admit, often formally (that one has done wrong, committed a crime, etc.) 承认；供认
deficit	/'defisit/	*n.*	[C] amount by which sth. is too small or smaller than sth. else 不足；缺少
competent	/'kɔmpitənt/	*a.*	(of people) having the necessary ability, authority, skill, knowledge, etc. (指人) 有能力的；能胜任的
span	/spæn/	*n.*	[C] length of time over which sth. lasts or extends from beginning to end 时间段
roughly	/'rʌfli/	*a.*	approximately 大概地；大约地
rationale	/ˌræʃə'nɑ:l/	*n.*	[C] fundamental reason for or logical basis of sth. 基本原理
feature	/'fi:tʃə(r)/	*vt.*	to give a prominent part to (sb./sth.) 给……以显著地位
		n.	[C] distinctive characteristic 特征；特色；特点
scope	/skəup/	*n.*	1. [*sing.*] range of matters being dealt with, studied, etc. 范围 2. [U] opportunity to do or achieve sth. 机会，余地
veteran	/'vetərən/	*a.*	with much or long experience 经验丰富的
		n.	[C] person with much or long experience, esp. as a soldier 经验丰富的人；老手；(尤指) 老兵
occupational	/ˌɔkju'peiʃənl/	*a.*	of, caused by or connected with a person's job 职业的；职业造成的
proclaim	/prə'kleim/	*vt.*	to make (sth.) known officially or publicly; to announce 宣告，公布
assignment	/ə'sainmənt/	*n.*	1. [C] a task or piece of work that sb. is given to do, usually as part of their job or studies 工作，任务 2. [U] the act of giving sth. to sb.; the act of giving sb. a particular task 分派，布置
excavation	/ˌekskə'veiʃn/	*n.*	[U] activity of making (a hole or channel) by digging; removing (soil, etc.) by digging 挖掘
staple	/'steipl/	*n.*	[C] main or principal item or element 主要成分；主要内容
primarily	/'praimərəli/	*a.*	mainly 主要地
adequate	/'ædikwət/	*a.*	satisfactory in quantity or quality; sufficient 足够的，充足的
exposure	/ik'spəuʒə(r)/	*n.*	[U] the act of showing sth. that is usually hidden 显露
novice	/'nɔvis/	*n.*	[C] person who is new and inexperienced in a job, situation, etc.; beginner 新手；生手；初学者
flexibility	/ˌfleksə'biləti/	*n.*	1. [U] the ability to change to suit new conditions or situations 适应；灵活性 2. [U] the state of bending easily without breaking 柔韧性；弹性
pique	/pi:k/	*vt.*	to arouse (a person's interest or curiosity) 引起

condense	/kən'dens/	*vt.*	to put sth. into fewer words 简缩；简述
		v.	to (cause sth. to) become thicker or more concentrated（使）变稠或变浓；浓缩
beneficial	/ˌbeni'fiʃl/	*a.*	having a helpful or useful effect 有益的；有用的
digest	/'daidʒest/	*vt.*	to take (information) in mentally; to fully understand 吸收；完全理解；彻底领会
		v.	to change (food) in the stomach and bowels so that it can be used by the body 消化（食物）

✪ New Expressions

fall in line with	be in agreement; not contradict sth. or each other 与……相一致；与……相符合
attract sb.'s attention	to arouse interest or pleasure in (sb./sth.) 吸引……兴趣
as to	with regard to sth.; regarding sth. 至于
distinguish between	to recognize the difference between (people or things) 区别，辨别
vary from... to...	change, esp. according to some factor 改变，变动
be pleased with	feeling or showing satisfaction or pleasure (with sb./sth.) 欣喜的，满意的，高兴的
be serious about	If you are serious about sth., you really mean it and are not joking or pretending. 对……是认真的
thrust sth. upon sb.	to force sb. to do or accept sth. 迫使某人做某事；迫使某人接受某事
equip... with	to provide sb. with the things that are needed for a particular kind of activity or work 装备……；配备……
prior to	before 在……之前
be obliged to	be compelled or required by law, agreement or moral pressure to do sth. 被强迫做……；被要求做……

〔Reading Comprehension〕

Understanding the text

I. Answer the following questions.

1. According to the text, what is a microlecture?

2. Why do microlectures fall in line with the concept of "flipping" the classroom?

3. What would most college students likely concur now according to the text?

4. With current research indicating that attention spans roughly mirror a students age, what question is aroused?

5. According to Shieh, what did school administrators at San Juan College do after the concept of microlecture was introduced to their college?

6. According to Penrose, instead of thrusting the knowledge upon students, what are teachers supposed to do during a microlecture?

7. How do the students in Animal Science at the University of Illinois learn adequate techniques through microlecture now?

8. According to the text, why are microlectures easy to be integrated into the curriculum?

Critical thinking

II. Work in pairs and discuss the following questions.

1. Have you ever participated in any form of microlecture? If yes, what do you think of it?

2. In your opinion, in what way can teachers improve the effectiveness of teaching?

3. How can students enhance their academic performance during studying process?

4. How can you improve yourself through microlectures?

Language Focus

Words in use

III. Fill in the blanks with the words given below. Change the form where necessary. Each word can be used only once.

deficit	brevity	exposure	condense	integrate
beneficial	competent	adequate	exceed	precisely

1. I think we can date back the decline of Western Civilization quite _____.

2. They have seen the change as unquestionably _____ to the country so they take a absolutely positive attitude towards it.

3. There's a(n) _____ of $3 million in the total needed to complete the project. How can you get that much money in such a short time?

4. All the candidates have been getting an enormous amount of _____ on television and in the press.

5. Little attempt was made to _____ the different parts into a coherent whole.

6. Most investigators _____ that certain facial expressions suggest the same emotions in all people.

7. Where payments _____ these limits they become fully taxable.

8. Most adults do not feel _____ to deal with a medical emergency involving a child.

9. People accused the ministry of failing to take _____ preventive measures to protect those war victims.

10. We have learned how to _____ serious messages into short, self-contained sentences.

Word building

The suffix -y can be added to verbs, nouns and adjectives to form new nouns. Nouns formed in this way refer to the circumstances, state, or conditions.

Examples

Words learned	Add -y	New words formed
minister	→	ministry
assemble	→	assembly

The suffix -al can be added to nouns to form adjectives. Adjectives formed in this way describe something that is connected with the thing referred to by the original noun. Sometimes, -ial is used instead of -al, especially for nouns ending in -er, -or and -ent. The suffix -al can also be added to verbs to form nouns.

Examples

Words learned	Add -al / -ial	New words formed
manager	→	managerial
editor	→	editorial
substance	→	substantial
survive	→	survival
tradition	→	traditional
margin	→	marginal

The suffix *-cy* can be added to adjectives and nouns to form new nouns. Nouns formed in this way refer to the state, quality, or experience described by the adjective or the noun. A final *t* or *te* is replaced by *–cy*.

Examples

Words learned	Add *-cy*	New words formed
consistent	→	consistency
accurate	→	accuracy

IV. Add -al / -ial, -cy, or -y to or remove them from the following words to form new words.

Words learned	New words formed
-y	
unite	
discover	
recover	
-al / ial	
clinic	
coastal	
norm	
influence	
memory	
finance	
-cy	
frequent	
efficient	
currency	

V. *Fill in the blanks with the newly-formed words in Activity IV. Change the form where necessary. Each word can be used only once.*

1. Interest-rate cuts have failed to bring about economic _____, so the economists have to find some other ways.

2. Those are our hopes; we are starting this _____ trial to investigate whether those hopes will be realized.

3. Traffic accidents are happening with increasing _____, which has aroused great concern from the authorities.

4. Chinese economists have made important contributions to the field of _____ and corporate economics.

5. Senior politicians met today to discuss the future of European political _____, but unfortunately, no agreement was made.

6. Foreign _____ depreciation is a result of economic depression in the country concerned.

7. In November, Clean's bakery produced 50 percent more bread than _____.

8. Charlie Chaplin was not just a genius. He was among the most _____ figures in film history.

9. The institutions have realized they need to change their culture to improve _____ and service to attract more customers.

10. More than fifteen thousand people took part in the _____ activity.

11. My films try to describe a journey of _____, both for myself and the watcher.

12. The government is allowing the areas of inshore _____ waters to be explored for oil and gas.

Banked cloze

VI. *Fill in the blanks by selecting suitable words from the word bank. You may not use any of the words more than once.*

A. benefiting	B. instead	C. integrate	D. challenge	E. inside
F. technological	G. unprepared	H. price	I. motivated	J. embrace
K. learn	L. afford	M. current	N. academic	O. educational

New technologies are changing the way we learn and they have also changed the process of teaching. Both teachers and students are using these new 1) _____ technologies to archive

specific academic goals. The only 2) _____ is that Information Technology comes at a cost, so those who can not 3) _____ the price tend to have difficulties in 4) _____ from the opportunities of Information Technology in education.

Students are more engaged and 5) _____ to learn when they use mobile devices, and research shows that 6) _____ performances can improve. We as educators need to take note of this, and look for safe, productive ways to 7) _____ mobile learning devices into our curriculum. For Lisa Nielsen, the author of the Innovative Educator blog, few things are more important.

"When the world 8) _____ schools looks so different from the world outside of schools, what are we really preparing students for?" she asks. "When we ban, rather than 9) _____, real-world technologies, we leave students ill-equipped to know how to harness the power of technology for learning, 10) _____ to develop a respectable digital footprint and lack of adequate knowledge to safely navigate the social web."

Expressions in use

VII. Fill in the blanks with the expressions given below. Change the form where necessary. Each expression can be used only once.

attract our attention to	distinguish between	varying from... to...
be pleased with	be serious about	thrust sth. upon sb.
equip... with	prior to	as to
be obliged to		

1. Success was given to the strong, failure _____ the weak.

2. Local inhabitants haven't the slightest doubt _____ who is the rightful owner.

3. Most of the time, no one will care about natural disasters, and they won't _____ avoiding disasters till one has really struck.

4. Research suggests that babies learn to see by _____ areas of light and dark.

5. He was _____ resign when one of his own assistants was involved in a financial scandal.

6. They become obsessed with trying to _____ their vehicles _____ gadgets to deal with every possible contingency.

7. A man seen hanging around the area _____ the shooting could have been involved.

8. The author used an ambiguous title to _____ the picture.

9. I was totally _____ his performance on Saturday—everything went right.

10. The importance of being an Olympian will _____ athlete _____ athlete.

Structure Analysis and Writing

Structure Analysis

Move from paragraph to essay

Starting from this book, you are moving from paragraph writing to short essay writing. Precisely, students at this level will learn how to write a short essay composed of 3–5 paragraphs, with no less than 150 words. An essay has three main parts: Introduction, Body, and Conclusion.

Introduction: The introduction part introduces the topic of an essay and usually contains a thesis statement. The introduction rouses the reader's interest and secures his/her attention to the subject matter of the essay or provides necessary background information. You can start the introduction with a dramatic incident, a famous quote, a thought-provoking question, or a general statement to interest or attract your readers.

Body: The body gives a clear and logical presentation of the facts and ideas the writer intends to put forth. It may consist of several paragraphs. Each body paragraph should address a specific point related to the thesis statement. You can develop ideas by way of examples, cause and effect, comparison and contrast, classification, narration or description, and argumentation.

Conclusion: The conclusion winds up the essay often with an emphatic and forceful statement to influence the reader's final impression of the essay and shows the implication or consequences of the argument. The conclusion of an essay is important because it is often the part that gives the reader the deepest impression. Not every essay needs a separate concluding paragraph. For a short composition, the last paragraph of the body, even the last sentence of that paragraph, may serve as the end, so long as it can give the reader a feeling of completeness. Concluding paragraphs should be short, forceful, substantial, and thought-provoking, made up mainly of restatements or summaries of the points that have been discussed. No new ideas should be introduced in a concluding paragraph. Sometimes it is good to link the concluding paragraph to the introductory. If, for instance, a question is raised in the introductory paragraph, an answer should be given in the concluding paragraph.

Now, let's start with a brief structure analysis of the text "Microlecture—Knowledge Burst".

Introduction: Bring out the topic and the thesis statement of the essay: microlectures fall in line with the concept of "flipping" the classroom—changing the format of the classroom so that students complete their homework in class with instructor support after watching the lecture at home. (Para. 1)

Bodys: Reasons for microlectures of various forms to appear and how popular they have become. (Paras. 2–5)

Examples of microlectures include some famous public microlecture sites and the microlectures are employed in some colleges and universities. (Paras. 6–10)

Conclusion: The format would soon become a critical component of every online course. (Para. 11)

Structured Writing

Read the sample essay and see how the introduction, body, and conclusion are developed.

Topic	Sample essay
Knowledge economy	Knowledge economy, which emphasizes knowledge and people of talent, is gradually replacing the industrial economy and becoming the dominant economic form. It is playing a more and more important role in our economic life in recent years.
Introduction	
Thesis statement: Knowledge economy is playing a more and more important role in our economic life in recent years.	
Body	Knowledge economy has fundamentally transformed our ways of work, business and education. To start with, with the development of knowledge economy, more and more people are transformed from traditional manufacturing industries to new fields such as the Internet and computer science area. Secondly, knowledge economy has given rise to the boom of electronic commerce and online trade, so you can do business anytime and anywhere. Besides, people have to keep learning something new to adapt to this explosive knowledge society.
Argument 1: With the development of knowledge economy, more and more people are transformed from traditional manufacturing industries to new fields.	
Argument 2: Knowledge economy has given rise to the boom of electronic commerce and online trade.	
Argument 3: People have to keep learning something new to adapt to this explosive knowledge society.	
Conclusion	In my opinion, we should insist on developing knowledge economy and make efforts to educate the young generation, to contribute to the progress of knowledge economy.
We should insist on developing knowledge economy.	

VIII. Write an essay of no less than 150 words on one of the following topics. One topic has an outline that you can follow.

Topic
The subject of computer science, a headache to me
Introduction

Thesis statement: The subject of computer science is a big headache to me.

Body

Example: The difference between the *theory* and the *practical use*

Conclusion

I'll try my best to learn it well.

More topics:

• Will traditional ways of learning be replaced by modern ones?

• The advantages / disadvantages of modern ways of teaching

Translation

IX. Translate the following paragraph into Chinese.

Microlectures are typically produced by an instructor, who might begin by drafting a rough script—containing just an introduction, a list of key points to cover, and a conclusion—perhaps with help from instructional technologists. The lecture is then recorded, often with a webcam but possibly with only a microphone. Video content may feature the instructor as a talking head or may display other types of visual information to accompany a voice-over, a slide presentation, a screencast (截屏视频), or perhaps an animation. The result is uploaded to the LMS, a dedicated media server, or a public site like YouTube, Vimeo, or iTunes U, depending on campus infrastructure options. The title of each microlecture can be specific to the concepts discussed to ensure students to locate the lectures they need, and keywords and meta tags can also be added.

X. Translate the following paragraph into English.

长城是中国古代规模浩大的军事防御工程。修筑长城最初是为了抵御北方游牧民族（nomadic groups）的入侵。长城东西绵延上万华里，跨越 17 个省份，主要由城墙、关隘、烽火台（watchtower）组成。今天我们看到的长城多数可追溯到明朝。保存最完好、最为壮观的部分是北京的八达岭长城。长城已有两千多年历史，某些部分现已毁坏或消失，然而它仍然是世界上最吸引人的景观之一。长城是耗时最长的建筑工程。它位列世界新七大奇观，当之无愧。

Section
B

Reading Skills: *Fact and Opinion*

A fact is the information that can be proved true through objective evidence. This evidence may be physical proof or the spoken or written testimony of witnesses.

An opinion is a belief judgment, or conclusion that cannot be objectively proved true. As a result, it is open to question. For instance, on my great-grandmother's gravestone, we are told that she is "sweetly sleeping". Of course I certainly hope that she is sleeping sweetly, but I have no way of knowing for sure. The statement is a opinion.

The amount of fact and opinion in a piece of writing varies, depending on the author's purpose. For example, news articles and scientific reports, which are written to inform readers, are supposed to be as factual as possible. On the other hand, the main points of editorials, political speeches, and advertisements—materials written to persuade readers—are opinions. Such writings may contain facts, but, in general, they are facts carefully selected to back up the authors' opinions.

Both facts and opinions can be valuable to readers. However, it is important to recognize the difference between the two.

Here is one example from Text A.

While one minute lectures may be beyond the scope of imagination for any veteran teacher, Shieh reports on the piloting of the concept at San Juan College in Farmington, N.M. The concept was introduced as part of a new online degree program in occupational safety last fall. According to Shieh, school administrators were so pleased with the results that they are spreading the micro-lecture concept to courses in reading. (Para. 4)

Which sentence contains a fact?

To sharpen your understanding of fact and opinion, read the following statements and decide whether each is a fact or opinion. Put F (for "fact") or O (for "opinion") before each statement. Put F+O before the statement that is a mixture of fact and opinion.

_____ 1. Last night, a tree outside our house was struck by lightning.

_____ 2. The waiters at that restaurant are rude, and the food costs twice as much as it's worth.

_____ 3. Ostriches do not hide their heads in the sand.

_____ 4. Tom Cruise and Halley Berry are the most gorgeous movie stars in Hollywood today.

_____ 5. It's a fact that the best of the fifty states to live in is Hawaii.

_____ 6. Installing a new sink is an easy job for the do-it-yourselfer.

_____ 7. The Grimm brothers collected their fairy tales from other storytellers.

_____ 8. There is nothing like a bottle of Coca-Cola to satisfy thirst.

_____ 9. In the late 1890s, when Coke was first sold, it included a small amount of cocaine, which was then legal.

_____ 10. One of the most delicious of soft drinks, Coca-Cola was first intended to cure various ills, including headaches.

Mobile Learning Technologies for 21st-Century Classrooms

1. The mobile revolution is here. More and more schools are moving toward mobile learning in the classroom as a way to take advantage of a new **wave** of electronic devices that offer portability and ease of use on a budget. Netbooks, iPads, cell phones, e-readers and even PDAs are increasingly becoming the tools of choice for today's educators. We cannot **ignore** the **mainstream** and it is easy to see why.

2. Mobile learning technologies offer teachers and students a more convenient approach to learn. Computer labs are great, but do your students use technology in the classroom, in the school garden, in the study hall, in the gym, and on field trips? Don't be **confused**. With mobile learning devices, you can do all this, and more.

3. It can be **recalled** that Marc Prensky has warned us in 2001, "Our students have changed **radically**. Today's students no longer apply to our educational system that was designed to teach." He went on to **depict** how these "digital natives" were being exposed to more gadgets and technology than was ever thought possible. It makes much sense to change the ways in which children learn. They are more engaged in learning when using the latest technological gadgets, because it is what they are most used to interacting with, not a **mysterious** field. Our students don't just want mobile learning, they need it.

4. The education system we work in is not always known for its speed at latching on to new ideas and methodologies, but with mobile learning it is catching up quickly. For instance, you can use the dictionary on Dictionary.com, **explore** the world with Google Earth, or **plot** equations with Quick Graph.

5. The research that has been done on the use of mobile apps like these has been very **promising**. For example, a study, conducted at the Abilene Christian University, centered upon the use of the Statistics 1 app. Students used it in and out of the classroom and remarked that they

understood the content better, and were more **motivated** to do well, when using the app. The instructors agreed with this observation, and added that the students were also better prepared for classes.

6. Studies like this help underline the academic potential that mobile learning devices can enrich the learning process for students. They are versatile, motivating, and active learning tools. Deidra Hughey, an instructor who teaches students with special needs, likes mobile learning devices because of the **accessibility** they have to a wide **range** of students. "Students with learning differences benefit greatly from mobile learning, as such opportunities allow them to feel more like their peers, and foster a sense of **normalcy specifically**," she said. "This is very important for social development that can be seriously affected due to late or slow academic development." One example of mobile technology for children with special needs is Proloquo2go, an app available on iTunes. Students with autism spectrum disorders, and others who may have difficulty speaking, can use the app's library of symbols and text-to-speech shift to communicate easily and naturally with others. This type of app helps broaden students' **horizons** both in and out of the classroom.

7. So what about e-readers? Is there really a place for these in the classroom? E-books are **portable**, easy to update, and cost-effective, and can be read on net-books, e-readers, laptops, and more. Can you imagine a world where students can carry around all their textbooks in one easy-to-read, lightweight device? I can.

8. Kelly Tenkely, the author of the iLearn Technology blog, has recently **submitted** a **proposal** to use the iPad in a one-to-one learning environment at her elementary school. She sees it as a **marvelous** way to improve the reading, math, and science skills of the students at her school.

9. "It provides the potential to **empower** and uplift students in their learning," she said. "To improve effectiveness, education in the 21st century has to be active, and engaging. Students must have universal access to mobile technologies that will enable **critical** thinking, **differentiation**, problem solving and language learning. It is our belief that the technology in Apple's iPad meets these needs and more."

10. The same thing happened to cell phones. Speaking of cell phones, traditionally they have a bad reputation at schools, but that is starting to change. Instead of banning cell phones, some forward-thinking educators are actively using them. The National Council for Curriculum and Assessment in Ireland, for instance, is currently in phase 3 of an interesting experiment with the use of cell phones at a number of Irish schools. Most students speak English as their first language, but Irish language lessons are encouraged to maintain a link to Ireland's cultural past. The NCCA program aims to increase the level of oral **fluency** in Irish by providing students with cell phones to support them in language classes. Students are sent text messages with Irish vocabulary words to use during classes, and call a number with a voice-response system to leave answers to teachers' questions.

11. Other creative uses of cell phones in education involve websites like Poll Everywhere and Text the Mob, which allow a teacher to **devise** a set of questions that the students can respond to with a text message. The results can be displayed **instantly** as a graph **via** an LCD projector, or on an interactive whiteboard, and the teacher can **gauge** the level of students' understanding very quickly. A class set of student response systems can be an expensive outlay, but to some extent, it can be **negotiated**. If your students already brought their cell phones to school, we might as well have put them to use in the classroom.

12. Mobile learning is an exciting opportunity for educators, but in many ways we are just scratching the surface of all that can be achieved with it. With proper training, and time to explore these high-tech gadgets, teachers will soon be able to make rapid **strides** with them, and be able to support and instruct the use of such devices in the classroom on a regular basis. Now is the time to act. Our digital natives are counting on us.

(1019 words)

Notes

Digital natives: people who are characterized as having access to network digital technologies and the skills to use those technologies. Major parts of their life and daily activities are mediated by digital technologies.

Dictionary.com: an online dictionary whose domain was first registered on May 14, 1995.

Google Earth: a virtual globe, map and geographical information program that was originally called EarthViewer 3D created by Keyhole, Inc, a Central Intelligence Agency (CIA) funded company acquired by Google in 2004.

Abilene Christian University: a private, non-profit university in Abilene, Texas, affiliated with Churches of Christ. ACU was founded in 1906, as Childers Classical Institute. In 2014, Abilene Christian University's fall enrollment was 4,427 students of which 777 were graduate students.

Proloquo2Go: an award-winning symbol-supported communication app providing a voice to over 150,000 individuals who cannot speak. It is designed to promote the growth of communication skills and foster language development through research-based vocabularies.

Autism spectrum disorders: a range of conditions classified as neurodevelopmental disorders in the fifth and most recent revision of the American Psychiatric Association's *Diagnostic and Statistical Manual of Mental Disorders* published in 2013.

Poll Everywhere: a privately held company headquartered in San Francisco, California. The company, founded on April, 2007 is an online service for classroom response and audience response systems.

🔊 New Words

wave	/weiv/	*n.*	[C] 1. a sudden increase in a particular activity or type of behavior, especially an undesirable or unpleasant one（活动或行为的）突然爆发；浪潮　2. a raised mass of water on the surface of water, especially the sea, which is caused by the wind or by tides making the surface of the water rise and fall 波浪；(尤指)海浪
		v.	to move your hand from side to side in the air, usually in order to say hello or goodbye to someone. 挥（手以示意）
ignore	/ig'nɔːr/	*vt.*	to intentionally not listen or give attention to 不理睬，忽视
mainstream	/'meinˌstriːm/	*n.*	[C] **(the ~)** ideas, methods, or people that are considered ordinary or normal and accepted by most people 主流
		a.	*(only before noun)* considered ordinary or normal and accepted or used by most people 主流的
confused	/kən'fjuːzd/	*a.*	unable to think clearly or to understand something 迷惑的；糊涂的
recall	/ri'kɔːl/	*v.*	to remember a particular fact, event, or situation from the past 回想；回想起
radically	/'rædikəli/	*a.*	in a radical manner 根本地；彻底地；完全地
depict	/di'pikt/	*vt.*	*(fml.)* to describe sth. or sb. in writing or speech, or show them in a painting picture, etc. 描写；描述；描绘
mysterious	/mi'stiəriəs/	*a.*	difficult to explain or understand 神秘的；难以解释的
explore	/ik'splɔː/	*v.*	1. to examine (sth.) thoroughly in order to test or find out about it 仔细检查（某事物）；探索；探究　2. to travel into or through (a place, esp. a country) in order to learn about it 勘探；探测；探险，考察
plot	/plɔt/	*v.*	to make a plan or map of (sth.) 绘制
		n.	[C, U] (plan or outline of the) events in the story of a play or novel（戏剧或小说的）故事情节
promising	/'prɔmisiŋ/	*a.*	seems likely to be very good or successful 有望成功的；前景很好的
motivated	/'məutiveitid/	*a.*	provided with a motive or given incentive for action 有动机的；有积极性的
accessibility	/əksesə'biləti/	*n.*	1. [U] the quality of being at hand when needed 可接近；可得到　2. [U] the attribute of being easy to meet or deal with 便利性；可理解性
range	/reindʒ/	*n.*	[C] limits between which sth. varies; extent（种类或变化的）限度，范围，幅度，程度
normalcy	/'nɔːmlsi/	*n.*	[U] the state of being normal 正常状态，常态
specifically	/spə'sifikli/	*a.*	1. relating to or intended for one particular type of person or thing only 特定地；具体地；专门地　2. in a detailed or exact way 详尽地；明确地

horizon	/hə'raizn/	*n.*	1. [C] the limit of one's ideas, knowledge, and experience 范围、界限；眼界　2. [C] [*sing.*] the line far away where the land or sea seems to meet the sky 地平线
submit	/səb'mit/	*vt.*	to give or offer something for a decision to be made by others 提交；呈递
proposal	/prə'pəuzəl/	*n.*	1. [C] a suggestion, sometimes a written one 建议；计划；　2. [C] an offer of marriage 求婚
marvelous	/'mɑːvələs/	*a.*	extremely good, enjoyable, impressive, etc. 极好的；绝妙的；了不起的
empower	/im'pauə/	*vt.*	to give someone official authority or the freedom to do something 赋予……权力；授权；使自主
critical	/'kritikl/	*a.*	looking for faults; pointing out faults 找出毛病的；指出缺点的；批评的
differentiation	/ˌdifərenʃi'eiʃn/	*n.*	1. [C] 区别，区分，辨别　2. [U] the process of becoming or making something different 差异化
fluency	/'fluːənsi/	*n.*	[U] fluent speech or writing is smooth and confident, with no mistakes（语言或文字）流利、流畅
devise	/di'vaiz/	*vt.*	to plan or invent a new way of doing sth. 想出；设计；发明
instantly	/'instəntli/	*a.*	at once; immediately 立刻；马上；瞬即
via	/'viə/	*prep.*	through; using 经由；通过
gauge	/geidʒ/	*vt.*	1. to make a judgment about (sth.) 判断　2. to measure (sth.) esp. accurately 测量
negotiate	/ni'gəuʃiˌeit/	*v.*	to have formal discussions with someone in order to reach an agreement with them 谈判，磋商
stride	/straid/	*n.*	1. [C] an important positive development 进展，进步　2. [C] a long step when walking or running 大步；阔步　3. [C] the distance covered by a step 步幅
		vi.	to walk with long steps 大步行走
		vt.	to cover or traverse by taking long steps 跨过

❂ New Expressions

take advantage of	to use the good things in a situation 利用；利用……的机会
engage in	to take part in sth. 参加；参与；从事
be/get used to	to be familiar with sth. because you do it or experience it often 习惯于；适应
center upon/on	to be or make sb./sth. become the person or thing around which most activity, etc. take place 把……当作中心；（使）成为中心
apply to	to be relevant to a particular person or thing 适宜；适用

count on	to be confident that you can depend on sb. or sth. 依靠；指望
be exposed to	to put sb. or sth. in a place or situation where they are not protected from sth. harmful or unpleasant 面临，遭受
latch on to	1. to understand an idea or what sb. is saying 理解，懂得，领会 2. to become attached to sb./sth. 依附于 3. to join sb. and stay in their company, especially when they would prefer you not to be with them 纠缠，缠住
speak of	to talk about 提到；提及
scratch the surface	to deal with, understand, or find out about only a small part of a subject or problem 浅尝辄止；隔靴搔痒

Reading Comprehension

Understanding the text

I. Choose the best answer to each of the following questions.

1. What does the word "mainstream" (Para. 1) imply?

    A. Mobile phones are becoming more and more popular among individuals.

    B. More and more schools are moving toward mobile learning in the classroom.

    C. More and more people are using mobiles to learn English.

    D. More and more apps have been created for students to learn languages.

2. What is the result of the research on the Statistic 1 app?

    A. Students master more skills and knowledge about the app.

    B. Teachers are more motivated to do well when using the app.

    C. Teachers do not agree to use this app in classroom.

    D. Students can understand the content better, and are more motivated to do well when they are using the app.

3. Why does Deidra Hughey like mobile learning devices?

    A. Because students like them.

    B. Because students have more passion to use them in classroom.

    C. Because of the accessibility they have to a wide range of students.

    D. Because of the function they have to students.

4. What is the effect of auxiliary app on students?

    A. It helps improve students' ability of writing.

    B. It helps broaden students' horizons both in and out of the classroom.

C. It helps motivate students' interest in classroom.

D. It helps improve students' ability of listening.

5. Which one of the following is NOT the feature of e-books?

   A. Portable.   B. Easy to update.

   C. Cost-effective.   D. High-speed.

6. What does Kelly Tenkely think of using the iPad in a one-to-one learning environment?

   A. She sees it as a marvelous way to improve the students' skills at her school.

   B. She regards it as a good way to train teachers in daily classroom.

   C. She sees it as an effective method to improve students' confidence.

   D. She regards it as a great approach to teach languages.

7. How did NCCA program increase students' level of oral fluency in Irish?

   A. Provided students with cell phones to support them in language classes.

   B. Provided students with computers to support them in language classes.

   C. Provided students with electronic dictionary to support them in language classes.

   D. Provided students with multimedia to support them in language classes.

8. What is the author's attitude toward the development of mobile learning?

   A. Optimistic.   B. Pessimistic.

   C. Neutral.   D. Ironic.

Critical thinking

II. Work in pairs and discuss the following questions.

1. What do you think of mobile learning technologies?

2. Have you ever used any apps to improve your language skills in your daily life?

3. Do you agree that students bring their cell phones to school and apply them to classroom study? Why or why not?

4. Are there any mobile learning technologies used in your daily classroom study? If yes, what are they?

5. With the mobile learning technologies, how can you improve your academic performance?

Language Focus

Words in use

III. Fill in the blanks with the words given below. Change the form where necessary. Each word can be used only once.

recall	ignore	negotiate	confused	mysterious
devise	specifically	depict	foster	via

1. His mother _____ later, "he used to stay up until two o'clock in the morning playing these war games."

2. Being equipped with one of the most recent cutting-edge IT products could just help a college or university _____ a cutting-edge reputation.

3. Educators may fear that children hearing two languages will become permanently _____ and thus their language development will be delayed.

4. The patient's brain activity is monitored _____ electrodes taped to the skull.

5. The carvings cover hundreds of square meters and also _____ battles and scenes from Hindu mythology.

6. The _____ snowy mountains, vast grassland, and groups of yaks form a unique plateau scenery.

7. That scholar has _____ a new method of teaching foreign languages, which is welcomed by most of his students.

8. You do not have to _____ program these features into your application. It's not necessary.

9. For all the contemporary problems cars bring, no one can deny the convenience cars bring to us and _____ the effort we make to solve these problems.

10. The president also called on nations to redouble their efforts to _____ an international trade agreement.

Expressions in use

IV. Fill in the blanks with the expressions given below. Change the form where necessary. Each expression can be used only once.

speak of	take advantage of	engage in	apply to
count on	latch on to	be (get) used to	scratch the surface
be (get) exposed to		center on	

1. When people _____ his father, words like courageous and dogged flow from the lips.

2. To be honest, I really don't _____ to what he said.

3. Film studios are _____ the new-found enthusiasm for dinosaurs to rush out monster movies.

4. Ben could always _____ his sister to help him out of trouble.

5. Similar arrangements _____ students who choose to stay in Scotland for a long time.

6. Industry leaders want scientists to _____ fundamental research, not applied one.

7. This essay is so short that it can only _____ of the topic.

8. In the worst cases, a person must not _____ sunlight and must use protection.

9. I found the job tiring at first but I soon _____ it.

10. His problems _____ allegations that his family and inner circle used their positions for personal financial gains.

Sentence structure

V. Rewrite the following sentences by using "make (no / any / much) sense".

> **Model:** It is very meaningful to change the ways in which children learn.
>
> → It makes much sense to change the ways in which children learn.

1. There is no sense in buying expensive clothes for children, as they soon grow out of them.

   _____

2. It's too late to change your mind now; so there is no point in shedding tears.

   _____

3. Whatever the boss says, it is unreasonable to ask me to work without pay.

   _____

VI. Complete the following sentences by translating the Chinese into English, using "might as well + present perfect" to say that it would not make any difference if you did something else.

> **Model:** _____ (我们还不如将它们用在课堂上).
>
> → We might as well have put them to use in the classroom.

1. The weather was so bad, _____

   (我们还不如待在家里呢).

2. I already knew the truth, _____

   (所以你还不如早点告诉我).

3. It was too far from the destination, _____

   (我们还不如像你建议的那样骑车去呢).

Unit 2
My Learning Experience
—Discovery of an
IT Course

Measuring programming progress by lines of code is like measuring aircraft building progress by weight.

— *Bill Gates (American business magnate, investor, author and philanthropist)*

Writing in C or C++ is like running a chain saw with all the safety guards removed.

— *Bob Gray (American data analyst and author)*

As an IT learner, learning to program isn't something you can do in an afternoon, and it doesn't have to be a life's work, either. There are lots of things you can do to make it easier for yourself when you are learning to program. The first step of learning to program is to understand programming languages. What are the programming languages and who created them? How could we use them to program? What are the differences among different programming languages? During the programming, which coding styles will you choose? Maybe these questions have bothered you for a long time. Digging into Text A and Text B, you will find the answer.

Section

Pre-reading Activities

I. *Listen to a talk about a college student who majors in computer science. He and his classmates created a program which helped his father sleep better. Choose the best answer to each of the following questions.*

1. When did Patrick return after serving as a convoy commander in the US army?

    A. In 2007.   B. In 2016.   C. In 2010.

2. What did Patrick suffer from after he returned?

    A. Heart disease.   B. Physical injury.   C. Sleep panic attacks.

3. What did Tyler think he could do to help his father?

    A. To learn some medical knowledge.

    B. To make a computer program.

    C. To take his father to see a doctor.

4. Where did the name of the program come from?

    A. Bivouac, a medical term for a safe place to sleep in.

    B. Bivouac, a military term for a safe place to sleep in.

    C. Bivouac, a scientific term for a safe place to sleep in.

5. What are the main components of the program?

    A. A smart watch.   B. A smart phone.   C. A and B.

6. How much money did Tyler and his team win in the contest held in Washington?

    A. $25,000.   B. $1,500.   C. $10,000.

II. Work in pairs and discuss the following questions.

1. What do you know about programming languages?

2. What do you know about the position of programming in IT companies?

3. In your opinion, what is the most effective way to learn programming languages?

Learn a C-style language

1. A C-style language, just like millions of developers learned before you, went back to the 1980s and earlier. It's not a **mystery**; it's not **brilliant**; it's usually not cutting **edge**, but it is smart. Even if you don't stick with it, or program in it on a daily basis, having a C-style language in your **repertoire** is a necessary if you want to be taken seriously as a developer.

2. Why? The answer to that depends on who you ask, because there's almost nothing developers enjoy more than arguing over the influences and **derivation** of languages—except maybe arguing over which language is the best. Despite all the arguing, there's pretty **solid** agreement that C, C++, Java, C#, and Objective-C are all C-style languages.

3. The broadest definition is if the language uses curly braces "{}" to set aside blocks of functionality, it's a C-style language. Many, but not all, C-style languages are strongly typed. Many of the more popular C-style languages are object-oriented (C++, Java, C#), but C itself is not. Many of the other big names, such as Python, Perl, and PHP also have a C-style **influence**, although how important that is, and to what degree, depends on who you ask. JavaScript has a C-like syntax, but is **substantially** different once you get past the surface.

4. What you get out of learning a C-style language is the **fundamentals** of programming that are common to many other languages: variables, values, types, assignments and expressions, functions, **parameters**, and return values, control flow and program progression. These are basic concepts that any programmer will be expected to know, and if you learn them in a C-style language, you'll have the mode of thinking in common with most other developers you meet.

5. It is not suggesting that you learn any particular C-style language, just that you learn one of them. Which one is the best really depends on your particular job situation. If you're programming in Microsoft shop, learn C#. If you need to make Android apps, learn Java. If you're working on **embedded** systems, or anything close to the hardware, good old C is probably most useful. If

you're working anywhere else, C++ has a good **prospect**.

6. The **magical** thing about learning a C-style language is that once you know one of them, the rest are easier to learn. Nobody speaks Latin anymore, but it still captures people's **imagination** to learn; among other reasons, you get a jump on learning Italian, Spanish, and French for free. Knowing one C-style language doesn't **automatically** give you expert-level skills in the others, but it reduces the learning **curve** quite a bit. It's a safe **bet** that if you know C#, you can read Java with little trouble. Learning to write it requires a crash course in syntax, but that takes days, not months. Of course, being truly **fluent** in a programming language requires time, effort, and practice, but that's true of any language.

7. The term "polyglot programmer" gets thrown around a lot as a good **trait** for a developer. While that phrase usually means "I have some **insights** other than C-style languages," having the base of a C-style language is the foundation that you build your polyglot street cred on. The C-style language **represents** the basic mode that most programmers think in. Once you have that, you can branch out to functional, or other kinds of languages in the form of extending and associating the basic mode. Switching to another language paradigm means changing the way you think about programming which is not **liable** to do, and that's often challenging, but that's a good experience as well. That doesn't mean that starting with a C-style language has a terrible **defect**; if the first language you learn is functional, you'll need to change your way of thinking to learn to write **imperatively**. It is **bound** to have a learning **curve** when you change your fundamental habits, which is why it is **recommended** to start at the most common starting language.

8. For those of you who are making language choices to help your career, you need to be **conversant** in the languages where the jobs are. You can debate the correctness of any index you like, but in the **aggregate**, you get a pretty good **indication** of what employers are looking for. There are some flexible employers who don't **persist** that you know their language of choice when you start, but they will look for candidates with the shortest learning curve, and fluency in a C-style language gives you an advantage there.

9. Even if you're further along in your career, knowing a C-style language provides a nice safety net if you have an unexpected job change. You may have spent years programming in a company and loving it, but barriers can strike at any time, and if you have a C-style language in your **arsenal**, you are better off than a suddenly unemployed programmer who doesn't. If nothing else, you'll save a lot of time in interviews explaining why you never learned C++ or Java.

10. In the final **analysis**, your choice of a programming language to learn will almost certainly be based on what problems you need to solve, or what language your employer tells you to use. That decision is going to be based on the current "hotness" as often as any other reason. There's no denying that it's cool to be one of the few programming in the new language that everybody's talking about. If you're lucky, the language will be a hit, and you'll be one of the first to be able to

claim **extensive** experience in it when the **headhunters** come looking.

11. Having experience in a C-style language is more like brushing your teeth every day. It's not **glamorous**, and nobody will give you a reward for doing it, but someday down the road, you may be really happy that you did.

(982 words)

Notes

Latin: a classical language belonging to the Italic branch of the Indo-European languages. Latin was originally spoken in Latium. Through the power of the Roman Republic, it became the dominant language, initially in Italy and subsequently throughout the Roman Empire.

Perl: a family of high-level, general-purpose, interpreted, dynamic programming languages. The languages in this family include Perl 5 and Perl 6.

PHP: a server-side scripting language designed primarily for web development but is also used as a general-purpose programming language. PHP originally stood for Personal Home Page, but it now stands for the recursive acronym PHP— Hypertext Preprocessor.

◉ New Words

mystery	/ˈmɪstəri/	*n.*	[C, usu. *sing.*] sth. that you are not able to understand, explain, or get information about 无法解释的事物；谜
brilliant	/ˈbrɪliənt/	*a.*	very bright; sparkling 非常明亮的；光辉夺目的
edge	/edʒ/	*n.*	1. [C] a slight competitive advantage 优势　2. [C] sharp cutting part of a blade, knife, sword, or some other tool or weapon 锋利部分；刀口；锋
repertoire	/ˈrepətwɑː(r)/	*n.*	[C] all the plays, songs, pieces, etc. which a company, actor, musician, etc. knows and is prepared to perform 全部节目
derivation	/deriˈveɪʃn/	*n.*	[U] development or origin (esp. of words) 发展；起源
solid	/ˈsɒlɪd/	*a.*	1. in complete agreement; unanimous 一致的　2. that can be depended on; reputable and reliable 牢靠的；有信誉的；可靠的　3. strong and firm in construction; able to support weight or resist pressure; substantial 坚固的；结实的；耐压的
influence	/ˈɪnfluəns/	*n.*	[U] power to produce an effect; action of natural forces 影响力；作用
		vt.	to have an effect or influence on (sb./sth.); to cause (sb./sth.) to act, behave, think, etc. in a particular way 影响

substantially	/səb'stænʃ(ə)li/	*a.*	1. very much; a lot 大量地；相当多地 2. (*fml.*) mainly; in most details, even if not completely 大体上；本质上
fundamental	/ˌfʌndə'mentl/	*n.*	[C] the main or most important rules or parts 基本原则；基础
		a.	being or involving basic facts or principles 基础的，根本的
parameter	/pə'ræmitə/	*n.*	[C] quantity that does not vary in a particular case but does vary in other cases 参量；参数
embedded	/im'bedid/	*a.*	1. fixed into the surface of something 嵌入的 2. If an emotion, opinion, etc. is embedded in someone or something, it is a very strong or important part of him, her, or it. (感情、态度等) 深切的；根深蒂固的
prospect	/'prɔspekt/	*n.*	[C, U] sth. that is possible or likely to happen in the future, or the possibility itself 前景
magical	/'mædʒikl/	*a.*	1. (*infml.*) wonderful; very enjoyable 不可思议的 2. containing magic; used in magic 魔术的
imagination	/iˌmædʒi'neiʃn/	*n.*	[C, U] ability to form mental images or pictures 想象力
automatically	/ɔːtə'mætikli/	*a.*	(of actions) done without thinking, esp. from habit or routine; unconscious 不假思索而做出的；无意识的
curve	/kɜːv/	*n.*	[C] line of which no part is straight and which changes direction without angles 曲线；弧线
bet	/bet/	*n.*	1. [C] an opinion about what is likely to happen or to have happened 预计；估计 2. [C] arrangement to risk money, etc. on an event of which the result is doubtful 赌博
fluent	/'fluːənt/	*a.*	(of speech, a language or an action) expressed in a smooth and accurate way (指言语、语言) 流利而通顺的；(指动作) 灵活而准确的
trait	/treit/	*n.*	[C] element in sb.'s personality; distinguishing characteristic 个性；显著的特点
insight	/'insait/	*n.*	1. [U] the ability to see and understand the truth about people or situations 洞察力；深刻的了解 2. [C, U] ~ (**into sth.**) an understanding of what sth. is like 见解
represent	/repri'zent/	*vt.*	to stand for or to be a symbol or equivalent of (sb./sth.); to symbolize 代表
liable	/'laiəbl/	*a.*	(**be ~ to do sth.**) likely to do sth. in a particular way because of a fault or tendency 可能 (易于) 做某事的
defect	/'diːfekt/	*n.*	[C] fault or lack that spoils a person or thing 缺点；不足之处；毛病；瑕疵
		vi.	~ (**from sth.**) (**to sth.**) to leave a party, cause, country, etc. and go to another 背叛；变节

imperatively	/im'perətivli/	*a.*	in an imperative and commanding manner 命令式地
bound	/baund/	*a.*	(**~ to**) sth. that is bound to happen will almost certainly happen 一定的；几乎肯定的
recommend	/ˌrekə'mend/	*vt.*	1. to suggest (a course of action, treatment, etc.); advise 建议；劝告 2. **~ sb./sth. (to sb.) (for sth./as sth.)** to praise sth. as suitable for a purpose; to praise sb. as suitable for a post, etc.; to speak favorably of sb./sth. 推荐；赞许
conversant	/kən'vɜːsnt/	*a.*	(*fml.*) having knowledge of sth.; familiar with sth. 精通，熟悉
aggregate	/'æɡriɡeit/	*n.*	[C] total amount; mass or amount brought together 总计；合计；总量
		v.	1. **~ sb. (to sth.)** (*fml.*) to be formed or bring sb. into an assembled group or amount（使）聚集；（使）集合 2. (*infml.*) amount to (a total) 总计；合计
indication	/ˌindi'keiʃn/	*n.*	[C, U] a remark or sign that shows that sth. is happening or what sb. is thinking or feeling 指出；迹象；指示
persist	/pə'sist/	*vi.*	to continue to do sth., esp. in an determined way and in spite of opposition, argument or failure 坚持；执意
arsenal	/'ɑːsənl/	*n.*	[C] a place where weapons and ammunition are made or stored 军械场；军火库
barrier	/'bæriə(r)/	*n.*	[C] anything that prevents progress or makes it difficult for sb. to achieve sth. 障碍
analysis	/ə'næləsis/	*n.*	[C, U] a process of studying or examining sth. in detail in order to understand it or explain it 分析
extensive	/ik'stensiv/	*a.*	1. large in amount; wide-ranging 大量的；广泛的 2. large in area; extending far 广大的；广阔的
headhunter	/ 'hedhʌntə(r)/	*n.*	[C] a person whose job is to find people with the necessary skills to work for a particular company and to persuade them to join this company 猎头者（专门负责延揽人才）
glamorous	/'ɡlæmərəs/	*a.*	especially attractive and exciting, and different from ordinary things or people 富有魅力的；迷人的

✪ New Expressions

stick with	to keep to; to stay close to 紧跟；持续，坚持
set aside	to move sth. to one side until you need 把……放到一旁
depend on/upon	to rely on sb./sth. and be able to trust them 依靠；信赖
argue over	to argue on 辩论某事，为……争论
in common with	like sb./sth.; the same as 像……一样

capture one's imagination	to make sb. feel very interested in sth. 引起……的想象；吸引……的注意
build on	to base sth. on sth. 把……作为……的基础
branch out	to do something that is different from their normal activities or work 扩充范围，扩充
in the form of	in the way sth. is or appears to be 以……形式；以……方式
be bound to	to be certain to 必然；一定；注定
be better off	to be in a better situation, if or after something happens 境况更好；处境更好
be based on	to build on 根据，以……为基础；建立在……基础上

Reading Comprehension

Understanding the text

I. Answer the following questions.

1. What is the broadest definition of C-style language?

2. According to the text, how to know which C-style language is the best to learn?

3. If you're working on embedded systems, which C-style language is probably the most useful for you?

4. What is the magical thing about learning a C-style language?

5. What is required to become truly fluent in a programming language?

6. What's the meaning of "polyglot programmer" in Para. 7?

7. What does "switching to another language paradigm" mean in Para. 7?

8. Why is it important for programmers to learn a C-style language?

Critical thinking

II. Work in pairs and discuss the following questions.

1. In your opinion, which programming language will you choose to learn? And why?

2. Do you have any interest in learning a C-style language? Why or why not?

3. Do you think mastering a language is helpful for you to learn a programming language? Why or why not?

4. If you were a software developer, what kind of IT company would you want to work in?

Words in use

III. Fill in the blanks with the words given below. Change the form where necessary. Each word can be used only once.

prospect	mystery	analysis	glamorous	derivation
insight	barrier	defect	persist	solid

1. Factual and forensic evidence makes a suicide verdict the most compelling answer to the _____ of his death.

2. As an impartial observer my _____ is supposed to be objective.

3. Unfortunately, there is little _____ of seeing these big questions answered.

4. Some people experience shyness as a(n) _____ to communication, but this can be broken down gradually.

5. He urged the United States to _____ with its efforts to bring about peace.

6. She is not _____ but she's happier because her life is relatively less stressful.

7. He was a man of forceful character, with considerable _____ and diplomatic skills.

8. The new car had to be withdrawn from the market because of a mechanical _____.

9. This word is a(n) _____. Can you point out its root, prefix and suffix?

10. All substances, whether they are gaseous, liquid or _____, are made of atoms.

Word building

When the suffix *-ing* combines with the base form of verbs to form nouns, they are used to refer to the activity described by the verb. When the suffix *-ing* combines with the base form of verbs to form adjectives, they are used to describe a continuing process or state.

Examples

Words learned	Add *-ing*	New words formed
interest	→	interesting
follow	→	following
live	→	living

The suffix *-ive* combines with the base form of verbs and sometimes nouns to form adjectives which mean "with the tendency of, having the property of, or belonging to".

Examples

Words learned	Add -*ive*	New words formed
act	→	active
represent	→	representative
create	→	creative
attract	→	attractive
impress	→	impressive

The suffix -*ify* combines with nouns or adjectives to form verbs, which describe the process by which a state, quality, or condition is brought about.

Examples

Words learned	Add -*ify*	New words formed
pure	→	purify
diverse	→	diversify
quality	→	qualify

IV. Add -ing, -ive, or -ify to or remove them from the following words to form new words.

Words learned	New words formed
-ing	
develop	
miss	
disturbing	
-ive	
effect	
offensive	
collective	
product	
protective	
-ify	
simplify	
intense	

V. Fill in the blanks with the newly-formed words in Activity IV. Change the form where necessary. Each word can be used only once.

1. We will _____ cooperation with fellow developing countries, and to support their greater say in international affairs.

2. Today, any data that is _____ about us in one place or another—and for one reason or another—can be stored in a computer bank.

3. No _____, but if you want good quality, you have to pay for it.

4. In some _____ countries more and more people migrate to urban areas.

5. The Secretary General says they have taken _____ measures to preserve natural resources.

6. The regulations are made to _____ women's and children's rights and interests.

7. She has been ferreting around among her papers for the _____ letter.

8. The room, the view, and the two people, seemed so peaceful that I did not want to _____ them.

9. Buddhist ethics are _____ but its practices are very complex to a western mind.

10. This commercial forest is very _____ and can generate good economic returns.

Banked cloze

VI. Fill in the blanks by selecting suitable words from the word bank. You may not use any of the words more than once.

A. quickly	B. adhere	C. replace	D. invested	E. exceptions
F. programming	G. specific	H. logical	I. posed	J. applied
K. boost	L. intended	M. developed	N. dominant	O. promote

C is a 1) _____ language which was born at "AT & T's Bell Laboratories" of US in 1972. It was written by Dennis Ritchie. This language was created for a 2) _____ purpose: to design the UNIX operating system (which is used on many computers). From the beginning, C was 3) _____ to be useful—to allow busy programmers to get things done.

Because C is such a powerful, 4) _____ and supple language, its use 5) _____ spread beyond Bell Labs. In the late 70's C began to 6) _____ widespread well-known languages of that time like PL/I, ALGOL etc. Programmers everywhere began using it to write all sorts of programs. Soon, however, different organizations began applying their own versions of C with a subtle difference. This 7) _____ a serious problem for system developers. To solve this problem, the American National Standards Institute (ANSI) formed a committee in 1983 to establish a standard definition of C. This committee approved a version of C in 1989 which is known as ANSI C. With few 8) _____, every modern C compiler has the ability to 9) _____ to this standard. ANSI C was then approved by the International Standards Organization (ISO) in 1990.

Now, what about the name? Why was it named C, why not something else? The C language is so named because its predecessor was called B. The B language was 10) _____ by Ken Thompson of Bell Labs.

Expressions in use

VII. Fill in the blanks with the expressions given below. Change the form where necessary. Each expression can be used only once.

argue over	in common with	branch out	in the form of
stick with	capture attention	be better off	be based on
depend on	be bound to		

1. The person you have the most _____ is the one who can make you feel truly happy.

2. When you read something you know will show up on a test, write it down _____ a question.

3. Once you have set a simple and clear view of the world, _____ it.

4. Sometimes we _____ football but it's never anything too serious.

5. After you've accomplished that, you can _____ to other technologies.

6. We _____ see some ups and downs along the road to economic recovery.

7. Decisions about your children should _____ the practicalities of everyday life.

8. We would _____ if we lowered our expectations about the results of decisions.

9. Success doesn't _____ what you do. What you don't do is equally important.

10. How can you effectively _____, present your topic, establish credibility, and preview your major points in just a few minutes.

Structure Analysis and Writing

Structure Analysis
Focus on a cause-and-effect essay

In this unit, you'll learn how to write a cause-and-effect essay. Cause-and-effect essays are concerned with why things happen (causes) and what happens as a result (effects). When we write a cause-effect paper, we are actually making a causal analysis.

Two questions should be answered in a causal analysis:

1) What is the cause of something that has happened?

2) What effect will follow if something has happened?

In other words, a cause deals with the question "Why?" and an effect, the question "What if?". In answering the first question we reason from effect backward to cause, and in answering the second, from cause forward to effect. Cause and effect is a common method of organizing and discussing ideas. Look at the examples below.

Causes:

I like English in high school.

I want to be a teacher in the future.

I like to communicate with others.

Effect:

I choose English as my major.

Cause:

Being laid off

Effects:

Less monthly income

Increased pressure

Change in life style

Since an essay of 150 words is hard to include both causes and effects, you are required to focus on either causes or effects instead of both. To write such an essay, look at the following steps.

1. Choose an appropriate topic

Cause-effect essays typically examine either causes or effects. Choose an interesting subject and brainstorm the reasons for—or causes of—a specific outcome or effect.

2. Develop a strong thesis

Create an effective thesis statement—a single sentence explains the causes or effects you focus on and why they matter. Look at the examples.

Bank failures, governmental economic policies and drought were the primary causes of the Great Depression.

3. Develop and organize the body

Set up the body of the essay so you have one paragraph for each of the causes or effects from your thesis. If your paper explains a chain of events, you might organize the paragraphs chronologically. For example, you might write that the first effect of a polluted water supply in a town was minor illness, then more serious illness and, eventually, death. You might begin with the most blatant causes or effects and move to the less obvious. Another option is to arrange causes and effects by significance, by putting the most important one first. An essay about the causes of the American Civil War could begin with slavery and then move on to other ideas, such as states' rights. Include transition words such as "since", "therefore" and "because" to clarify the causal relationship among the ideas you present.

4. Develop a powerful introduction and conclusion

Begin your analysis with a vivid hook that gets the reader interested in your topic, such as a quote, statistic or brief story. At the end of the paper, add a concluding paragraph to summarize the causal relationship and return to your hook, connecting all the concepts in the analysis.

Now, let's take a look at an example in Text A.

1) *The answer to that depends on who you ask, because there's almost nothing developers enjoy more than arguing over the influences and derivation of languages—except maybe arguing over which language is the best.* (Para. 2)

Cause: There's almost nothing developers enjoy more than arguing over the influences and derivation of languages—except maybe arguing over which language is the best.

Effect: What C-style language is depends on who you ask.

2) *It is bound to have a learning curve when you change your fundamental habits, which is why it is recommended to start at the most common starting language.* (Para. 7)

Cause: It is bound to have a learning curve when you change your fundamental habits.

Effect: It is recommended to start at the most common starting language.

Structured Writing

Read the sample essay and see how it develops in the pattern of cause-and-effect.

Topic	Sample essay
Why do people like to travel? **Introduction**	Today people are so fond of traveling that tourism has become one of the fastest growing industries in most countries.

Thesis statement: There are two reasons to explain why people like to travel: relaxation and learning **Body** Cause 1: Relaxation Cause 2: Learning **Conclusion** Relaxation and learning are the reasons to explain why people like to travel.	Why do people like to travel? There are two major reasons: relaxation and learning. The first reason why people travel is for relaxation. For example, having worked hard throughout the weekdays, people will find a widened trip to the nearby mountains or beaches. For another example, spending an annual holiday traveling abroad is an especially satisfying experience for those who do not have much of an opportunity to be away from their homelands. When people return from the travel, they will generally feel fresh and energetic, ready to work harder. Another reason for people to travel is learning. You may have read or heard about something but you can never get an accurate picture of it until you see it for yourself. Seeing is believing. Furthermore, if you are a careful observer, you can learn much during your travel about the geography, biology, and history of the places you visit. No matter how well educated you are, there is always a lot for you to learn through traveling. The knowledge acquired from travel, as you will have found in your life, is no less valuable than that from any influential reference book. To conclude, relaxation and learning are the reasons why people like to travel. When you are in travel, enjoy yourself and experience more.

VIII. Write an essay of no less than 150 words on one of the following topics. One topic has an outline that you can follow.

Topic

Why do college students have difficulties finding jobs?

Introduction

Thesis statement: There are some reasons to explain this phenomenon.

Body

Cause 1: More students, less chances

Cause 2: The development of technology

Cause 3: Great guilds have raised barriers to entry

Conclusion

To conclude, if students want to find an ideal job, they need to improve their abilities and lower their expectations about job hunting.

More topics:

● The effects of mobile phone addiction

● What causes generation gap?

Translation

IX. Translate the following paragraph into Chinese.

The Internet has been used for public service in China for about twenty years. So far, the number of Chinese Internet users is over 700 million. Being widely used in China, the Internet has pervaded all aspects of life. The Internet businesses most frequently used by Chinese Internet users are email, news, search engine, web browsing, online music, instant message, online entertainment and so on. The Internet has been changing people's consumption concept, ways of entertainment and socializing, as well as modes of thinking. Now the Internet information technology has been affecting people's life more deeply than any other scientific invention in human history.

X. Translate the following paragraph into English.

远程教育（distance learning）属于正规教育，它打破了传统的课堂教学模式。一般而言，远程教育有三种基本的传输模式：电视现场直播、完整的或经过压缩的信息传输和基于计算机的教学。另外，师生间的互动以及学生之间的互动也是学习过程的重要组成部分。这些技术包括电子公告板、互联网、电子邮件、传真、互联网聊天、电话以及普通邮件。

Section

Reading Skills: *Argument*

Many of us enjoy a good argument. A good argument is not an emotional experience in which people's feelings get out of control, leaving them ready to start throwing things. Instead, it is a rational discussion in which each person advances and supports a point of view about some matter. We might argue with a friend, for example, about where to eat or what movie to see. We might argue about whether a boss or a parent or an instructor is acting in a fair or an unfair manner. We might argue about whether certain performers or sports stars deserve to get paid as much as they do. In a good argument, the other person listens carefully as we state our case, waiting to see if we really have solid evidence to support our point of view.

Argumentation is a part of our everyday dealings with other people. It is also an important part of what we read. When we read, there are three important steps we can do.

1. Recognize the point the author is making.

2. Decide if the author's support is relevant.

3. Decide if the author's support is adequate.

The basics of argument: point and support

A good argument needs a strong point and then provides persuasive and logical evidence to back it up.

Here is the example from Text A.

Point: *C is your safety net.*

Support:

A. *The employers will look for candidates with the shortest learning curve, and fluency in a C-style language gives you an advantage there.* (Para. 8)

B. *If you have a C-style language in your arsenal, you are better off than a suddenly unemployed programmer who doesn't.* (Para. 9)

C. *If nothing else, you'll save a lot of time in interviews explaining why you never learned C++ or Java.* (Para. 9)

The details provide solid support for the point. They give us a basis for understanding and agreeing with the point.

Read the following sentences from Text B and identify which one is the point and which one is the support.

1. *To be sustainable, new software and new businesses need to grow slowly and with loving care.* (Para. 14)

2. *We are transitioning from an industrial age and an economic era defined by growth to an age of sustainability.* (Para. 14)

Slow Life, Slow Programming

Listen to the song.

You'd better slow down.

Don't dance so fast.

Time is short; the music won't last.

Do you run through each day on the fly?

When you ask "How are you?", do you hear the reply?

When the day is done, do you lie in your bed with the next hundred **chores**

running through your head?

You'd better slow down.

Don't dance so fast.

Time is short; the music won't last.

When you run so fast to get somewhere, you miss half the fun of getting there.

Life is not a race. Do take it slower.

1. My dad used to say: "Slow down, son. You'll get the job done faster."

2. I've worked in many high-tech startup companies in the San Francisco Bay area. I am now 52, and I program slowly and **thoughtfully**. I'm kind of like a designer who writes code; this may become **apparent** as you read on.

3. Programming slowly was a **prime** problem for me when I recently worked on a project with some young coders who believed in making really fast, small **repetitive** changes to the code. At the job, we were encouraged to work in the same codebase, as if it were a big pot of soup, and if we all just kept **stirring** it continuously and **vigorously**, a fully-formed thing of wonder would emerge.

4. When it comes to the programming, many coders believed in the **fallacy** that all engineers are **replaceable**, and that no one should be responsible for any particular aspect of the code; any

coder should be able to change any part of the code at any time. After all, we have **awesome** services like Github which can be available to manage, **evaluate** and **merge** any number of **asynchronous contributions** from any number of coders. As long as everyone makes frequent commitment, and doesn't break anything, everything will come out just fine.

5. **Nonsense**.

6. You can't wish away design process. It has been in **existence** since the dawn of **civilization**. And the latest clever development tools, no matter how clever, cannot replace the best practices and real-life **collaboration** that built **cathedrals,** railroads, and feature-length films. Nor can any amount of programming ever result in a tool that reduces the time of software development to the speed at which a team of code monkeys can type.

7. According to Wikipedia, the slow programming movement is described as part of the slow movement. It is a software development **philosophy** that emphasizes careful design, quality code, software testing and thinking. It **strives** to avoid kludges, buggy code, and overly quick release cycles.

8. This also has something much to do with "Slow Software Development". As part of the quick software development movement, groups of software developers around the world look for more predictive projects, aiming at a more **stable** career and work-life balance. In addition, they **propose** some practices such as pair programming, code reviews, and code refactorings that result in more reliable and **robust** software applications.

9. Venture-backed software development in the San Francisco Bay area is on a **fever-pitch** fast-track. Money **dynamics** puts unnatural demands on a process that would be best left to the natural circadian **rhythms** of design **evolution**. Fast is not always better. In fact, slower sometimes actually means faster—when all is said and done. The subject of how digital technology is **usurping** our natural temporal rhythm is addressed in Rushkoff's *Present Shock*.

10. There's another problem: the almost **religious obsession** with technology—and a fetish-like love for tools. People wonder why software sucks. Software sucks because of navel-gazing. Fast programmers build hacker tools to get around the hacker tools that they built to get around the hacker tools that they built to help them code.

11. This is why I believe that we need older people, women, and educators inside the software development cycle. More people-people, fewer thing-people. And I don't mean on the outside, sitting at help desks or doing flower arranging. I mean on the inside—making sure that software accords with **humanity** at large.

12. A friend of mine who is a mature, female software engineer made an interesting **quip**: "software programming is not typing." Everyone knows this, but it doesn't hurt to remind ourselves every so often. The fact that we programmers spend our time **jabbing** our fingers at keyboards makes it appear that this physical activity **accords** with programming. But programming

is actually the act of bringing thought, design, language, logic, and mental construction into a form that can be stored in computer memory.

13. My wife often comes out into the yard and asks me: "are you coding?" Often my answer is "yes". Usually I am cutting twigs with a garden clipper, or moving **compost** around. Plants, dirt, and clippers have just as much to do with programming as keyboards and glowing screens.

14. We are transitioning from an industrial age and an economic era defined by growth to an age of sustainability. Yes, new software and new businesses need to grow. But to be sustainable, they need to grow slowly and with **sufficient** and loving care. Like good wine. Like a baby.

(755 words)

Notes

San Francisco Bay area: a populous region surrounding the San Francisco and San Pablo estuaries in Northern California. The region encompasses the major cities and metropolitan areas of San Jose, San Francisco, and Oakland, along with smaller urban and rural areas.

Github: a web-based Git repository hosting service. It offers all of the distributed version control and source code management (SCM) functionality of Git as well as adding its own features.

Rushkoff: (Douglas Rushkoff, born February 18,1961) an American media theorist, writer, columnist, lecturerand novelist. He is best known for his association with the early cyberpunk culture, and his advocacy of open source solutions to social problems.

UI: the space where interactions between humans and machines occur.

New Words

chore	/tʃɔː(r)/	*n.*	[C] unpleasant or tiring task 讨厌的或累人的工作
thoughtfully	/ˈθɔːtfəli/	*a.*	1. in a thoughtful manner 沉思地 2. showing consideration and thoughtfulness 体贴地，考虑周到地
apparent	/əˈpærənt/	*a.*	clearly seen or understood; obvious 清楚易见或易懂；明显的；显然的
prime	/praim/	*a.*	(*only before noun*) most important 首要的；最重要的
repetitive	/riˈpetətiv/	*a.*	characterized by repetition 重复的；反复的
stir	/stɜː(r)/	*vt.*	1. to move a liquid or substance around with a spoon or stick in order to mix it together 搅；搅动；搅拌 2. to make sb. have a strong feeling or reaction 激发、激起；引起
vigorously	/ˈvigərəsli/	*a.*	with vigor; in a vigorous manner 精神旺盛地；活泼地
fallacy	/ˈfæləsi/	*n.*	[C, U] false or mistaken belief 错误的见解；谬见

replaceable	/ri'pleisəbl/	*a.*	that can be used instead of sb./sth. else; that sth. can be done instead of sb./sth. else 可替换的；可代替的
awesome	/ɔːsəm/	*a.*	very good, enjoyable 很好的
evaluate	/i'væljueit/	*vt.*	(*fml.*) think carefully about sth. before making a judgment about its value, importance, or quality 评价；评估
merge	/mɜːdʒ/	*v.*	1. to (cause two things to) come together and combine 合并 2. ~ **(into sth.)** to fade or change gradually (into sth. else) 逐渐消失或变成
asynchronous	/ə'siŋkrənəs/	*a.*	not occurring or existing at the same time or having the same period or phase 异步的；不同时的；不同期的
contribution	/kɔntri'bjuːʃn/	*n.*	[U] action of contributing 捐款；捐助；贡献
nonsense	/'nɔnsns/	*n.*	[U, *sing.*] foolish talk, ideas, etc. 胡说；废话
existence	/ig'zistəns/	*n.*	[U] state or fact of existing 存在
civilization	/sivəlai'zeiʃn/	*n.*	[U] state of human social development 文明，文明阶段
collaboration	/kə,læbə'reiʃn/	*n.*	1. [C, U] ~ **(with sb.) (on sth.);** ~ **(between A and B)** the act of working with another person or group of people to create or produce sth. 合作 2. [C] a piece of work produced by two or more people or groups of people working together 合并
cathedral	/kə'θiːdrəl/	*n.*	[C] main church of a district under the care of a bishop 大教堂
philosophy	/fi'lɔsəfi/	*n.*	[U] search for knowledge and understanding of the nature and meaning of the universe and of human life 哲学
strive	/straiv/	*vi.*	(*fml.*) 1. ~ **(for/after sth.)** to try very hard (to obtain or achieve sth.) 努力，奋斗 2. ~ **(against/with sb./sth.)** to carry on a conflict; struggle 进行斗争；争斗
stable	/'steibl/	*a.*	firmly established or fixed; not likely to move or change 稳定的；稳固的；牢固的
propose	/prə'pəuz/	*vt.*	to offer or put forward (sth.) for consideration; to suggest 提议，建议
robust	/rəu'bʌst/	*a.*	1. firm and determined 坚定的；强硬的 2. (of a person) strong and healthy (人) 强壮的；健壮的
fever-pitch	/'fiːvəpitʃ/	*n.*	[C, U] a very high level of excitement or activity 狂热；极度兴奋
dynamic	/dai'næmik/	*n.*	[C] force that produces change, action, or effects 产生变化、行动或影响的力量
		a.	1. of power or forces that produce movement 动力的 2. (of a person) energetic and forceful (指人) 精力充沛的，有力的

rhythm	/'riðəm/	*n.*	1. [C, U] constantly recurring sequence of events or processes（事件或过程）有规律地反复出现 2. [U] pattern produced by emphasis and duration of notes in music or by stressed and unstressed syllables in words（音乐或词语的）节奏
evolution	/ˌiːvə'luːʃn/	*n.*	[U] process of gradually developing; evolving 演化；演进；演变
usurp	/juː'zɜːp/	*vt.*	(*fml.*) to take (sb.'s power, right, position) wrongfully or by force 篡夺或武力夺取
religious	/ri'lidʒəs/	*a.*	believing in and practicing a religion; devout 笃信宗教的，虔诚的
obsession	/əb'seʃn/	*n.*	1. [U] the state in which a person's mind is completely filled with thoughts of one particular thing or person so that they cannot think of anything else 无法摆脱的念头；沉迷 2. [C] a person or thing that sb. thinks about too much 念念不忘的事（或人）
humanity	/hjuː'mænəti/	*n.*	[U] 1. human nature; being human 人性 2. being humane; kind-heartedness 人道；仁慈 3. human beings collectively; the human race; people 人（总称）；人类
quip	/kwip/	*n.*	[C] witty or sarcastic remark 妙语；讽刺话
jab	/dʒæb/	*v.*	to poke or push at sb./sth. roughly, usu. with sth. sharp or pointed 捅，刺，戳
accord	/ə'kɔːd/	*v.*	(~**with sth.**) to agree with or be the same as sth. else 与……一致；与……相符
compost	/'kɔmpɒst/	*n.*	[C, U] mixture of decayed organic matter, manure, etc. added to soil to improve the growth of plants 混合肥料；堆肥
sufficient	/sə'fiʃnt/	*a.*	as much as is needed; enough 足够的；充足的

☺ New Expressions

slow down	to go or to make sth./sb. go at a slower speed or be less active（使）放慢速度，减缓，松劲
kind of	(*infml.*) slightly; in some ways 稍微；有点儿
work on	to do sth. that involves physical or mental effort especially as part of a job 致力于；从事于
be responsible for	to have control and authority over sth. or sb. and the duty of taking care of it, him, or her 负责……；掌管……
be able to do	to have the necessary physical strength, mental power, skill, time, money, or opportunity to do sth. 能够做……
be available to	to be able to be obtained, taken, or used 可获得；可利用
as long as	only if 只要

wish away	to do nothing and hope that a problem will disappear 希望……消失
result in	to cause a particular situation to happen 导致；结果造成
describe sb./sth. as	to say what sb. or sth. is likely by giving details about them. 把……说成；把……称为
have (much/little/nothing) to do with sb./sth.	to be related to sb. or sth., or be involved with sb. or sth. 与……有关；与……有联系
aim at	to plan, hope, or intend to achieve something 目的在于，旨在；致力于
in addition	used for adding an extra piece of information to what has already been said or written 另外
at large	generally; in detail 普遍地；全体地；详尽地

〔Reading Comprehension〕

Understanding the text

I. *Choose the best answer to each of the following questions.*

1. What is the author's profession?

   A. He is a writer.   B. He is a dancer.

   C. He is a coder.   D. He is a journalist.

2. What is the author's programming style?

   A. He programs slowly and thoughtfully.

   B. He programs slowly and hastily.

   C. He programs quickly and thoughtfully.

   D. He programs quickly and hastily.

3. What was the problem for the author when he worked with some young coders?

   A. The author programmed too quickly.

   B. The author programmed very slowly compared with those young coders.

   C. The author coded too thoughtfully.

   D. The author coded in a hasty way.

4. According to Wikipedia, which is NOT correct about the slow programming movement?

   A. The slow programming movement is the part of the slow movement.

   B. The slow programming movement is a software development philosophy.

   C. The slow programming movement is related to "Slow Software Development".

   D. The slow programming movement is a software development revolution.

5. According to the author, why does software suck?

   A. Because it is navel-gazing.　　　　B. Because it is fever-pitch.

   C. Because of high-tech.　　　　　　D. Because it is venture-backed.

6. What is the meaning of the phrase "on the inside" in Para. 11?

   A. To make sure that software can make self-recovery.

   B. To make sure that software can be downloaded.

   C. To make sure that software resonates with humanity at large.

   D. To make sure that software resonates with philosophy at large.

7. According to the author, what is programming?

   A. It is a kind of physical activity.

   B. It is an act of bringing thought, design, language, logic, and mental construction into a form that can be stored in software.

   C. It is a sort of typing.

   D. It is an act of bringing thought, design, language, logic, and mental construction into a form that can be stored in computer memory.

8. To be sustainable, what should new software and new businesses do?

   A. They need to grow slowly and with sufficient and loving care.

   B. They need to grow quickly and with sufficient and loving care.

   C. They need to grow slowly and with considerable care.

   D. They need to grow quickly and with less care.

Critical thinking

II. Work in pairs and discuss the following questions.

1. According to your understanding, what is programming?

2. How do you understand the sentence "new software and new businesses need to grow slowly like good wine, like a baby"?

3. What do you think about the profession of programmer?

4. Do you want to be a programmer in the future? If yes, what kind of programmer do you want to be?

Words in use

III. Fill in the blanks with the words given below. Change the form where necessary. Each word can be used only once.

prime	thoughtfully	sufficient	accord	religious
merge	robust	humanity	obsession	evaluate

1. The result can _____ with the actual circumstance, so this method is viable and valid.

2. His courage in defending _____ and civil rights inspired many outside the church.

3. Many companies _____ and few separate, therefore the directors have decided to combine the two small firms together.

4. Our research attempts to _____ the effectiveness of the different drugs.

5. Almost never has anyone intentionally and _____ designed an organization to achieve planned growth and stability.

6. He is so _____ and never has a trace of weariness.

7. It is for his _____ as much as his music that his numerous friends and pupils will remember him.

8. Most plants grow well where there is _____ moisture and when there is good sunshine.

9. The new government's _____ task is to reduce the level of inflation.

10. Although naturalism had not become a(n) _____ among American writers by 1914, it clearly commanded the allegiance of a majority of serious young writers.

Expressions in use

IV. Fill in the blanks with the expressions given below. Change the form where necessary. Each expression can be used only once.

aim at	describe... as	result in		at large
in addition	slow down	have something to do with		be available to
be encouraged to		be responsible for		

1. This service should _____ everybody, irrespective of whether they can afford it.

2. He believes that students should _____ experiment with bold ideas.

3. In software development, we _____ getting the architecture designed, implemented, and tested early in the project.

4. Doing so, however, will often _____ an immediate and positive impact to your project and your environment.

5. Part-time English classes are offered. _____, students can take classes in word-processing and computing.

6. We know exactly who _____ the execution of the whole business process.

7. Churchill accepted the gift. He _____ the painting _____ "a remarkable example of modern art", which drew loud laughter.

8. Are you implying that I _____ those attacks? If positive, please show some evidence.

9. The threat of global warming will eventually force the country to _____ its energy consumption.

10. I think the chances of getting reforms accepted by the community _____ remain extremely remote.

Sentence structure

V. Rewrite the following sentences by using "There is no denying that...".

> **Model:** It is no doubt that it's cool to be one of the few programming in the new language that everybody's talking about.
>
> → There's no denying that it's cool to be one of the few programming in the new language that everybody's talking about.

1. There is no doubt that computer crime is a very serious problem, so people think that all hackers need to be punished for their actions.

   _____

2. There is little doubt that recycling is good for the environment.

   _____

3. There is no question that today we are under constant pressure to work longer hours.

   _____

VI. Complete the following sentences by translating the Chinese into English, using "no matter how/what/where".

Model: And the latest clever development tools, _____ (无论多么灵巧), cannot replace the best practices and real-life collaboration that built cathedrals, railroads, and feature-length films.

→ And the latest clever development tools, <u>no matter how clever</u>, cannot replace the best practices and real-life collaboration that built cathedrals, railroads, and feature-length films.

---

1. A teacher cannot teach his students everything they want to know _____ (无论他多么博学).

2. (无论你去哪里旅游)_____, you can always find someone to communicate with in English since English is an important language.

3. (不管发生了什么)_____, I will not say a word.

Unit 3
Walk over the Cloud

I think there's a world market for about five computers.

—Thomas J. Watson (Chairman of the Board, IBM)

640K ought to be enough for anybody.

— Bill Gates (American business magnate, investor, author and philanthropist)

You must have had such experiences: you upload photos and videos to a website to share with friends; you have a mail box of which the capacity is dynamically changing in accordance with your needs; you store contact information of schoolmates on a website instead of an address book...You know what I am talking about: personal homepage of Tecent Traveler—Q-zone, video sharing websites Youku. com and Yudou.com. These are all manifestations of online storing and sharing functions of cloud computing. There is a proper analogy: the function of data storing is just like putting our saving money in banks instead of purchasing a safe box to store it.

Section

Pre-reading Activities

I. Describe the picture below to see how cloud computing works.

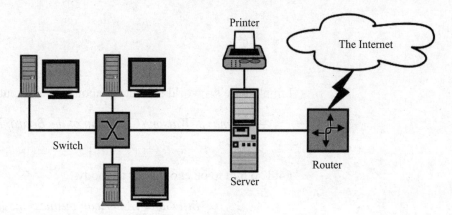

II. Work in pairs and discuss the following questions.

1. What ideas can you get from the picture above?

2. On storing data information, do you like to put your data in computer hard drive or use the technology of cloud computing? Tell the reasons for your choice.

What Cloud Computing Brings to Us?

1. With holiday coming soon, are you going to have a journey? Then how are you going

to tell your friends about your traveling plan? Resort to the telephone? It's the way prior to the computer and your friends will wonder at your **obsolescence**! What you need to do is to login to Google Docs with your Google **account** number, create a new document, make your plan and send this URL to your friends. Then they can request the URL and read your plan. And no matter how many of your friends are sharing the plan, they can edit the document with you. What's more, the URL can **witness** the **scenery** and your feelings in your journey which you want to share with everyone. If you are gone on this experience of editing documents, well then, you are enjoying a new network application pattern—cloud computing. What is the cloud? Where is the cloud? Are we in the cloud now? These are all questions you've probably heard or even asked yourself.

2. In the simplest terms, cloud computing is a new commercial computational model which means **storing** and accessing data and programs over the Internet instead of your computer's hard drive. It makes use of **transmission** capability of the high-speed broadband network to **transfer** the process of data processing from personal computer to computer groups on the net. These computers are ordinary industry standard servers which are managed by a large-scale DPC (data processing center). The DPC **distributes** computing capability according to the clients' need and **eventually** brings about the same efficiency with a super computer.

3. Companies around the world have witnessed this technology. To most people, cloud computing is an unfamiliar, **peculiar** and even **mystic** concept. In fact, we are **unconsciously** enjoying the **convenience** brought by cloud computing. On office software, Google Apps, **released** by Google, have already got a number of users. While, as the leader of office software market, Microsoft, unwilling to give way to Google, has released its online equivalent office software Office Live Workspace. Let's leave the final result of their **competition** unsaid. As end users, we do have enjoyed the convenience and benefits brought by cloud computing.

4. Cloud computing is referred to as the next technological revolution as it will have an radical effect on our business model and working way. Thomas Watson, founder of IBM, said that the world will then need five computers in all. And Bill Gates **claimed** in a speech that individual users will need only 640KB RAM (random access memory).

5. Cloud computing provides us with a good data storing center. Many parallel cloud storage to bank service. Just like money being saved in banks, our data will be protected by the most professional team. Strict access **ensures** that only **specified** persons can share the data. We needn't to worry about losing the data.

6. Cloud computing reduces hardware requirement to the lowest level. We no longer need to update our computer configuration for using a new OS; we no longer need to ferret about on the net for **proper** software for editing files of certain format. What we need is just to enter an URL and then enjoy the fun of cloud computing.

7. With the powerful processing capability of a large number of servers' union, cloud

computing **promotes** working efficiency and reduces the costs greatly. *New York Times* once **rented** Amazon's cloud computing server, using the cloud computing software to transfer its reports since 1851 into searchable **digital** documents within one day. While in traditional methods, this task would be finished in several months.

8. Although cloud computing is used everywhere, a **major** barrier to it is the interoperability of applications. While it is possible to insert an Adobe Acrobat file into a Microsoft Word document, things get a little bit more difficult when we talk about web-based applications. This is where some of the most attractive elements to cloud computing—storing the information on the web and allowing the web to do most of the "computing"—becomes a barrier to getting things done.

9. Apart from the fact that Google probably doesn't want you to have the ability to insert a competitor's document into their spreadsheet, this creates a ton of data security issues. So not only would we need a standard for web "documents" to become web "objects" capable of being **generically** inserted into any other web document, we'll also need a sensible system to **maintain** a certain level of security when it comes to this type of data sharing.

10. In February 2015, one of Amazon's services Simple Storage Service had a fault which lasted for four hours. Besides having heard about clients' **complaints**, people began to worry about the security of cloud computing. How to ensure users' data safely is an **urgent** problem. So, although enjoying the convenience and benefits of cloud computing, we **hesitate** on the safety issue. But remember it takes banking industry almost half of a century to drag their customers into its hall, why cannot we make allowances for **immaturity** of cloud computing and give it a transition. Since we believe that cloud computing can change IT world by its charm, we shouldn't back off.

11. Cloud computing changes everything. We can predict we could get the same information and **perform** the same tasks whether we are at work, at home, or even a friend's house. Not that we would want to take a break between rounds of Texas Hold'em to do some work for the office—but the prospect of being able to do it is pretty cool.

(915 words)

Notes

URL: (Uniform Resource Locator) a reference to a web resource that specifies its location on a computer network and a mechanism for retrieving it. A URL is a specific type of Uniform Resource Identifier (URI), although many people use the two terms interchangeably.

Microsoft Office Live: a discontinued web-based service providing document sharing and website creation tools for consumers and small businesses. Office Live consists of two services, Office Live Workspace, which is superseded by OneDrive, and Office Live Small Business, which is superseded by Office 365.

New York Times: an American daily newspaper, founded and continuously published in New York City since September 18, 1851, by the *New York Times* Company.

Amazon: an American electronic commerce and cloud computing company that was founded on July 5, 1994 by Jeff Bezos and is based in Seattle, Washington.

Simple Storage Service: an web service offered by Amazon Web Services. Amazon S3 provides storage through web services interfaces. Amazon launched S3 on its fifth publicly available web service, in the United States in March 2006 and in Europe in November 2007.

Texas Hold'em: (also known as Texas holdem, hold'em, and holdem) a variation of the card game of poker.

New Words

obsolescence	/ˌɔbsə'lesns/	*n.*	[U] (*fml.*) the state of becoming old-fashioned and no longer useful 过时；废弃；淘汰
account	/ə'kaunt/	*n.*	[C] arrangement made with a bank, firm, etc. allowing credit for financial or commercial transactions (used esp. as in the expressions shown) 账户，户头
witness	/'witnis/	*vt.*	to be present at (sth.) and see it 目击
scenery	/'si:nəri/	*n.*	[U] general natural features of an area, eg. mountains, valleys, rivers, forests 景色；风景
store	/stɔ:/	*vt.*	to collect and keep sth. for future use 储备或储存某物
		n.	[C] quantity or supply of sth. kept for use as needed 储存；储藏；储备
transmission	/trænz'miʃn/	*n.*	[U] action or process of transmitting or being transmitted 传送；传播
transfer	/træns'fɜ:(r)/	*vt.*	to copy (recorded material) using a different recording or storage medium 转录或转存
distribute	/di'stribju:t/	*vt.*	to spread (sth.); to scatter; to place at different parts 使……散开；散布
eventually	/i'ventʃuəli/	*a.*	in the end; at last 最后；终于
peculiar	/pi'kju:liə(r)/	*a.*	special or particular 专门的；特别的
mystic	/'mistik/	*a.*	of hidden meaning or spiritual power 神秘的
unconsciously	/ʌn'kɔnʃəsli/	*a.*	done or spoken, etc. without conscious intention 无意地
convenience	/kən'vi:niəns/	*n.*	[U] quality of being suitable; freedom from trouble or difficulty 方便
release	/ri'li:s/	*vt.*	to make sth. available to the public 向公众提供……
competition	/ˌkɔmpə'tiʃn/	*n.*	[C, U] competing; activity in which people compete 竞争；角逐
claim	/kleim/	*vt.*	to state or declare (sth.) as a fact 声称；宣称
ensure	/in'ʃuə/	*vt.*	to make sure; to guarantee 确保；保证

specified	/'spesifaid/	*a.*	clearly and explicitly stated 规定的；详细说明的
proper	/'prɔpə/	*a.*	that fits, belongs or is suitable; fitting or appropriate 适合的；适当的；适宜的；适用的；恰当的
promote	/prə'məut/	*vt.*	to help the progress of (sth.); to encourage or support 促进，增进
rent	/rent/	*vt.*	to pay for the occupation or use of (land, premises, a telephone, machinery, etc.) 租借或租用
		n.	[C, U] regular payment made for the use of land, premises, a telephone, machinery, etc.; sum paid in this way 租金；地租；房租
digital	/'didʒitl/	*a.*	showing amounts by means of numbers 数字的；数字显示的
major	/'meidʒə/	*a.*	(more) important; great(er)（较）重要的；（较）大的；主要的
		n.	[C] principal subject or course of a student at college or university（大专院校学生的）主修科目，主修课程；专业
generically	/dʒi'nerikli/	*a.*	shared by or including a whole group or class; not specific 类别地；一般地
maintain	/mein'tein/	*vt.*	to cause sth. to continue; to keep sth. in existence at the same level, standard, etc. 保持；维持
complaint	/kəm'pleint/	*n.*	[C, U] a statement that sb. makes saying that they are not satisfied 抱怨；埋怨
urgent	/'ɜːdʒənt/	*a.*	needing immediate attention, action or decision 紧急的；迫切的
hesitate	/'heziteit/	*v.*	to be slow to speak or act because one feels uncertain or unwilling; to pause in doubt 犹豫；踌躇；迟疑
immaturity	/imə'tjuərəti/	*n.*	[U] not (yet) fully developed or grown 不成熟；未完全
perform	/pə'fɔːm/	*vt.*	to do (a piece of work, sth. one is ordered to do, sth. one has agreed to do) 做，执行，履行（某事）
		vi.	to work or function（指机器等）工作，运转

✿ New Expressions

resort to	to make use of sth. for help; to adopt sth. as an expedient 求助于，诉诸于
wonder at	to be very surprised by sth. 感到诧异；非常惊讶
make use of	to use sb. or sth., especially to get an advantage 使用
according to	in a manner that is consistent with (sth.) 按照，依照
bring about	to make sth. happen 导致；引起
give way to	to be replaced by sth. else 被……取代
have an effect on	to make a change that is produced in one person or thing by another 对……产生作用
ferret about	to search for sth. that is lost or hidden among a lot of things 搜索，四处搜寻

| **apart from** | in addition to sb. or sth. 除……之外；此外 |
| **back off** | to stop supporting sth., or decide not to do sth. you were planning to do 放弃；退出 |

Reading Comprehension

Understanding the text

I. Answer the following questions.

1. According to the author, what is cloud computing?

2. What's the function of DPC according to the text?

3. What does Thomas Watson mean by saying that "the world will then need five computers in all" in Para. 4?

4. What did Microsoft do after Google released its Google Apps?

5. What is the major barrier for us to use cloud computing everywhere? Give an example to illustrate it.

6. What's the consequence of the accident happened to one of Amazon's services—Simple Storage Service?

7. What do you think of the author's attitude toward cloud computing?

Critical thinking

II. Work in pairs and discuss the following questions.

1. Do you think cloud computing can totally change the ways we store data information? Why or why not?

2. How do you evaluate the effect cloud computing brings to our lives?

3. What's your attitude toward the technology of cloud computing?

4. What prospect can you predict about cloud computing?

Language Focus

Words in use

III. Fill in the blanks with the words given below. Change the form where necessary. Each word can be used only once.

| equivalent | parallel | sensible | peculiar | maintain |
| convenience | predict | witness | label | radical |

1. I can't bear those people who make judgments and _____ me.

2. You can improve your chances of profit by _____ planning.

3. These economies will no doubt _____ their dominance of financial markets.

4. Friends of the dead lawyer were quick to draw some _____ points between two murders.

5. Many of these poems bear _____ to his years spent in India and China.

6. Even the cheapest car costs the _____ of 5 years' salary for a government worker.

7. Please return at your earliest _____ the manuscript submitted to you for approval.

8. We observe that the first calls for _____ transformation did not begin until the period of the industrial revolution.

9. It is yet premature to _____ the possible outcome of the dialogue.

10. He has _____ features and penetrating views in literary creation.

Word building

The suffix *-ic* combines with nouns to form adjectives. Adjectives formed in this way describe something as resembling, involving, or being connected with the thing referred to by the original noun.

Examples

Words learned	Add *-ic*	New words formed
chaos	→	chaotic
drama	→	dramatic
academy	→	academic
atom	→	atomic
electron	→	electronic

The suffix *-ion* combines with verbs to form nouns. Nouns formed in this way refer to the state or process described by the verb, or to an instance of that process.

Note: There are a number of variations of the spelling of *-ion*. The most common ones are *-ation*, *-ition*, *-sion* and *-tion*.

Examples

Words learned	Add *-ion*	New words formed
depress	→	depression
detect	→	detection
erode	→	erosion

The suffix *-ist* occurs in nouns which refer to a person whose behavior is based on a particular belief or a person who does a particular kind of work. For example, a feminist is someone who believes that women should have the same rights, power and opportunities as men; a scientist is someone who works in the field of science.

Examples

Words learned	Add *-ist*	New words formed
social	→	socialist
piano	→	pianist
human	→	humanist
right	→	rightist

IV. Add -ic, -ion, or -ist to or remove them from the following words to form new words.

Words learned	New words formed
-ic	
economy	
history	
artist	
-ion	
compensate	
contribute	
classify	
confusion	
cooperation	
dictation	

Continued

Words learned	New words formed
-ist	
economy	
capital	
novel	

V. Fill in the blanks with the newly-formed words in Activity IV. Change the form where necessary. Each word can be used only once.

1. The _____ building is as much part of our heritage as the paintings.

2. Ask for an extra _____ payment to make up for the stress you have suffered.

3. His competence as a(n) _____ had been reinforced by his successful fight against inflation.

4. The writer has sold out his _____ standards and now just writes for a living.

5. Developing of production and promoting of social progress are common target for both _____ and workers.

6. As _____ can improve students' comprehensive language ability, it has been widely applied in English teaching.

7. We are doing this work in the context of reforms in the _____, social and cultural spheres.

8. Only by writing things down could I bring some sort of order to the _____.

9. A great _____ or non-fiction writer who died at 28 might not have yet produced her or his magnum opus.

10. Such policies would require unprecedented _____ between these two nations.

11. Other successful countries like India and Brazil have made a big _____ to that result as well.

12. This article discussed two data mining algorithms: the _____ tree and clustering.

Banked cloze

VI. Fill in the blanks by selecting suitable words from the word bank. You may not use any of the words more than once.

A. equivalent	B. offered	C. superior	D. reinforce	E. favorite
F. sensible	G. upload	H. security	I. sharing	J. acceptable
K. crashes	L. sitting	M. far	N. creating	O. acquaint

The simplest thing that a computer does is to allow us to store and retrieve information. We can store our family photographs, our 1) _____ songs, or even save movies on it. This is also the most basic service 2) _____ by cloud computing.

Flickr is a great example of cloud computing as a service. While Flickr started with an emphasis on 3) _____ photos and images, it has emerged as a great place to store those images. In many ways, it is 4) _____ to storing the images on your computer.

First, Flickr allows you to easily access your images no matter where you are or what type of device you are using. While you might 5) _____ the photos of your vacation to Greece from your home computer, you can easily access them from your laptop while on the road or even from your iPhone while 6) _____ in your local coffee house. Second, Flickr lets you share the images. There's no need to burn them to a compact disc or save them on a flash drive. You can just send someone your Flickr address. Third, Flickr provides data 7) _____. If you keep your photos on your local computer, what happens if your hard drive 8) _____? You'd better hope you backed them up to a CD or a flash drive! By uploading the images to Flickr, you are providing yourself with data security by 9) _____ a backup on the web. And while it is always best to keep a local copy—either on your computer, a compact disc or a flash drive—the truth is that you are 10) _____ more likely to lose the images you store locally than Flickr is of losing your images.

Expressions in use

VII. Fill in the blanks with the expressions given below. Change the form where necessary. Each expression can be used only once.

wonder at	make use of	back off	resort to
give way to	have an effect on	ferret about	apart from
bring about	according to		

1. Human beings in all times and places think about their world and _____ their place in it.

2. You can offer your help to others but _____ if they appear to be offended by your persistence.

3. The individual colors within the light spectrum are believed to _____ health.

4. _____ criminal investigation techniques, students learn forensic medicine, philosophy and logic.

5. The testers also can _____ his expertise and experience to determine weak spots and

high-risk areas.

6. The move stopped the pound's decline but failed to _____ a significant rally.

7. It helps if we remember that life is one phase after another and that this difficult time will inevitably _____ something new and different.

8. We should apply advanced experience _____ local conditions and shouldn't apply it mechanically.

9. She nonetheless continued to _____ for possible clues.

10. They have responsibility to ensure that all peaceful options are exhausted before the army _____ war.

Structure Analysis and Writing

Structure Analysis

Focus on an advantage / disadvantage essay

In Unit 1, you learned about the structure of an essay that contains introduction, body, and conclusion. Starting from this unit, you will focus on a particular writing method to write about a certain topic. This time you will expect to learn how to write an advantage / disadvantage essay.

Generally speaking, the outline of writing an advantage / disadvantage essay falls in one of these three formats: 1) advantages and disadvantages; 2) advantages only; 3) disadvantages only. When you write such an essay, remember that you are giving information, a method that is called exposition or expository writing.

Begin your essay by introducing your topic and explaining that you are exploring the advantages or disadvantages of the topic. Mention in your thesis statement the advantages or disadvantages you will discuss in the essay. Use transitions to make your ideas flow smoothly. The following transitional words are very common when writing an advantage / disadvantage essay.

Firstly, ...

Another advantage is that...

In other words,...

Finally, ...

This means that...

In conclusion, ...

It is also...

To sum up, ...

Conclude your essay with the summary of the advantages and / or disadvantages. Even though you are not persuading your readers when you write this type of writing, you are required to add your opinion at the end as your final comment on the topic. For example, if you're talking about the advantages of employing cloud computing in your daily life, you may say the following in your conclusion.

To sum up, by employing cloud computing, we are provided with a sage data storing center. Hardware requirement is reduced to the lowest level, working efficiency is promoted, and the costs is greatly reduced. We should be aware of the significance of employing cloud computing.

You can always choose a position when you write about an advantage / disadvantage essay. For instance, you don't have to talk about both advantages and disadvantages of something or doing something. Instead, you can only focus on one, the advantages or disadvantages of that or doing that.

Now, examine how this method of writing is reflected in Text A, especially Paragraphs 4–11.

Introduction: *Regarded as the next technological revolution, cloud computing will have an radical effect on our business model and working way. And many IT tycoons speak very highly of it.* (Para. 4)

Body (advantages and disadvantages of employing cloud computing):

Cloud computing provides us with a safe data storing center. (Para. 5)

Cloud computing reduces hardware requirement to the lowest level. (Para. 6)

With the powerful processing capability of a large number of servers' union, cloud computing promotes working efficiency and reduces the costs greatly. (Para. 7)

Although cloud computing is used everywhere, a major barrier to it is the interoperability of applications. (Para. 8)

Apart from the fact that Google probably doesn't want you to have the ability to insert a competitor's document into their spreadsheet, this creates a ton of data security issues. (Para. 9)

Conclusion: *Cloud computing changes everything. We can predict we could get the same information and perform the same tasks whether we are at work, at home, or even a friend's house.* (Para. 11)

From what is listed above, we can see that writing an essay about the advantages or disadvantages of an issue requires supporting points. If your essay focuses on advantages or disadvantages of employing cloud computing in daily life, then several advantages or disadvantages should be provided to support your points.

Structured Writing

Read the sample essay and see how the advantages and disadvantages are introduced.

Topic	Sample essay
The advantages and disadvantages of technological change	Nowadays, our society develops very rapidly accompanied by the changes of technology, which lead to the appearance of both various kinds of new products and problems. While some people hold the idea that the technological changes make our life more convenient, some people think that technological changes make our life worse.
Introduction	As for the advantages, firstly, we cannot deny the fact that our life has become more and more convenient thanks to those technological inventions. Nowadays, many modern traffic means enable us to travel all over the world in much less time than ever before. Computers—the most widely used tool currently enable us to communicate with other people as convenient as possible and make us work with more efficiency. Secondly, technological changes have cleared up many matters that were mysterious to us in the past. We now know that volcanic eruption, thunder and lightening are not caused by the angry god but the normal natural phenomena. As a result, a large number of harmful superstitions have disappeared and we can try our best to minimize the damage of some natural disasters.
Thesis statement: While some people hold the idea that the technological changes make our life more convenient, some people think that technological changes make our life worse.	
Body	
Advantage 1: We cannot deny the fact that our life has become more and more convenient thanks to those technological inventions.	
Advantage 2: Technological changes have cleared up many matters that were mysterious to us in the past.	
Disadvantage 1: We can easily find that the more we use technology the worse of environment and human health would be.	In terms of disadvantages, firstly, we can easily find that the more we use technology the worse of environment and human health would be. The more cars in the streets the more harmful gas will be released and will descend the air quality. The most important is that we cannot live without technology like computer, mobile phone, and nuclear power plant which is used to generate electricity for our daily use and can also produce a lot of harmful radiation. And all the above disadvantages are bad to our health. Secondly, technological changes have been accompanied by a decline in the traditional culture, which means the gradual destruction of our unique civilization.
Disadvantage 2: Technological changes has been accompanied by a decline in the traditional culture.	
Conclusion	
If we could fully recognize the problems, minimize the destruction as much as much, and make a great use of the benefits, we would live a happy and beautiful life without any regrets for now and most importantly, for the future.	

	In conclusion, everything has two sides. If we could fully recognize the problems, minimize the destruction as much as possible, and make a great use of the benefits, we would live a happy and beautiful life without any regrets for now and most importantly, for the future.

VIII. Write an essay of no less than 150 words on one of the following topics. One topic has an outline that you can follow.

Topic

Advantages and disadvantages of mobile phones

Introduction

Thesis statement: Some people think that mobile phones bring more disadvantages than its benefits whist others think with opposite trend.

Body

Advantage 1: Mobile phones make everyone closer only by a click of the key.

Advantage 2: Mobile phones provide us with more convenient way of entertainment.

Advantage 3: Mobile phones enable us to search and find answers as quickly as possible.

Disadvantage 1: Sometimes we get phone harassment in our daily life.

Disadvantage 2: With the focus on mobile phones we neglect our family and friends.

Disadvantage 3: We become lazier with the use of mobile phones.

Conclusion

We should take an objective angle to treat mobile phones.

More topics:

● Advantages and disadvantages of Facebook

● Advantages and disadvantages of the Internet

Translation

IX. Translate the following paragraph into Chinese.

A MOOC (massive open online course) is an online course aimed at unlimited participation and open access via the web. MOOCs are a recent development in distance education and have now become a surging trend in higher education. These classes are aimed at expanding a university's reach from thousands of tuition-paying students who live in town, to millions of students around the world. In addition to traditional course materials, MOOCs provide interactive user forums to support interactions between students and professors. MOOCs can encourage communication among participants who bring a variety of viewpoints, knowledge, and skills to the course, inspire people to "try on" subjects that they wouldn't otherwise pursue or even try on education itself, provide multiple ways to engage with course material, encourage multi-modal learning that can address the needs of learners with a variety of learning styles, and inspire better teaching and use of technologies for face-to-face courses.

X. Translate the following paragraph into English.

饺子（Jiaozi）是人们在北方常年吃的主要食物之一。饺子的发音听起来与最早的纸币的名字相似，所以吃饺子被认为会带来幸运。很多家庭在除夕夜吃饺子。有些厨师会藏一枚干净的硬币在里面，让幸运的人找到它。常见的饺子肉馅包括猪肉、牛肉、鸡肉以及鱼肉，这些肉馅通常会与切碎的蔬菜混合在一起。

Section

Reading Skills: *Understanding Figurative Language*

To make language more interesting and entertaining, we often use expressions which are not literally true. For example, we use figurative language in speaking and writing. Figurative language can be confusing if it is understood literally. The ability to recognize and interpret or explain figurative language can help us fully understand a writer's point.

There are different ways of using figurative language. Listed below are just a few of them.

1. Simile (明喻 / 直喻): a figurative expression which directly compares one thing to another by using the words *as* or *like*, such as *as white as snow*.

2. Personification (拟人化): a figurative expression which compares non-human things to human.

3. Parallelism (平行结构): also known as parallel structure or parallel construction; a balance within one or more sentences of similar phrases or clauses that have the same grammatical structure.

Now, let's take a look at the following examples from Text A.

Example 1:

Companies around the world have witnessed this technology. (Para. 3)

Example 2:

Just like money being saved in banks, our data will be protected by the most professional team. (Para. 5)

Example 3:

We no longer need to update our computer configuration for using a new OS; we no longer need to ferret about on the net for proper software for editing files of certain format. (Para. 6)

From the three examples we can see the first one is personification because the sentence compares non-human things (companies) to humans (only living things can witness). The second one is definitely a simile since it compares saving information through cloud computing to saving money in banks directly using the phrase *just like*. The third one is a parallelism because the two sentences use the same "*we no longer need to...*" structure.

The following sentences are from Text B. Fill in the blanks with your own words to explain the figurative language and also indicate in brackets which particular way is used.

1. *While Homer's Trojan War was fought to determine the future of trade across the Hellespont, today's cyber war will determine the future of e-commerce and IT services in the cloud.* (Para. 3)

   Explanation:

   _____

   _____ (   )

2. *This approach is equivalent to modern day email phishing attacks.* (Para. 4)

   Explanation:

   _____

   _____ (   )

3. *For many cloud systems and applications, passwords are like the Achilles heel.* (Para. 6)

   Explanation:

   _____

   _____ (   )

4. *Helen was famed for her beauty, so much so that her face launched a thousand ships.* (Para. 9)

   Explanation:

   _____

   _____ (   )

Text B

Securing the Cloud: How to Avoid a Greek Tragedy?

1. In early 2014, *Cloud Odyssey: A Hero's Quest*—a movie about the heroic journey of an ordinary man embracing the cloud was released. While the movie is set in the future, the name of the movie **alludes** to Homer's epic tale, *the Odyssey*, which **chronicles** the journey of Odysseus, king of Ithaca, returning home from the Trojan War.

2. With the cloud technology becoming more and more important, like Odysseus, IT organizations preparing to adopt cloud solutions must have a **feasible** strategy and battle plan to secure the cloud. Today's cloud heroes—the CIOs and IT staffers who are **venturing** bravely into the cloud—must put controls in place to secure private information and applications from the possible **siege** of hostile users and hackers.

3. While Homer's Trojan War was fought to determine the future of trade across the

Hellespont, today's cyber war will determine the future of e-commerce and IT services in the cloud. In *Iliad* (the prequel to *Odyssey*), the most valuable assets were **precious** metals and jewels; today our valuable assets are customer data, financial data, **commercial** data and intellectual **property**. Indeed, there are lessons to be learned from the siege of ancient Troy that can be applied to securing the cloud.

Beware of Greeks bearing gifts

4. After realizing the walls of Troy could not be **breached**, Odysseus created a giant **hollow** wooden horse, hiding attackers within, as a victory gift to the Trojans. The Trojans accepted the gift without **hesitation** and brought the horse inside the walls of Troy only to awake and find the city sacked. This approach is equivalent to modern day email **phishing** attacks.

5. Today we use the term "Trojan" to describe **malware** that gains special access to a system or application. Researchers at the University of Wisconsin have shown how software in one part of the cloud can be used to spy on tenants in another part of the cloud. To detect these, organizations can use access management software, which can find **anomalous** activities and privileged access control software to manage **administrative** and super user accounts in systems and applications. By applying adaptive access, organizations can **dramatically** reduce their attack surface.

Protect the Achilles heel

6. Achilles, the greatest hero of the war, is famous for being **invulnerable** except for his heel. For many cloud systems and applications, passwords are like the Achilles heel. Eighty percent of attacks target weak passwords and that's a problem because 40 percent of users don't use strong passwords. It is **demonstrated** that passwords are a frequent cause and target when databases are attacked because stolen passwords can be used to follow on attacks. Based on the estimate from multiple sources, so far more than 60 million passwords have been stolen from cloud applications. The weakness is **compounded** by the transmission of passwords in clear text behind the firewall where we assume they are safe. This problem is easily addressed with a few simple controls like regular password changes, strong password policies, multi-factor authentication and step-up authentication. According to Verizon, 76 percent of network **intrusions** use weak or stolen **credentials**.

Heed the warnings of Cassandra

7. The princess of Troy, Cassandra, warned the Trojans not to bring the horse into the city, only to be ignored. The term Cassandra has become a metaphor when valid warnings are disbelieved or ignored, and many security professionals know the feeling. With many cyber attacks the evidence was in plain sight only to be lost in the trifles of data. For example, in 69 percent of breaches the victim organization was informed of the attack by a third party. Yet, despite these statistics, 35 percent of organizations adopting SaaS applications do not evaluate application security. Organizations shouldn't **surrender** themselves to a **series** of attacks. With a few simple solutions on attacks, they can regain control.

Protect the crown jewels

8. After the fall of Troy, the Greek armies **plundered** the **miserable** city. Today, the motive for cyber attackers is often economic. Hackers take any data that may be of economic value from credit cards and social security numbers to intellectual property. **Perimeter** security isn't enough. For most organizations, 66 percent of the most valuable data reside in databases. Despite this, a recent PWC study showed that 53 percent of organizations don't take special measures to secure their databases. At the same time, 43 percent of the most serious attacks are SQL injection attacks aimed at relational databases. That's a recipe for disaster. The most effective solution is a **comprehensive** database security suite with **preventive**, detective and administrative solutions to secure your most valuable assets. According to a recent Gartner forecast, **encryption** can reduce the cost of cloud security by 30 percent.

Don't launch a thousand ships

9. The Trojan War began when Paris of Troy stole Helen, the wife of Menelaus, who was the king of Sparta. Helen was famed for her beauty, so much so that her face launched a thousand ships. Today that kind of excess is out of the question. If the cost of securing the cloud **outweighs** the economic benefits gained, the business case will be **derailed**. Cloud security requires good identity and access governance and database security.

10. The moral to this story is that the success of the IT journey to the cloud depends on reliable security. The good news is that 97 percent of security risks are preventable and with a few properly exercised controls, cloud environments can be made more secure than the "topless towers of Ilium".

(906 words)

Notes

Homer: a name ascribed by the Ancient Greeks to the semi-legendary author of the two epic poems, *Iliad* and *Odyssey*, the central works of Greek literature.

Homer's Trojan War: In Greek mythology, the Trojan War was waged against the city of Troy by the Achaeans (Greeks) after Paris of Troy took Helen from her husband Menelaus, king of Sparta. The war is one of the most important events in Greek mythology and has been narrated through many works of Greek literature, most notably through Homer's *Iliad*. *Iliad* relates a part of the last year of the siege of Troy; *Odyssey* describes the journey home of Odysseus, one of the war's heroes. Other parts of the war are described in a cycle of epic poems, which have survived through fragments. Episodes from the war provided material for Greek tragedy and other works of Greek literature, and for Roman poets including *Virgil* and *Ovid*.

University of Wisconsin: a public research university in Madison, Wisconsin, United States.

Hellespont: a narrow, natural strait and internationally-significant waterway in northwestern

Turkey that forms part of the continental boundary between Europe and Asia, and separates Asian Turkey from European Turkey.

Achilles: a Greek hero of the Trojan War and the central character and greatest warrior of Homer's *Iliad*.

Verizon: a broadband telecommunications company and the largest US wireless communications service provider.

SaaS: (Software as a service) a software licensing and delivery model in which software is licensed on a subscription basis and is centrally hosted.

Face launched a thousand ships: a figure of speech that stands for Helen of Troy. Helen of Troy (formerly of Sparta) was so beautiful that Greek men went to Troy and fought the Trojan War to win Helen back from Paris. The thousand ships refer to the Greek troops that set sail from Aulis to Troy where the Trojan prince Paris had taken Menelaus' wife, Helen.

🔊 New Words

allude	/ə'luːd/	*vi.*	(*fml.*) to mention sb. or sth. without talking about them directly 影射，暗指
chronicle	/'krɒnikl/	*vt.*	to record (sth.) in a chronicle 将⋯⋯载入编年史
		n.	[C] a written record of historical events 编年史；年代记；大事记
feasible	/'fiːzəbl/	*a.*	possible or likely to succeed 可行的；可能的
venture	/'ventʃə(r)/	*v.*	to risk going somewhere or doing sth. that might be dangerous or unpleasant, or to risk saying sth. that might be criticized 冒险
		n.	[C] a new activity, usually in business, which involves risk or uncertainty 企业；投机活动；商业冒险
siege	/siːdʒ/	*n.*	[C, U] the surrounding of a place by an armed force in order to defeat those defending it 围攻；包围
precious	/'preʃəs/	*a.*	of great value (and beauty) 贵重的；宝贵的
commercial	/kə'mɜːʃl/	*a.*	related to business and the buying and selling of goods and services 商业的；商务的
property	/'prɒpəti/	*n.*	1. [U] an object or objects that belong to someone 所有物；财产；资产 2. [C, U] a building or area of land, or both together 房产；地产；房地产 3. [U] specialized the legal right to own and use something 财产权；所有权
breach	/briːtʃ/	*vt.*	1. to make an opening in a wall or fence, especially in order to attack someone or something behind it 突破；攻破 2. to break a law, promise, agreement or relationship 破坏，违犯；违反
		n.	[C] an act of breaking a law, promise, agreement or relationship 破坏；违反

hollow	/'hɔləʊ/	*a.*	1. empty inside 空的；中空的；空心的 2. with no real meaning 无意义的；虚有其表的
hesitation	/ˌhezi'teiʃn/	*n.*	[C, U] when you pause before doing something, especially because you are nervous or not certain 犹豫，踌躇
phishing	/'fiʃin/	*n.*	[U] an attempt to trick someone who has an internet bank account into giving information that would allow someone else to take money out of the account "网络钓鱼"（骗取他人网上银行账户的有关信息从而盗取他人资金的行为）
malware	/'mælweər/	*n.*	[U] computer software that is designed to damage the way a computer works 恶意软件
anomalous	/ə'nɔmələs/	*a.*	deviating from the general or common order or type 异常的；不规则的；不恰当的
administrative	/əd'ministrətiv/	*a.*	relating to the arrangements and work which is needed to control the operation of a plan or organization 管理的；行政的
dramatically	/drə'mætikli/	*a.*	1. suddenly or obviously 剧烈地；明显地 2. acting in a play 戏剧性地；夸张地
invulnerable	/in'vʌlnərəbl/	*a.*	impossible to damage or hurt in any way 无法伤害的；无法损坏的
demonstrate	/'demənˌstreit/	*vt.*	1. to show or prove sth. clearly 说明；证明；证实；论证 2. to show or describe how to do sth. or how sth. works 示范；演示
compound	/'kɔmpaʊnd/	*vt.*	1. to make a problem or difficult situation worse 使加重，使加剧，使恶化 2. to mix two things together 使混合；使复合
		n.	[C] (*fml.*) something consisting of two or more different parts 复合物；混合物
		a.	consisting of two or more substances or ingredients or elements or parts 复合的；混合的
intrusion	/in'truːʒn/	*n.*	[C, U] the act of entering a place which is private or where you may not be wanted 闯入；侵入
credential	/kri'denʃl/	*n.*	[C] document showing that a person is what he claims to be, is trustworthy, etc. 证明书、证件
surrender	/sə'rendə/	*vi.*	to say officially that you want to stop fighting, because you realize that you can't win 投降
series	/'siəriːz/	*n.*	[C, usu. *sing.*] (*pl.* series) (a ~ of) a set of similar things that follow one after another 系列
plunder	/'plʌndə/	*vt.*	1. to steal goods violently from a place, especially during a war 掠夺，抢劫，劫掠 2. to steal or remove something precious from something, in a way that does not consider moral laws or is more severe than it need be 骗取；窃取；侵吞，侵占
miserable	/'miz(ə)rəbl/	*a.*	extremely unhappy or uncomfortable 苦恼的；痛苦的；难受的

perimeter	/pə'rimitə(r)/	*n.*	[C] boundary of an area 周围的界限
comprehensive	/kɔmpri'hensiv/	*a.*	complete and including everything that is necessary 全面的；综合的；详尽的
preventive	/pri'ventiv/	*a.*	intended to stop something before it happens 防止的，预防的
encryption	/in'kripʃn/	*n.*	[U] the action of encrypting 编密码；加密
outweigh	/ˌaut'wei/	*vt.*	to be greater in weight, value or importance than (sth.) 超过
derail	/di'reil/	*v.*	to (make a train) run off the track（使）（火车）出轨

✿ New Expressions

be equivalent to	equal to 等（同）于；相等（当）于……
spy on	to keep watch secretly 暗中监视；侦察；窥探
be famous for	widely known and esteemed 因……而著名
in plain sight	as plain as the nose on your face 显而易见；一览无遗
surrender oneself to	to allow oneself to be controlled or influenced by sth. 听任某事摆布；屈服于某事
a series of	a sequence of 一系列的；一连串的
reside in	to dwell 居住；存在于
be aimed at	to have sth. as an aim 目的是；旨在
out of the question	totally unlikely 不可能；不知底细；根本谈不上

Reading Comprehension

Understanding the text

I. Choose the best answer to each of the following questions.

1. According to the text, the term "Trojan" is cited by the author _____.

    A. to mean the malware that gains privileged access to a system or application

    B. to mean the software that supports a system or application

    C. to mean a war that was fought to determine the future of trade

    D. to mean a geographical name

2. By means of _____, an organization can dramatically reduce their attack surface.

    A. supporting a new program   B. applying adaptive access

    C. setting a new password   D. offering effective anti-virus software

3. For many cloud systems and applications, what do the passwords mean?

    A. They mean the Warnings of Cassandra.   B. They mean Odysseus's gifts.

    C. They mean the Achilles heel.   D. They mean the Crown Jewels.

4. Why is password a frequent cause and target?

    A. Because passwords can be changed.

    B. Because passwords are easy to attack.

    C. Because stolen passwords can be used to steal money.

    D. Because stolen passwords can be used to follow on attacks.

5. Today, which of the following is the metaphor of Cassandra?

    A. Distrust of anyone.   B. Valid warnings that are disbelieved or ignored.

    C. A beautiful woman.   D. A fatal weakness.

6. What is probably the incentive for cyber attackers?

    A. Economic value.   B. Social value.

    C. Political value.   D. Environmental values.

7. What is the most effective solution to protecting a database?

    A. Encrypting databases.

    B. Building a comprehensive database security suite with preventive, detective and administrative solutions to secure all the things.

    C. Installing security system.

    D. Building a comprehensive database security suite with preventive, detective and administrative solutions to secure the most valuable assets.

8. Cloud security requires the following factors EXCEPT _____ .

    A. good identity   B. access governance

    C. database security   D. policy support

Critical thinking

II. Work in pairs and discuss the following questions.

1. What do you know about the importance of cloud security?

2. In your opinion, what are the incentives for hackers?

3. Have you ever experienced hackers' attacks to your IT products?

4. In your opinion, what can you do to secure your cloud?

Language Focus

Words in use

III. Fill in the blanks with the words given below. Change the form where necessary. Each word can be used only once.

hesitation	invulnerable	comprehensive	demonstrate	miserable
commercial	valid	feasible	surrender	hollow

1. London in its heyday was a major center of industrial and _____ activities.

2. He should have fought for his rights, but he _____ to political pressure.

3. She questioned whether it was _____ to stimulate investment in these regions.

4. Space scientists believe that the black hole is _____, and would draw everything toward its center.

5. They were born with magic power and were as _____ as the immortals of Olympus.

6. I use this example to simply _____ the principle.

7. A really bad cold pulls you down and leaves you feeling very _____.

8. He promised there would be no more _____ in pursuing reforms.

9. We need a(n) _____ assessment of the issue of DNA combination, preferably under the auspices of the federal government.

10. Most designers share the unspoken belief that fashion is a(n) _____ form of visual art.

Expressions in use

IV. Fill in the blanks with the expressions given below. Change the form where necessary. Each expression can be used only once.

be equivalent to	in plain sight	aim at
a series of	reside in	be famous for
out of the question	spy on	surrender oneself to

1. Sometimes nodding your head _____ saying " yes".

2. The fountain of Rome _____ their architectural beauty.

3. She _____ despair and committed suicide eventually.

4. For the homeless, private medical care is simply _____.

5. When the cloud is public, the enterprise and provider _____ different networks.

6. I can't believe I left my diary _____, what if my girlfriend reads it?

7. In his latest collection of poems readers are confronted with _____ reflections on rebirth.

8. I thought you were a new customer and now I know that you only came to _____ me and my menu.

9. Republican strategists are taking particular _____ Democratic senators.

Sentence structure

V. Rewrite the following sentences by using the independent structure "with + n. + v.-ing". Make changes where necessary.

> **Model:** As the cloud technology has become more and more important, IT organizations preparing to adopt cloud solutions must have a feasible strategy and battle plan to secure the cloud.
>
> → With the cloud technology becoming more and more important, IT organizations preparing to adopt cloud solutions must have a feasible strategy and battle plan to secure the cloud.

1. As more and more Chinese people buy cars, much more oil will be consumed.

    _____

2. As the Internet has become increasingly popular for young people to connect with their friends, letter writing is becoming less and less common.

    _____

3. She stood there chatting with her friend, and her child was playing beside her.

    _____

VI. *Complete the following sentences by translating the Chinese into English, using the independent structure "with + n. + prepositional phrase".*

> **Model:** _____ (通过几个解决入侵的方法), they can regain control.
>
> → <u>With a few solutions on attacks</u>, they can regain control.

1. He sat there thinking, _____ (手托着下巴).

2. _____ (这种大衣已过时了), people don't wear them any more.

3. _____ (在人生观和价值观上存在差异), the couple seemed to live in two different worlds.

Unit 4
Information Leaks
—So Many "Yous"
in Your Life

To err is human, but to really foul things up you need a computer.

— *Paul Ehrlich (German physician and scientist)*

A computer lets you make more mistakes faster than any invention in human history—with the possible exceptions of handguns and tequila.

— *Mitch Radcliffe (American computer scientist)*

Preview

With the rapid development of computer technology, information leakage has been a real and growing problem which can cause a lot of trouble. For example, we may get lots of junk messages which are not welcomed. What's worse, we may lose our money or leak important personal information which can be used by identity thieves to commit crimes. Facing these information security problems, how can we protect our privacy? If our personal information leaks, what should we do to deal with it? Should we pay attention to it or just ignore it? Consider your own feelings about information leakage and get ready to give your insights to respond to these questions.

Section

Pre-reading Activities

I. *Look at the set of pictures regarding the ways of information leakage. Match the number of each picture in the left column with the particular way of information leakage in the right column.*

Pictures	Types
2	online shopping
1	online registration
4	applying for VIP or membership cards
3	online banking

II. Work in pairs and discuss the following questions.

1. Have you ever experienced personal information leakage? If yes, how does it impact your life?

2. Besides the four ways in the above pictures, do you know any other ways that may cause information leakage?

To Catch an Identity Thief (Part I)

1. Karen Lodrick ordered a latte at Starbucks while waiting nervously for the bank on San Francisco's Market Street to open. She displayed her anxiety and was **distracted** but couldn't help noticing the **scruffy**-looking pair standing next to her: a tall man wearing a navy baseball jacket and a large woman in jeans and Gucci glasses, carrying a brown suede coat and a Prada purse. Karen stared at the woman for a while because she looked **vaguely** familiar.

2. That coat! A cold **tingle** of fear ran through Karen as she took it all in. The distinctive fur trim along its edges looked as **unkempt** as the woman who held it. And then—bingo—she knew. Karen's ID had been stolen five months before. Her bank account had been emptied, and her life sent reeling out of control. The coat she was looking at was the same one she'd seen in the bank surveillance tape, worn by the woman who'd stolen Karen's ID.

3. Karen followed the pair onto the **patio** and watched as they settled at a round table under a window **awning**. She called 911, asked a police officer meet her, and then settled at the next table, pretending not to watch and wait.

4. A cell call from her friend Ed Fuentes interrupted her thoughts. She walked toward the **hedges** that bordered the Starbucks patio, out of earshot of the pair, and told him her **suspicions**.

5. The large woman and her **companion** stole glances at Karen, looking increasingly nervous and **cautious**. Then they got up from the table and separated, which didn't take Karen by surprise. The man turned south. The woman **proceeded** to north.

6. "Ed, I've got to go," she told her friend. "I've got to follow her."

7. "Don't take the **liberty** of doing anything crazy, Karen," said Fuentes. "She could have a gun."

8. "I've got to do it." She feared that if she didn't **commence** to act, the identity thief would disappear, along with any hope of ending her bad dream. The chase was on.

9. For five months, the thief had dipped into Karen's accounts like they were her own private bank. She got a **scam** of thousands of dollars more, using credit cards she opened in Karen's name. The banks were unable to stop her. The police could do nothing. Creditors demanded payment for the thief's transactions. Consequently, Karen closed her accounts, only to have the **criminal** crack open the new ones she'd opened and **drain** those too.

10. The woman turned a corner. Karen's phone rang. The caller ID said "unknown caller". Karen looked up the street and saw that the woman had her cell phone out. Could she be checking to see if the real Karen Lodrick was on her tail? And where were the police?

11. Karen again called 911 as the woman took off up the hill, looking over her shoulder at Karen every few seconds.

12. "I need somebody to come to Buchanan and Market," Karen **lodged** a request to the 911 operator who answered. "She is running. I need the police."

13. "What's the problem, ma'am?"

14. "This woman has been taking my identity. For the last five months, I have started to be **pessimistic** about my life. It's been a living hell."

15. There was a **weird** voice mail from Karen's bank when she returned home to San Francisco in November from a family **reunion** in Michigan. Karen called back, and the service rep asked if she'd made any large **withdrawals** and mentioned one in the amount of $600. Karen assumed it was a bank error and asked the rep to check the **debit** card number.

16. "That's not my card," she said.

17. The bank representative insisted—**mistakenly**, as Karen later learned—that someone had called from Karen's phone to order the new debit card. After much back-and-forth, Karen **convinced** the rep that it wasn't hers, and he **canceled** it. What he failed to make clearer was that a second new debit card had been issued on her account. And it was still open.

18. Concerned after the bank rep told her the order that came from her phone, Karen started to remember several months ago, she used her phone number to register an email account which was bound to receive the emails from the bank. For the last five months, when Karen logined the email account, the same message always appeared showing that her email account was possibly logined at another site, therefore suggested Karen change the email password to avoid leaking important information. She didn't pay any attention to it or did anything about it. The identity thief had **apparently** hacked into Karen's email account and stolen at least four envelopes: two with debit

cards and two that provided the debit card PINs.

19. As far as Karen knew, the thief had stolen $600. Bad enough, but not life-altering. It wasn't until she got to the bank, and a **representative** turned the computer screen around for her to see, that she understood what had occurred. Screen after screen showed dozens of withdrawals, just over the past few days. About $10,000 was gone. Karen's balance was zero. Her **overdraft** protection plan had automatically **deducted** another $1,200 from savings to cover the shortfall after the thief had cleaned out the checking account.

20. Karen filed a police report, closed her now-empty account and submitted a claim. She tried her best to be immune to the troubles, but with no money to cover checks, she couldn't pay her bills, her rent. She couldn't even buy **groceries**. Late fees were compounded by black marks on her credit report. She didn't **deserve** to suffer all of that, but it was just the beginning.

(to be continued)

(938 words)

☉ New Words

distracted	/dɪˈstræktɪd/	*a.*	unable to pay attention to sb./sth., because you are worried or thinking about sth. else 心烦意乱的，思想不集中的
scruffy	/ˈskrʌfi/	*a.*	dirty or untidy 邋遢的
vaguely	/ˈveɪgli/	*a.*	1. slightly 稍微地 2. in a way that is not detailed or exact 不清晰地；模糊地 3. in a way that shows that you are not paying attention or thinking clearly 含糊地
tingle	/ˈtɪŋgəl/	*n.*	1. [C] an exciting or uncomfortable feeling of emotion 激动 2. [U] a slight stinging or uncomfortable feeling in a part of your body 刺痛
		vi.	1. (of a part of your body) to feel as if a lot of small sharp points are pushing into it 感到刺痛 2. ~ **with sth.** to feel an emotion strongly 强烈地感到
unkempt	/ʌnˈkempt/	*a.*	not kept tidy; looking disheveled or neglected 不整洁的；凌乱的；疏于整理的
patio	/ˈpætiəʊ/	*n.*	1. [C] paved area next to a house where people can sit, eat, etc. outdoors 露台 2. [C] roofless courtyard within the walls of a Spanish or Spanish-American house (西班牙式或拉丁美洲式住宅的) 院子，天井
awning	/ˈɔːnɪŋ/	*n.*	[C] canvas or plastic sheet fixed to a wall above a door or window and stretched out as a protection against rain or sun 遮篷
hedge	/hedʒ/	*n.*	[C] row of bushes or shrubs planted close together and forming a boundary for a field, garden, etc. 树篱
suspicion	/səˈspɪʃn/	*n.*	[U] suspecting or being suspected 怀疑；涉嫌

companion	/kəm'pænɪən/	*n.*	[C] person or animal that goes with, or spends much time with, another 同伴
cautious	/'kɔːʃəs/	*a.*	~ (**about/of sb./sth.**) showing or having caution; careful 小心的；谨慎的；细心的
proceed	/prə'siːd/	*vi.*	1. to move in a particular direction 前进；移动 2. (*fml.*) to continue to do sth. that has already been planned or started 继续进行着；继续做
liberty	/'lɪbəti/	*n.*	1. [U] sth. you do without asking permission, esp. which may offend or upset sb. else 擅自的行为；冒犯的举动；放肆的行为 2. [C, U] the freedom and the right to do whatever you want without asking permission or being afraid of authority 自由；自由权
commence	/kə'mens/	*v.*	(*fml.*) to begin or start sth. 开始；着手
scam	/skæm/	*n.*	[C] dishonest scheme 骗局；欺诈
criminal	/'krɪmɪnəl/	*n.*	[C] person who commits a crime 罪犯；犯罪者
		a.	[only before noun] connected to the laws that deal with rime: criminal law 犯罪的
drain	/dreɪn/	*vt.*	to make sb./sth. weaker, poorer, etc. by gradually using up his/its strength, money, etc. 消耗；耗尽
		n.	[C] pipe or channel that carries away sewage or other unwanted liquid 下水管；下水道
lodge	/lɔdʒ/	*vt.*	to formally make sth. such as a complaint or claim 提出投诉、要求
		v.	to live somewhere temporarily; to pay rent to live in someone else's house, or provide sb. with a place to live 借住；提供住宿
pessimistic	/ˌpesə'mɪstɪk/	*a.*	~ (**about sth.**) expecting bad things to happen or sth. not to be successful 悲观的；悲观主义的
weird	/wɪəd/	*a.*	(*infml.*) very strange and unusual, and difficult to understand or explain 古怪的；奇异的
reunion	/riː'juːnjən/	*n.*	1. [U] reuniting or being reunited 再联合 2. [C] social gathering of people who were formerly friends, colleagues, etc. 团聚 , 联谊活动
withdrawal	/wɪθ'drɔːəl/	*n.*	1. [C] the act of taking an amount of money out of your bank account 提款，取款 2. [C, U] the act of moving or taking sth. away or back 撤走；收回；取回
debit	/'debɪt/	*n.*	[C] a written note in an account of a sum owed or paid out 收方；借方
mistakenly	/mɪs'teɪkənli/	*a.*	in a mistaken manner 错误地；误解地
convince	/kən'vɪns/	*vt.*	to make sb. feel certain; to cause sb. to realize 使某人确信
cancel	/'kænsl/	*v.*	to say that (sth. already arranged and decided upon) will not be done or take place; to call off 取消；废除

apparently	/ə'pærəntli/	*a.*	according to what you have heard or read; according to the way sth. appears 显然地
representative	/ˌrepri'zentətiv/	*n.*	1. [C] person chosen or appointed to represent another or others; delegate 代表　2. [C] typical example of a class or group 典型；有代表性的人或事物
		a.	1. serving to show or portray a class or group 有代表性的；典型的　2. consisting of elected deputies; based on representation by these 由选出之代表组成的；代议制的
overdraft	/'əuvədrɑːft/	*n.*	[C] amount of money by which a bank account is overdrawn 透支；透支额
deduct	/di'dʌkt/	*vt.*	~ **sth. (from sth.)** to take away (an amount or a part) 减去；扣除
grocery	/'grəusəri/	*n.*	[*pl.*] food and other goods sold by a grocer or at a supermarket 食品杂货
deserve	/di'zɜːv/	*vt.*	1. have earned sth. by good or bad actions or behavior 应得，应受到　2. If a suggestion, idea, or plan deserves consideration, attention, etc., it is good enough to be considered, paid attention to, etc. 值得考虑；值得注意

✪ New Expressions

can't help doing sth	used to say that it is impossible to prevent or avoid sth. 忍不住做……；不可避免做……
stare at	to look at sth. or sb. with one's eyes widely open for a long time without moving 凝视；盯着看
out of control	to lose control of 失控，失去控制
pretend to do sth.	to behave as if sth. is true when in fact you know it is not 假装……；装作……
out of earshot of	too far away to hear sb./sth. or to be heard 无法听到
steal glances at	to peep sb. or sth. 偷看
take sb. by surprise	to do sth. to make sb. feel surprised 使……出乎意料
take the liberty of doing sth.	to do sth. without permission 擅自做……
along with	in addition to sb./sth.; in the same way as sb./sth. 除……以外（还）；与……同样
dip into	to put your hand into a container to take sth. out 把手伸进……
on one's tail	to pursue or stalking sb. so closely 紧追
look over one's shoulder at	to keep watch for danger or threats to oneself 警惕
be pessimistic about	to have a pessimistic view of sth. 对……持悲观看法
immune to	not affected by sth. 不受……影响的；对……有免疫力的

Reading Comprehension

Understanding the text

I. Answer the following questions.

1. Why did a cold tingle of fear run through Karen when she saw the coat?

2. What did "the large woman" and her companion do after they stole glances at Karen?

3. Why did Karen decide to chase the large woman and her companion?

4. How did Karen react when the service rep asked if she'd made any large withdrawals?

5. What did the rep fail to clarify after he canceled Karen's new debit card?

6. In what way did the identity thief steal Karen's bank information?

7. What is the exact meaning of "life-altering" in Para. 19?

8. What did Karen do after she got to the bank and understood what had occurred?

Critical thinking

II. Work in pairs and discuss the following questions.

1. Have you ever received any messages claiming your email account was possibly logined at another site? If yes, what did you do?

2. If your personal information was stolen, how would you do?

3. Why has information leakage become more and more common nowadays?

4. How to solve the problem of information leakage individually and socially?

Language Focus

Words in use

III. Fill in the blanks with the words given below. Change the form where necessary. Each word can be used only once.

display	proceed	cancel	cautious	suspicion
commence	deserve	lodge	criminal	pessimistic

1. They are seeking permission to begin _____ proceedings against him for breaking the law on financing political parties.

2. Department stores _____ their goods in the windows to attract the potential consumers' attention.

3. Someone who is _____ thinks that bad things are going to happen.

4. Under the agreement, Britain will _____ hundreds of millions of pounds in debts owed to it by some of world's poorest countries.

5. American analysts have been somewhat _____ in estimating the size of the B2B market.

6. Although the new tax is already in force, you have until November to _____ an appeal.

7. It will be hard to overcome decades of mistrust, but we will _____ with courage, rectitude and resolve.

8. The next stage of work on constitutional development cannot _____ without first resolving the issues of legislative process.

9. Government officials clearly _____ some of the blame as well.

10. He has been questioned on _____ of slandering the Prime Minister.

Word building

The suffix *-ed* combines with base form of most verbs to form the past participles, which are used as adjectives indicating that something has been affected in some way.

Examples

Words learned	Add *-ed*	New words formed
exhaust	→	exhausted
learn	→	learned
clarify	→	clarified
approve	→	approved

The suffix *-ion* combines with verbs to form nouns. (For explanation, refer to Word building in Unit 3.)

Examples

Words learned	Add *-ion*	New words formed
appreciate	→	appreciation
contribute	→	contribution

Continued

Words learned	Add -*ion*	New words formed
clarify	→	clarification
distract	→	distraction
simply	→	simplification
educate	→	education
limit	→	limitation
definite	→	definition
describe	→	description
translate	→	translation

IV. Add -ed or -ion to or remove them from the following words to form new words.

Words learned	New words formed
-ed	
impress	
compressed	
disappoint	
-ion	
identify	
celebrate	
comprehend	
illustrate	
exhibition	
collaborate	
operate	
interpret	
perceive	

V. Fill in the blanks with the newly-formed words in Activity IV. Change the form where necessary. Each word can be used only once.

1. It is impossible to _____ the story of the First World War into a few pages.

2. They are notorious for resorting to trickery in order to _____ their clients.

3. A spokesman for UNHCR said he was surprised and _____ by the decision made by the General Assembly.

4. If you change your attitude, you change your _____, change your actions, and change your life.

5. That couple always holds a little _____ every year on their wedding anniversary.

6. The woman who was on passport control asked me if I had any further _____.

7. The course also features creative writing exercises and listening _____.

8. I was frankly astonished at the degree to which different singers can affect the _____ of a song.

9. Cheaper energy conservation techniques have been put into _____ in the developed world.

10. The scientist hopes the work done in _____ with other researchers may be duplicated elsewhere.

11. _____ by example is better than explanation in words.

12. His work was _____ in the best galleries in America, Europe and Asia.

Banked cloze

VI. Fill in the blanks by selecting suitable words from the word bank. You may not use any of the words more than once.

A. Sensitive	B. intelligence	C. reveals	D. necessarily	E. tempting
F. plain	G. limited	H. usernames	I. facilitate	J. charm
K. useful	L. range	M. local	N. components	O. display

Information leakage occurs when a web site 1) _____ sensitive data, such as developer comments or error messages, which may aid an attacker in exploiting the system. 2) _____ information may be present within HTML comments, error messages, source code, or simply left in 3) _____ sight. There are many ways a web site can be coaxed into revealing this type of information. While leakage does not 4) _____ represent a breach in security, it does give an attacker 5) _____ guidance for future exploitation. Leakage of sensitive information may carry various levels of risk and should be 6) _____ whenever possible.

In the first case of information leakage (comments left in the code, verbose error messages, etc.), the leak may give 7) _____ to the attacker with contextual information of directory structure, SQL query structure, and the names of key processes used by the web site. Often a developer will leave comments in the HTML and script code to help 8) _____ in debugging or integration. This information can 9) _____ from simple comments detailing how the script works, to, in the worst cases, 10) _____ and passwords used during the testing phase of development.

Expressions in use

VII. Fill in the blanks with the expressions given below. Change the form where necessary. Each expression can be used only once.

immune to	dip into	stare at
take sb. by surprise	out of control	out of earshot of
be pessimistic about	can't help doing	pretend to do sth.
take the liberty of		

1. A number of French players went nuts, completely _____ but we really don't know what have happened to them.

2. If you _____ know what you don't know, you'll only make a fool of yourself.

3. But he looked so different from his usual look that I stopped a moment to _____ him.

4. If this accounted for all the growth in Intra-Asian trade, then one should _____ the future.

5. We _____ approaching you this time to seek for the establishment of long-term business relations which is to our mutual benefit.

6. We shall not give them any notice. We must _____.

7. He is _____ chickenpox because he had it as a child.

8. The writer of the novel claimed the novel exhibited the ideal cultural personality attached to essential color of culture tradition, but we _____ suspicious of this.

9. Keep negative opinions to yourself, or between you and your friends, and _____ your children.

10. Just when she was ready to _____ her savings, Greg hastened to her rescue.

Structure Analysis and Writing

Structure Analysis

Focus on a narrative essay

In this unit, you will learn how to write a narrative. A narrative, in some sense, is simply a story that illustrates a point. That point is often about some emotion you feel: anger, jealousy, confusion, thankfulness, loneliness, sadness, terror, or relief. A narrative essay tells a story, usually concerning an event or issue in your life. The story must have a purpose, such as to describe how the event has changed your life, altered your outlook or taught you a lesson. In writing the essay, using vivid, detailed language and emphasizing conflict will draw readers into your narrative. When you write a narrative, you will go through several steps.

1. Pick a strong topic

You should choose a compelling topic to grab readers' attention. Centering your paper on a topic where there is conflict and growth making your readers want to finish reading your paper and see how your problems are resolved. Alternatively, you can amuse and intrigue your readers by writing about an exciting adventure or a funny event that happened to you.

2. Write chronologically

Once you have chosen a topic, you can begin to organize your essay. Since you are telling a story about an event or series of events in your life, the easiest way to structure your essay is to write it chronologically. This both provides a simple way to organize your thoughts and makes your essay easier for your readers to follow.

3. Use vivid language

You should tell your story with detailed, concrete language. Describe the environment in which your story takes place, including any sights, sounds and smells that you remember. Avoid general statements; every sentence in your story should describe something you specifically thought, felt or experienced. You should also avoid weak verbs and modifiers in your essay, as well as the passive voice. Words that skirt around the point you are trying to make will make your essay less exciting to read.

4. Provide conflict and resolution

The bulk of your essay should concentrate on the conflict of your story—the problem you are trying to resolve. The last few paragraphs should provide resolution for the conflict. The resolution allows your readers to see how you have changed as a result of the events described in the story.

Now, take a look at Paragraph 1 of Text A. From this paragraph, you can see how the story started.

> *Karen Lodrick ordered a latte at Starbucks while waiting nervously for the bank on San Francisco's Market Street to open. She displayed her anxiety and distracted but couldn't help noticing the scruffy looking pair standing next to her: a tall man wearing a navy baseball jacket and a large woman in jeans and Gucci glasses, carrying a brown suede coat and a Prada purse. Karen stared at the woman for a while because she looked vaguely familiar.* (Para. 1)

Structured Writing

Read the sample essay and see how the story develops with details.

Topic	**Sample essay**
An unforgettable day	I have never really understood my mother's love to me until that night.
Introduction	It was one night near the end of last summer vacation. At about half past nine, I wanted to visit a former classmate and have a chat with him because he would go abroad the next day. I thought I would return soon, so I left home without telling my mother. We talked until half past twelve. When I got back home, my mother was waiting for me anxiously. "I have been waiting for you on pins and needles until now. Do you know how much I have worried about you?" I explained where I had been and said sorry. She sighed, "You are going back to college soon. I hope you could stay home with me during the last few nights."
Thesis statement: I understood my mother's love to me after I left home to visit my former classmate without telling my mother.	
Body	
Detail 1: Where I went and what I did.	
Detail 2: How my mother reacted to me after I got back home.	
Detail 3: What I felt and how I reacted to my mother's love.	
Conclusion	I was shocked by these words. She had never said anything like that before. I always took mother's love for granted and never thought of the sacrifices she had made for me. I was ashamed of myself.
I was shamed of myself and I will understand my mother more.	But from that sleepless night, I know what I can do to make up for the past and I try to understand my mother more.

VIII. Write an essay of no less than 150 words on one of the following topics. One topic has an outline that you can follow.

Topic
A cheerful surprise
Introduction
Thesis statement: Because my friend Lucy was depressed, sad and downhearted recently, we, some of Lucy's friends decided to give a surprise to cheer her up.
Body
Detail 1: My friend Lucy had a terrible condition and had been hospitalized for over a month.
Detail 2: She was so moved after she found that we all crowded into her dorm to give her a surprise.
Conclusion
She recovered to be happy after that day.

More topics:

● My first day in college

● Attitude is everything

Translation

IX. Translate the following paragraph into Chinese.

There's no question that email is a huge source of risk for organizations today. In fact, the average employee sends and receives about 80 emails each day. One in every 20 of those emails contains "risky" data—from sensitive attachments to social security numbers to protected health information to valuable corporate secrets that set your organization apart. All of this risky data can become toxic to your company if it's hacked or suffers a breach (unintentionally through a data leak or otherwise)—causing reputation damage, customer loss, heavy fines and decreased competitive edge.

X. Translate the following paragraph into English.

信用卡 (credit card) 是银行创造出来的最便捷同时也是最危险的信用工具。通过信用卡，人们可以先用银行付账的方式购买那些负担不起的物品；同时，银行也将对此征收比一般贷款要高的利率 (interest rate)。信用卡现已成为社会体制 (social system) 的重要组成部分，而该体制还得依赖消费 (consumption) 的持续增长。

Section

Reading Skills: *Tone and Attitude*

> A writer's tone reveals the attitude that he or she has toward a subject, characters, or audience. Tone and attitude can be positive, negative, or neutral.
>
> A positive tone conveys "good" feelings including *happiness, pride, enthusiasm, humor…*
>
> A negative tone conveys "bad" feelings including *sadness, anger, hatred...*
>
> A neutral tone is neither positive or negative. Words used to describe this tone include *fair, balanced, objective, neutral, detached and etc.*
>
> Here are two examples from Text A.
>
> **Example 1:**
>
> *"Don't take the liberty of doing anything crazy, Karen," said Fuentes. "She could have a gun."* (Para. 7)
>
> Tone and attitude: Worried.
>
> **Example 2:**
>
> *She tried her best to be immune to the troubles, but with no money to cover checks, she couldn't pay her bills, her rent. She couldn't even buy groceries. Late fees were compounded by black marks on her credit report. She didn't deserve to suffer all of that, but it was just the beginning.* (Para. 20)
>
> Tone and attitude: Depressed, pessimistic, compassionate.

Read the following sentences from Text B and write down the tone and attitude.

1. *The thief ran into a busy intersection against the light and flagged down a taxi. Karen felt scared. "She is not going to get away," she cried to the operator. "I am not going to let her escape." She caught the taxi before the driver pulled out.* (Para. 5)

   Tone and attitude:

2. *"Don't let her go!" she implored. "She's an identity thief." The driver lifted his hands off the wheel and held them up.* (Para. 6)

   Tone and attitude :

3. *"Idiot! You should have kept running," Karen told her and had a feeling of release in the pit of her stomach.* (Para. 19)

   Tone and attitude:

Text B

To Catch an Identity Thief (Part II)

1. At five-two and 110 pounds, Karen Lodrick was tiny compared with the nearly six-foot-tall woman carrying the brown suede coat. Block after block in downtown San Francisco, Karen chased the woman, keeping the 911 operator on the phone to let her know exactly where they were.

2. She lost sight of the woman after she turned a corner. But as Karen looked through the French doors leading into a **stately** old apartment building, she was there again. One glance at Karen and the woman took off down the hill toward Market Street, a main **thoroughfare** with multiple lanes in either direction.

3. Traffic **whizzed** by. Locals **strolled** the tree-lined sidewalks and walked in and out of **funky** coffeehouses. Some, **toting** bags of bottles and **aluminum** cans, **meandered** toward the recycling center. People of every description moved along Market Street. But she didn't see any police officers.

4. As the identity thief passed an abandoned shopping cart, Karen saw her arm swing out. She **tossed** something inside **hastily**. Karen raced to the cart. "I got what she dropped," she told the 911 operator. "It's a wallet. A Prada wallet." Karen wanted to look inside, but she had no time.

5. The thief ran into a busy **intersection** against the light and flagged down a taxi. Karen felt scared. "She is not going to get away," she cried to the operator. "I am not going to let her escape." She caught the taxi before the driver pulled out.

6. "Don't let her go!" she **implored**. "She's an identity thief." The driver lifted his hands off the wheel and held them up. Her escape **thwarted**; the woman got out and **confronted** Karen.

7. "Why are you chasing me?" the woman **frowned** and asked Karen first.

8. For an instant, Karen felt doubt. What if this wasn't the thief? She tried to **conceal** her anger and convince the woman to wait for the police. But she was **indifferent** to Karen and took off down Market Street again, toward Octavia, where the freeway spilled out its traffic. Karen kept after her.

9. It drove Karen crazy that it took about two weeks for the bank's credit card division to process the problem and credit money to her account. Hard as it is, Karen felt hopeful when the bank called to tell her it had a surveillance video of the thief. On it Karen saw a big, dark-haired woman in a suede coat and sunglasses at an ATM. Karen **signed** an **affidavit** that she didn't know the woman, got a printout of her image, and that was it.

10. Meanwhile, the thief reached deeper into Karen's life. She used her Social Security number and other information to get a fake driver's license, showing Karen's license number but the thief's picture. With the license and the Social Security number, she reopened accounts that

Karen had closed years before.

11. One day, the Dell computer company made contact with Karen to confirm that it was all right to send "her" $7,000 order to an address different from the one on her account.

12. "Close that account and don't send those computers," she told Dell's rep, **conveying** someone had stolen her identity. She asked for the address the thief had wanted the equipment sent to. Dell refused to give her the address, saying if she put the request in writing, she would get it.

13. Karen placed **fraud** alerts with the credit reporting agencies. But that didn't stop the thief from opening more accounts in Karen's name. Again and again, she asked the bank to put an alert on her account, but when she checked, it wasn't there. The thief got into her new bank account, and the whole cycle began again. She was at her wit's end.

14. Now, with a **phony** driver's license, the thief was approaching her third checking account covertly.

15. For half an hour, up and down the streets, around corners and into alleyways, Karen Lodrick, defeated fears and pursued the woman with the suede coat. Karen lost her twice when she slid into buildings to hide. And then she lost her a third time at an indoor parking lot. "It's over," she told the 911 operator. **Exasperated** and exhausted, Karen zipped open the Prada wallet.

16. Two of her bank statements were tucked into one side of the large wallet. On the other were the two debit cards used to clean out her account in November. She also found one of her own paychecks. But what **exceedingly chilled** her were tiny "cue cards" with her name, Social Security number, driver's license number and address.

17. The 911 operator assured her that an officer would be there as soon as he finished an emergency call, and Karen agreed to wait by the entrance to the **garage**. When the cop arrived a few minutes later, Karen told him what had occurred, feeling little hope that he'd find the woman now.

18. But only moments later, the officer found her—**crouched** between a car and the building, smoking a cigarette.

19. "Idiot! You should have kept running," Karen told her and had a feeling of release in the pit of her stomach.

20. The arresting officer said the identity thief, Maria Nelson, had at least 60 prior arrests, was indeed on **probation** and was wanted in another **jurisdiction** for similar crimes. When Nelson came before a judge 44 days later, however, thanks to a **plea** deal with the **prosecutor**, she was **sentenced** to only time served plus probation.

21. Meanwhile, Karen keeps getting billed for phone service and items at a department store that she didn't buy. She is not **thrilled** after the identity thief was arrested because she fears her ID may have been sold on the black market, **prolonging** her nightmare.

(958 words)

⊙ New Words

stately	/'steitli/	*a.*	grand 堂皇的；宏伟的
thoroughfare	/'θʌrəfeə(r)/	*n.*	[C] public road or street that is open at both ends, esp. for traffic 大道；大街
whiz	/wiz/	*vi.*	to move very fast 高速移动
stroll	/strəul/	*vi.*	to walk in a slow leisurely way 散步；漫步；闲逛
funky	/fʌŋki/	*a.*	very modern; fashionable 新式的；新型的；时髦的
tote	/təut/	*vt.*	(*infml.*) to carry (sth.) 携带
aluminum	/ə'lu:minəm/	*n.*	[U] a silvery ductile metallic element found primarily in bauxite 铝
meander	/mi'ændə(r)/	*vi.*	1. (of a person) to wander aimlessly 漫步，闲逛 2. (of a river, etc.) to follow a winding course, flowing slowly（指河流等）蜿蜒；缓慢流动
toss	/tɔs/	*vt.*	1. to throw sth. lightly or carelessly or easily 扔；抛；掷 2. to jerk (one's head, etc.), esp. in contempt or indifference 猛然扭
hastily	/'heistili/	*a.*	quickly, perhaps too quickly 飞快地；仓促地
intersection	/ˌintə'sekʃən/	*n.*	1. [C] a place where two or more roads, lines, etc. meet or cross each other 十字路口 2. [C] the act of intersecting sth. 交集
implore	/im'plɔ:(r)/	*vt.*	to ask or beg (sb.) earnestly; to beseech 恳求，乞求
thwart	/θwɔ:t/	*vt.*	to prevent (sb.) doing what he intends; to oppose (a plan, etc.) successfully 阻挠；阻止
		n.	[C] seat across a rowing-boat for an oarsman 坐板
confront	/kən'frʌnt/	*vt.*	~ **(sb. with sb./sth.)** to make sb. face or consider sb./sth. unpleasant, difficult, etc. 面对；正视
frown	/fraun/	*vi.*	to make an angry, unhappy, or confused expression, moving your eyebrows together 皱眉
conceal	/kən'si:l/	*vt.*	(*fml.*) to hide your real feelings or the truth 隐藏，隐瞒
indifferent	/in'difrənt/	*a.*	having no interest in sb./sth.; neither for nor against sb./sth.; not caring about sb./sth. 不感兴趣；漠不关心
sign	/sain/	*vt.*	to write (one's name) on (a document, etc.), eg. to show that one has written it, that it is genuine, or that one agrees with its contents 签字
affidavit	/ˌæfi'deivit/	*n.*	[C] (*law*) written statement that can be used as evidence in court, made by sb. who swears that it is true 书面证词；宣誓书
convey	/kən'vei/	*vt.*	to communicate or express sth., with or without using words 表达；传达；传递
fraud	/frɔ:d/	*a.*	deceitful or dishonest 欺骗的；诈骗的；不诚实的
		n.	[C, U] (act of) deceiving sb. illegally in order to make money or obtain goods 欺骗；诈骗

phony	/'fəuni/	*a.*	not real or true; false, and trying to deceive people 假冒的
		n.	[C] (*fml.*) a person who is not honest or sincere; a thing that is not real or true 赝品；骗子
exasperated	/ig'zɑːspəreitid/	*a.*	extremely annoyed, especially if you cannot do anything to improve the situation 激怒的；恼火的
exceedingly	/ik'siːdiŋli/	*a.*	(*fml.*) extremely 非常；极其
chill	/tʃil/	*vt.*	1. to scare 使恐惧 2. to make (sb./sth.) cold 使……感到冷；使……冷却
garage	/'gærɑːʒ/	*n.*	[C] building in which to keep one or more cars, vans, etc. 汽车房；汽车库
crouch	/krautʃ/	*vi.*	to lower the body by bending the knees, eg. in fear or to hide 蹲；蹲伏
		n.	[*sing.*] crouching position 蹲着的姿势
probation	/prə'beiʃ/	*n.*	1. [U] (*law*) (system of) keeping an official check on the behavior of (esp. young) people found guilty of crime as an alternative to sending them to prison 缓刑：*sentenced to three years' probation* 被 判 处 缓 刑 三 年 2. [U] testing of a person's abilities or behavior to find out if he or she is suitable 试用（期）
jurisdiction	/ˌdʒuəris'dikʃn/	*n.*	1. [U] authority to carry out justice and to interpret and apply laws; right to exercise legal authority 司法；司法权 2. [U] limits within which legal authority may be exercised 管辖权限
plea	/pliː/	*n.*	1. [C] (*law*) statement made by or for a person charged with an offense in court 抗辩，答辩，辩护 2. [C] (*fml.*) ~ **(for sth.)** earnest request; appeal 恳求；请求：*a plea for forgiveness, money, more time* 恳求原谅、给予金钱、多给些时间
prosecutor	/'prɔsikjuːtə/	*n.*	[C] a public official who charges sb. officially with a crime and prosecutes them in a court of law 公诉人；检察官
sentence	/'sentəns/	*vt.*	to say officially in a court of law that sb. is to receive a particular punishment 判决；宣判；判刑
thrilled	/θrild/	*a.*	very excited, happy and pleased 非常激动的；非常幸福的
prolong	/prə'lɔŋ/	*vt.*	to make (sth.) longer, esp. in time; extend 延长；使延伸

⊛ New Expressions

flag down	signal to stop 打旗号，挥旗要求停车
pull out	to leave 离开
take the initiative	be in a position to control a situation and decide what to do next 采取主动；首先采取行动

indifferent to	not showing any interest or sympathy to（对……）不关心的，不在乎的
drive sb. crazy	to make sb. more and more angry or irritated, especially over a long period of time 使人受不了；让人十分恼火
make contact (with sb.)	to succeed in speaking to or meeting sb. 取得联系
ask for	to say that you would like sb. to give you sth. 请求
stop sb. from doing sth	to prevent sb. from doing sth. 阻止；阻碍
at one's wit's end	at the limit of one's mental resources; utterly at a loss 智穷计尽，毫无办法
slide into	to move in somewhere quietly and smoothly 悄悄移进
in the pit of one's stomach	If you feel an emotion in the pit of your stomach, you experience is strongly, often as a bad feeling in your stomach. 在胸口；在心窝

Reading Comprehension

Understanding the text

I. Choose the best answer to each of the following questions.

1. What did the identity thief drop?

   A. A ticket.　　　　　　　　　B. A watch.

   C. A wallet.　　　　　　　　　D. A mobile phone.

2. Why did Karen panic?

   A. Because the thief ran into a busy intersection against the light and flagged down a taxi.

   B. Because the thief ran into an shopping mall.

   C. Because the thief disappeared from Karen's sight.

   D. Because the thief ran into an alley.

3. What did Karen see in the surveillance video?

   A. A thin, dark-haired woman in a suede coat and designer sunglasses at an ATM.

   B. A big, dark-haired woman in a suede coat and designer sunglasses at an ATM.

   C. A big, blonde-haired woman in a suede coat and designer sunglasses at an ATM.

   D. A tall, blonde-haired woman in a suede coat and designer sunglasses at an ATM.

4. How did the thief use Karen's license and Social Security number?

   A. She opened a new credit card under Karen's account.

   B. She stole the money in Karen's Social Security card.

C. She sold the Karen's Social Security number on the black market.

D. She reopened accounts that Karen had closed years before.

5. Why did the company of Dell refuse to give Karen the thief's address?

   A. Because Karen didn't submit an application.

   B. Because Dell didn't have the address of the thief.

   C. Because Karen didn't put the request in writing form.

   D. Because Dell ignored the Karen's request.

6. What made Karen feel exceedingly chilled?

   A. Tiny "cue cards" with Karen's name.

   B. Karen's Social Security number.

   C. Karen's driver's license number and address.

   D. All mentioned above.

7. Where did the officer find the thief?

   A. Between a car and the building.   B. In a building.

   C. In an indoor parking lot.   D. In a bank.

8. Why didn't Karen feel thrilled after the identity thief was arrested?

   A. Because she feared the bank might not help her cancel her accounts.

   B. Because she feared her ID might have been sold on the black market.

   C. Because she was worried that her ID might be stolen by another identify thief.

   D. Because she was worried that she couldn't find her lost money.

Critical thinking

II. Work in pairs and discuss the following questions.

1. How do you deal with information security?

2. Do you think the problem of online information leakage can be solved? Why or why not?

3. Can you give some suggestions to organizations or individuals to prevent online information leakage?

Language Focus

Words in use

III. Fill in the blanks with the words given below. Change the form where necessary. Each word can be used only once.

hastily	frown	pursue	strolled	prolong
convey	exceedingly	implore	plea	thrilled

1. The smile disappeared to be replaced by a doleful _____.

2. We found out that he was _____ fond of fishing.

3. This train _____ over one thousand passengers every day.

4. Government intervention, like modern health-care, can _____ the inevitable, but only for so long.

5. The implication seems to be that it is impossible to _____ economic reform and democracy simultaneously.

6. I was _____ to hear that I had passed the entrance examination.

7. If you missed that post, I _____ you to go back and look at the comments.

8. James got to his feet and started to come over, but the girls _____ backed away.

9. The manager will make a special _____ to draft the player into his squad as a replacement.

10. They looked happy and relaxed as they _____ in the sunshine on a shopping trip.

Expressions in use

IV. Fill in the blanks with the expressions given below. Change the form where necessary. Each expression can be used only once.

flag down	take the initiative	slide into
indifferent to	make contact with	at one's wit's end
stop... from doing	drive... crazy	ask for
in the pit of one's stomach		

1. Against this backdrop, neither North Korea nor the United States wanted to _____ for a breakthrough.

2. Because I want to do the post concerning sale, I like to _____ market directly.

3. She is able to _____ a room without anyone noticing.

4. Being _____, he is asking anyone he can think of for help.

5. To be a kind person, how can you be so _____ the sufferings of these children?

6. Soaking wet, she decided to _____ the next car.

7. Suddenly he had a sinking feeling _____.

8. The ceaseless noise from that machine are going to _____ me _____.

9. When officials like gas and electricity men call to read the meter, _____ their identification.

10. You may grieve your losses, but don't let them _____ you _____ great things.

Sentence structure

V. Rewrite the following sentences by changing the "if" clause to a "with" phrase to indicate how a certain condition can affect a particular situation.

> **Model:** Dell refused to give her the address, saying if she put the request in writing, she would get it.
>
> → Dell refused to give her the address, saying with her request in writing, she would get it.

1. If you take this medicine, all your symptoms will fall away.

_____

2. If you keep doing exercise, you will gain more energy and keep a good health.

_____

3. If it's mobile learning, it doesn't require much study in a regular classroom but requires more time to study by yourself.

_____

VI. Complete the following sentences by translating the Chinese into English, using the inverted structure "a./ad. + as + main" clause.

Model: _____ (虽然很难), Karen felt hopeful when the bank called to tell her it had a surveillance video of the thief.

→ <u>Hard as it is</u>, Karen felt hopeful when the bank called to tell her it had a surveillance video of the thief.

1. _____ (尽管他很勇敢), he couldn't finish this difficult task.

2. _____ (尽管听起来很愚蠢), I was so in love with her that I believed everything she said.

3. _____ (虽然她精疲力竭), there was no hope of her being able to sleep.

Unit 5
IT Life

It would appear that we have reached the limits of what it is possible to achieve with computer technology, although one should be careful with such statements, as they tend to sound pretty silly in five years.

—*John Von Neumann (Hungarian-American mathematician, physicist, inventor, computer scientist, and polymath)*

Software suppliers are trying to make their software packages more "user-friendly"... Their best approach so far has been to take all the old brochures and stamp the words "user-friendly" on the cover.

— *Bill Gates (American business magnate, investor, author and philanthropist)*

> Nowadays, it is not rare to see a man walking on the sidewalks with a smart phone in his/her hand, completely absorbed in the digital world. Just as what computers once achieved, smart products have touched so many different areas in our life, and transformed our life in every possible way—how we socialize, entertain, and study. As mobile technology continues to become smarter and more helpful, smart products will continue to make a huge impact on the whole world. What have smart products brought to us? Can we live a day without smart products? Will you be a smart consumer when you want to buy a new smart product? These are good questions for you to consider.

Section

Pre-reading Activities

I. Listen to the news about the new development in IT industry and fill in the blanks in each sentence based on what you have heard.

1. Technology companies and experts from around the world come to the event to _____ _____.

2. Each year's show has specific trends, or popular items. These trends help companies _____ _____.

3. Another trend at the show is _____ _____.

4. One of the most popular categories of products in this year's show is _____. One such device is _____.

5. Robots were also shown at this year's show. Some of them helped children _____. Others _____, or "virtual," version of a person so _____ _____.

II. Listen to the news again and answer the following questions.

1. Where is the Consumer Electronics Show held every year? As one of the largest technology shows in the world, what do technology companies and experts from all over the world usually do in it?

2. How many people are expected to attend the show held this week?

3. In your opinion, what impact will the technology mentioned in the above show have on our daily life?

Living in Apple's World

1. According to *Bible*, long long ago when the world just started, apple was a **prohibited** fruit in the Garden of Eden where Adam and Eve lived with God, but the **serpent tempted** them into eating the fruit from the tree of knowledge of good and evil, which God had forbidden. After doing so, God **expelled** them from the Garden to prevent them eating from the tree of life and becoming **immortal**.

2. Many people believe in the Autumn of 1665, Newton was enlightened to **formulate** his theory of **gravitation** by watching the fall of an apple from a tree, which changed our opinions about nature and the way we think.

3. And today, another apple follows its two "**predecessors**".

4. **Dozing** on the couch on a lazy Sunday afternoon, barbecue potato chip crumbs **steeped** in tiny formations on my gray sweatshirt and a baseball game on TV, I was **startled** by my daughter Angela, 24, waving her wrist in front of me.

5. "Dad, I got one," she said, showing off a bright blue Apple Watch.

6. "Cool," I **mumbled** before asking her what she thought of it.

7. Shortly after she did, an Apple Watch ad popped up on the TV screen to **underscore** the point.

8. Even while on vacation, I can't escape from Apple.

9. It's Apple's world. We just happen to live in it.

10. That fact was driven home Monday, when the world's most-valued company announced another **sterling** financial quarter: Record income and earnings pushed the Apple machine to a market capitalization of about $800 billion with nearly $200 billion in cash. As our tech **columnist** John Shinal pointed out the value of Apple is more than Google and Microsoft combined. From the **perspective** of usage, the Apple symbol is **seemingly** everywhere—as **ubiquitous** as software giant Microsoft was in the 1990s and IBM in the 1980s.

11. From dawn, when we awake to our iPhone alarm, to work, where Macintosh laptops are common in the publishing industry, in which Apple ads frequently embed the broadcasts of sporting events, it's hard not to run across the familiar icon.

12. Throughout the day, whether at work or on vacation on the East Coast, I am reminded. People **intently** staring at their iPhone screens, **oblivious** to the world around them. I can see

MacBook Pros in the laps of students at the University. I can see headlines about Apple in newspapers and on tech blogs. I always end my day with my iPhone on the night stand.

13. Someday soon, perhaps, we'll drive to work in our Apple car and watch those ads on an Apple-branded TV. There is no shortage of these possibilities that seem **endless**, with the iPhone as the **hub** of our digital house.

14. If that isn't enough, when it refers to Apple, there are plenty of books and film treatments on Steve Jobs. Academy Award-winner Alex Gibney has completed a documentary on the Apple co-founder, and a major **motion** picture from director Danny Boyle and **screenwriter** Aaron Sorkin—both Oscar winners—is on the way.

15. Of course, I shouldn't be surprised. Apple is on track and has redefined the way the world communicates, **gleans** information and entertains itself.

16. Apple has done so—in a very visible way—by bridging the **gap** between less tech **savvy** individuals and products they might normally shy away from. Through design and ease of use, it manages to influence all age groups to try to use smart phones, tablets, music players and, now, the wearable.

17. And, as Angela reminded me Sunday, Apple is about to become even more **omnipresent**. For the first time, an Apple product is being worn as a fashion statement.

18. The new Apple Watch just may be the latest example of tech **zeitgeist intersecting** with pop culture. Apple (previously with iPhone and, briefly, iPad), Google (Chrome and driverless cars) and Microsoft (Windows) all did it to varying degrees. Whether wearing Apple's smart watch captures a moment in time or is merely a passing fancy is **secondary** to the company's **outsize** role in our society.

19. Perhaps Apple's influence is simply a **reflection** of its **status** as the world's most valuable company and one of its most respected brands, according to an annual ranking from **consulting** firm Interbrand. "Every so often, a company changes our lives—not just with its products, but with its **ethos**," said Jez Frampton, Interbrand's global CEO.

20. And with rumored new products—did someone say car or television? Apple's impact could deepen. Jobs famously said he wanted his company's cleanly designed products to meld into a home, offering functionality as well as form. In fact, an early influence for the young Jobs were the Eichler-style homes in his old neighborhood. Visit many American homes and you're apt to see iPhones, Macs and iPads in seemingly every room. You might even spot an Apple TV.

21. I know Apple will never be too far away from me. Our home is filled with iPhones, MacBook Pros and, when my daughter drops in, an Apple Watch.

22. Nothing manipulates me. I think, now, it's Apple's world, and we're all just part of it.

(843 words)

Notes

Bible: a collection of sacred texts or scriptures that Jews and Christians consider to be a product of divine inspiration and a record of the relationship between God and humans.

Garden of Eden: a beautiful garden where Adam and Eve were placed at the Creation; when they disobeyed and ate the forbidden fruit from the tree of knowledge of good and evil they were driven from their paradise.

Newton: an English physicist and mathematician who is widely recognized as one of the most influential scientists of all time and a key figure in the scientific revolution.

Macintosh: (branded as Mac since 1998) a series of personal computers (PCs) designed, developed, and marketed by Apple Inc. Steve Jobs introduced the original Macintosh computer on January 10, 1984.

Steve Jobs: an American businessman, inventor, and industrial designer. He was the co-founder, chairman, and chief executive officer (CEO) of Apple Inc.

Interbrand: a division of Omnicom, is a brand consultancy, specializing in areas such as brand strategy, brand analytics, brand valuation, corporate design, digital brand management, packaging design and naming. Interbrand has 29 offices in 22 countries.

Eichler-style homes: Between 1949 and 1966, Joseph Eichler's company, Eichler Homes, built over 11,000 homes in nine communities in Northern California and three communities in Southern California. Later, other firms worked with Eichler's company to build similar houses. Together, they all came to be known as Eichlers. During this period, Eichler became one of the nation's most influential builders of modern homes.

🔊 New Words

prohibited	/prəˈhibitid/	*a.*	excluded from use or mention 禁止的
serpent	/ˈsɜːpənt/	*n.*	1. [C] snake, esp. a large one 蛇　2. [C] person who tempts others to do wrong; sly person 诱人犯错的人；狡猾的人
tempt	/tempt/	*vt.*	1. ~ **sb. (into sth./doing sth.)** to persuade or try to persuade sb. to do sth., esp. sth. wrong or unwise 劝说或鼓动某人　2. to arouse a desire in sb.; attract sb. 引起某人的欲望；吸引某人
expel	/ikˈspel/	*vt.*	1. ~ **sb. (from sth.)** to force sb. to leave (esp. a country, school or club) 驱逐；赶走；开除　2. to send or drive (sth.) out by force 用力排出或驱出
immortal	/iˈmɔːtl/	*a.*	living forever; not mortal 不朽的；永世的
formulate	/ˈfɔːmjuleit/	*vt.*	to create (sth.) in a precise form 固定……格式
gravitation	/græviˈteiʃn/	*n.*	[U] (physics) a force of attraction that causes objects to move towards each other 引力，重力

predecessor	/'pri:disesə(r)/	*n.*	1. [C] thing that has been followed or replaced by sth. else 先前的事物；被取代的事物 2. [C] person who held an office or position before sb. else 前任者
doze	/dəuz/	*vi.*	to sleep lightly 小睡；打盹儿
steep	/sti:p/	*vt.*	to (be steeped in sth.) have a lot of a particular quality 饱含（某品质）
startle	/'sta:tl/	*vt.*	to give a sudden shock or surprise to (a person or an animal); to cause move or jump suddenly (from surprise) 使……惊吓
mumble	/'mʌmbl/	*v.*	~ (about sth.); ~ sth. (to sb.) to speak or say sth. unclearly and usu. quietly, so that people cannot hear what is said 咕哝；喃喃自语
		n.	[C] speech that is not heard clearly; noise like this 含糊的话或声音；咕哝
underscore	/ʌndə'skɔ:(r)/	*vt.*	1. (*fig.*) to reinforce (an attitude, a situation, etc.); emphasize 强化；加强；强调 2. to draw a line under (a word, etc.) 在……下面画线
sterling	/'stɜ:liŋ/	*a.*	admirable or excellent in quality 令人钦佩的，优秀的
columnist	/'kɔləmnist/	*n.*	[C] a journalist who writes regular articles, usually on a particular topic, for a newspaper or magazine 专栏作家
perspective	/pə'spektiv/	*n.*	[C] a way of thinking about sth. 角度，观点，想法
seemingly	/si:miŋli/	*a.*	appearing to be something, especially when this is not true 貌似；表面上
ubiquitous	/ju:'bikwitəs/	*a.*	(*fml.*) (seeming to be) present everywhere or in several places at the same time 普遍存在的，无处不有的
intently	/in'tentli/	*a.*	full of eager interest and concentration 专心地；渴望地，热切地
oblivious	/ə'bliviəs/	*a.*	~ (of/to sth.) unaware of or not noticing sth.; having no memory of sth. 未觉察；不注意；忘记
endless	/'endlis/	*a.*	without end 无止境的；无穷尽的
hub	/hʌb/	*n.*	1. [C] central point of activity, interest or importance 中心 2. [C] central part of a wheel from which the spokes radiate 轮毂
motion	/'məuʃn/	*n.*	1. [U] (manner of) moving 运动；移动；动态 2. [C] particular movement; way of moving part of the body; gesture 动作；姿态 3. [C] formal proposal to be discussed and voted on at a meeting 动议；提议
		vi.	~ (to sb.) to indicate to sb. by a gesture 以姿势向……示意
		vt.	to direct (sb.) in the specified direction by a gesture 用姿势给……指示方向
screenwriter	/'skri:nraitə(r)/	*n.*	[C] a person who writes screenplays 电影剧本作家，编剧家
glean	/gli:n/	*vt.*	~sth. (from sb./sth.) (*fig.*) to obtain (news, facts, information, etc.) usu. from various sources, in small quantities and with effort 收集（消息、资料、情报等）
		vt.	to gather (grain left in a field by harvest workers) 拾

gap	/gæp/	*n.*	1. [C] a big difference between two situations, amounts, and groups of people, etc. 差距；差额；差别　2. [C] a space between two objects or two parts of an object, esp. because sth. is missing 缺口；开口；裂缝
savvy	/'sævi/	*n.*	[U] common sense; understanding 常识；理解
omnipresent	/ˌɔmni'preznt/	*a.*	(*fml.*) present everywhere 无处不在的；普遍存在的
zeitgeist	/'zaitgaist/	*n.*	[*sing.*] spirit of a particular period of history as shown by the ideas, beliefs, etc. of the time 时代精神
intersect	/ˌintə'sekt/	*vi.*	~ **(sth.) (with sth.)** (of lines, roads, etc.) to meet and go past (another or each other) forming a cross shape（指线条、道路等）相交
		vt.	to divide (sth.) by going across it 横断，横切，横穿
secondary	/'sekəndri/	*a.*	1. ~ **(to sth.)** coming after sth. that is first or primary; of less importance, value, etc. than what is primary 第二的；次要的　2. dependent on, caused by or derived from sth. that is original or primary 从属的；引申出的；次生的　3. following primary or (in the US) elementary or junior high schools 中等教育的
outsize	/'autsaiz/	*a.*	(of clothing or people, etc.) larger than the standard sizes（指衣物或人等）大于标准大小的，特大的
reflection	/ri'flekʃn/	*n.*	[C, U] reflecting or being reflected 反映；反射；表现；沉思
status	/'steitəs/	*n.*	[U] high rank or social position 地位；身份
consult	/kən'sʌlt/	*vt.*	~ **sb./sth. (about sth.)** to go to (a person, book, etc.) for information, advice, etc. 请教，查阅
		vi.	~ **(with sb.)** to discuss matters with sb.; to confer with sb. 与……商量；与……磋商
ethos	/'i:θɔs/	*n.*	[U] (*fml.*) characteristic spirit, moral values, ideas or beliefs of a group, community or culture 气质；道德观；思想，信仰

✪ New Expressions

tempt sb. into sth./doing sth.	to persuade or try to persuade sb. to do sth., esp. sth. wrong or unwise 劝说、鼓动某人做某事
prevent sb. from doing sth.	to stop something from happening or someone from doing sth. 阻止，妨碍；预防
show off	a person who tries to impress other people by showing how good he or she is at doing sth. 炫耀；使显眼
pop up	to appear suddenly 突然出现
drive sth. home	to make sb. understand or accept sth. by saying it often, loudly, etc. 把……讲透彻；阐明
point out	to tell someone about some information, often because you believe they do not know it or have forgotten it 指出

run across sth./sb.	to meet someone you know when you are not expecting to 偶然遇到，偶然撞见
no shortage of	no lacking in 不缺少；不缺乏
refer to	mention or speak about sb. or sth. 提到；谈到
on track	in a situation that is likely to lead to success 在……轨迹上
shy away	to avoid doing sth. because you are nervous or frightened 回避；躲避；避免做
meld into	to combine with sth. else（使）融合，合并
be filled with	be full of 充满

Reading Comprehension

Understanding the text

I. Answer the following questions.

1. Who tempted Adam and Eve into eating the fruit from the tree of knowledge of good and evil?

2. After Adam and Eve left the Garden of Eden, what happened to them?

3. What was the influence of Newton's theory of gravitation?

4. What did the columnist John Shinal point out?

5. How did Apple, the company redefine the way the world communicates, gleans information and entertains itself in a very visible way?

6. How did Apple manage to influence all age groups to use its products?

7. What did Jez Frampton say about Apple?

8. What did Jobs want his company to be?

Critical thinking

II. Work in pairs and discuss the following questions.

1. What do you think about the Information Age that we live in?

2. Have you ever used an Apple product? Do you like Apple products? Why or why not?

3. Facing the slogan "boycotting foreign goods", "boycotting Apple products" proposed by some people, what idea do you have?

4. What do you think is the influence of Apple products on our life?

5. Do you agree with the author's opinion that "it's Apple's world, and we're all just part of it"? Why or why not?

Words in use

III. Fill in the blanks with the words given below. Change the form where necessary. Each word can be used only once.

endless	perspective	manipulate	consult	omnipresent
motion	immortal	startle	mumble	tempt

1. Beauty is _____, therefore everything is capable of giving us joy.

2. If someone has a great sense of humor, it means he is happy, socially confident and has a healthy _____ on life.

3. He _____ something to me which I didn't quite catch.

4. The Congress voted down a(n) _____ to change the union's structure.

5. Scientists would soon be able to _____ human genes to control the aging process.

6. I can't endure her _____ complaint noise a moment longer.

7. Reducing the income will further impoverish these families and could _____ an offender into further crime.

8. She was _____ by their daughter's request but trying hard not to show it.

9. I am going to _____ with my publisher about my forthcoming book.

10. The Nile River gave birth to the _____ civilization of the Egyptians.

Word building

The suffix *-er* combines with verbs to form nouns. Nouns formed in this way refer to people who do the action described by the original verb. The suffix *-er* also combines with verbs to form nouns that refer to things rather than people.

Examples

Words learned	Add *-er*	New words formed
compute	→	computer
drink	→	drinker
swim	→	swimmer
drive	→	driver

The suffix *-ion* combines with verbs to form nouns. (For explanation, refer to Word building in Unit 3.)

Examples

Words learned	Add *-ion*	New words formed
educate	→	education
definite	→	definition
express	→	expression
regulate	→	regulation
promote	→	promotion
populate	→	population

IV. Add -er or -ion to or remove them from the following words to form new words.

Words learned	New words formed
-er	
develop	
message	
consumer	
-ion	
admit	
react	
appreciate	
negotiate	
communicate	
cultivate	
cooperation	
formulation	
instruction	

V. Fill in the blanks with the newly-formed words in Activity IV. Change the form where necessary. Each word can be used only once.

1. A(n) _____ is someone who develops something such as an idea, a design or a product.

2. He _____ much time and energy in writing this book.

3. My son's _____ to the letter was somewhat indifferent.

4. Following this session, we shall _____ a series of laws.

5. In order to _____ the students to cooperate better, teachers should first learn how to cooperate.

6. We take this opportunity to express our sincere _____ of your help.

7. Technological innovation and talents _____ are the power for the increasing of knowledge-economy.

8. The UN had been _____ with the State Department on a plan to find countries willing to take the refugees.

9. One of the fundamental bars to _____ is the lack of a universally spoken, common language.

10. We have had meaningful _____ and I believe we are very close to a deal.

11. You can't blame the _____ for bringing the bad news.

12. The _____ notice he received from the university rejoiced his mother's heart.

Banked cloze

VI. Fill in the blanks by selecting suitable words from the word bank. You may not use any of the words more than once.

A. flooded	B. considering	C. leaders	D. submit	E. accessed
F. hub	G. prepared	H. mobile	I. motion	J. doze
K. advantage	L. populate	M. proper	N. difficult	O. underscore

The world of education is changing as the modern world continues to grow. With so much progress happening, it's important that education be able to reach students in new ways so that their students are 1) _____ for the future. The students of today are the 2) _____, inventors, teachers, and businessmen (and women) of tomorrow. Without the 3) _____ skills, these students will not have the preparation needed to survive.

With so much focus placed on education, it can sometimes be 4) _____ to hold a job and still get the training needed to get a better job. Information technology plays a key role in students being able to keep their jobs and go to school. Now, most schools offer online classes that can be 5) _____ on computers or laptops, tablets, and even 6) _____ phones. A busy student at work can easily check in or 7) _____ assignments while on their lunch break.

Teachers need to be prepared by staying up to date with information technology, and this can mean more than just reading about the latest gadgets. Using technology, teachers can prepare their students for a future 8) _____ with gadgets including tablets, mobile phones, computers, and so much more.

Information technology is helping to prevent more high school and college dropouts as well. Life events can happen to anyone at any time, and even high schools are taking 9) _____ of online classes so that students can continue their education instead of 10) _____ dropping out.

Expressions in use

VII. Fill in the blanks with the expressions given below. Change the form where necessary. Each expression can be used only once.

tempt sb. into doing sth.	show off	point out
no shortage of	prevent sb. from doing sth.	on track
be filled with	refer to	run across
shy away		

1. The woman used all her wiles to _____ him _____ running after her.

2. To keep economic reform _____, 60,000 public-sector jobs must be cut.

3. Her son _____ ambition to become a great inventor.

4. There's _____ skilled workers but there aren't enough jobs for them.

5. She likes to _____ her nice figure by wearing tight dresses.

6. That is why they tend to _____ this type of movement as scientific socialism.

7. They _____ going on holiday by their lack of money.

8. I _____ several old friends when I went back to my hometown.

9. He likes to _____ other people's shortcomings, but he means well.

10. Don't be like an arrogant self-centered person or those who _____ from others because of self-contempt.

Structure Analysis and Writing

Structure Analysis

Focus on a comparison / contrast essay

In this unit you will learn the comparison / contrast writing method. Comparison and contrast is a method that is often used by writers to analyze the similarities and differences between two subjects. To compare is to bring out the similarities between two things, while to contrast is to emphasize the differences between them. As a result, you can understand the two subjects better than you would do if you just examine the two individually. The comparison and contrast essay is assigned in almost any subject area to encourage students to analyze concepts on a deeper level. There are some points to remember when you write a comparison / contrast essay.

1. Choose a topic

When you choose a topic, be sure not to choose two totally unrelated subjects. You must start with subjects that have some basic similarities. For instance, you could choose to compare / contrast two movies, two authors, two modes of transportation, or two sports figures.

2. Choose an organizational format

There are two basic patterns to write the comparison / contrast essay: **point-by-point** and **subject-by-subject**. With the point-by-point format, you alternate back and forth between the ideas, focusing on one point of comparison at a time. The subject refers to the two items or people you want to compare or contrast. In this unit, you will learn how to use the point-by-point format. For instance, to show several differences between vacationing in the mountains and vacationing at the beach, you may organize the details as follows:

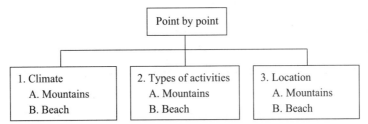

3. Use structure words

Comparison: similar to, like, both... and..., in addition, moreover, besides, likewise, similarly, in the same way, etc.

Contrast: different from, in contrast to, compared with, unlike, but, on the other hand, conversely, however, etc.

4. Points to Consider

1) Only subjects of the same general class can be compared and contrasted;

2) Compare and contrast according to a single principle and purpose;

3) Follow a clear pattern of organization. Choose either subject-by-subject pattern or point-by-point pattern;

4) Comparison and contrast should be supported by concrete and relevant facts or examples;

5) Deal equally with both subjects;

6) Compare and contrast significant points.

Now, take a look at a Para. 10 of Text A. From this part, you can see what is the comparison / contrast.

As our tech columnist John Shinal pointed out the value of Apple is more than Google and Microsoft combined. From the perspective of usage, the Apple symbol is seemingly everywhere—as ubiquitous as software giant Microsoft was in the 1990s and IBM in the 1980s.

Point: the perspective of usage

Apple vs. Microsoft vs. IBM

Conclusion: Apple icon is seemingly everywhere—as ubiquitous as software giant Microsoft was in the 1990s and IBM in the 1980s.

Structured Writing

Read the sample essay and see how it develops in the pattern of point-by-point comparison.

Topic	Sample essay
The differences between Japanese animation industry and American animation industry **Introduction** Thesis statement: They have some differences due to their cultural diversity. **Body** Point 1: Painting style	Recently, young people seem to be crazy about an activity which is called cosplay. In the activity they dress up in some wired clothes and pose themselves as a character in Japanese or American cartoons. As we all know, both Japanese and American cartoon are the most popular animation industry in the world. However, they have some differences due to their cultural diversity. Painting style is an obvious difference between Japanese and American cartoon. American painting style is usually realistic while Japanese is exaggerated. In American cartoon, the appearance of a man usually is strong and has lots of muscles

Japanese cartoon American cartoon Point 2: Industrial structure Japanese cartoon American cartoon **Conclusion** Although the two kinds of animation industry have developed to a high level in the world, there still are problems which prevent the industries from getting better.	and woman is sexy with her thick lip and electric eyes. Compared with American style, a girl in Japanese cartoon has exaggerated big eyes which have a size amount for half her face, and the small lip is painted into just one short line. Industrial structure is supposed to be another difference. Japanese cartoon has extended to various areas at the same time. For example, real-person films, dramas and PC games. Japanese cartoon has been a sign of Japanese cultural undertakings. It is welcomed by a large number of people around the world. However, a survey this year indicates that in the Europe cartoon market, the condition of Japanese cartoon is not ideal. More and more Japanese realize the problem that they have lots of good painter but are short of excellent marketers. To conclude, in contrast to Japanese cartoon, American cartoon has a complete nature industrial chain and perfect industrial structure. The Disney Company is a good example. The Disney Park built by the Disney Company has located in many countries. You can find all the characters of Disney cartoon in the park.

VIII. Write an essay of no less than 150 words on one of the following topics. One topic has an outline that you can follow.

Topic

McDonald's and Chinese restaurants

Introduction

Thesis statement: The differences between McDonald's and Chinese restaurants can be found in many aspects.

Body

Point 1: Food served

McDonald's

Chinese restaurants

Point 2: Service provided

McDonald's

Chinese restaurants

Point 3: Main consumers

McDonald's

Chinese restaurants

Conclusion

Although there are many differences between the McDonald's and Chinese restaurants, they are both popular among people.

More topics:

● An online class vs. a traditional face-to-face class

● High school vs. college

Translation

IX. Translate the following paragraph into Chinese.

Cambridge psychologists and computer scientists have developed a mobile phone technology which can tell if a caller is happy, angry, bored or sad. The Emotion Sense technology will enable psychologists to show links between mood, location and people. It uses speech-recognition software and phone sensors attached to standard smart phones to assess how people's emotions are influenced by day-to-day factors. The sectors analyze voice samples and then place them into 5 emotional categories: happiness, sadness, fear, anger and a neutral category (such as boredom or passivity). Scientists then cross-reference (注释) these emotions against surroundings, the time of day and the caller's relationship with the person they are speaking to. Result from a pilot scheme revealed that callers are happier at home, sadder at work and display more intense emotions in the evenings.

X. Translate the following paragraph into English.

当今世界，人类生活在不同文化、种族、肤色、宗教和不同社会制度所组成的世界里，各国人民形成了你中有我、我中有你的命运共同体。我们应该推动不同文明相互尊重、和谐共处，让文明交流互鉴成为增进各国人民友谊的桥梁、推动人类社会进步的动力、维护世界和平的纽带。我们应该从不同文明中寻求智慧，汲取营养，为人们提供精神支撑和心灵慰藉，携手解决人类共同面临的各种挑战。

Section

Reading Skills: *Purpose*

There is an author—a person with thoughts, feelings, and opinions—behind everything you read. Whether this person is a sports writer, a newspaper columnist, a novelist, or a friend sending you a letter, he or she works from a personal point of view. That point of view is reflected in the purpose of a piece of writing. Purpose is the reason why the author writes. Figuring out the author's purpose of writing can help you better evaluate the content of a whole essay. Three common purposes are as fellows.

Informative writing. It gives information about a subject. Authors provide facts / opinions that will explain or teach something to readers.

Example 1: The author of an informative paragraph about the definition of "brainstorm" might begin, "Process for generating creative ideas and solutions through intensive and freewheeling group discussion..."

Persuasive writing. It convinces the reader of a particular position or opinion. Authors with this purpose may give facts or opinions, but their main goal is to argue or prove a point to readers.

Example 2: The author of a persuasive paragraph about "Apple" might begin "I know Apple will never be too far away from me. Our home is filled with iPhones, MacBook Pros and, when my daughter drops in, an Apple Watch." (Para. 21, Text A)

Entertaining writing. It entertains readers, and appeals to the reader's sense and imagination. Authors with this purpose entertain readers in many ways including fiction and nonfiction.

Example 3. The author of an entertaining paragraph about "quit smoking" might be "It is easy to quit smoking. I've done it hundreds of times."

Read the three paragraphs below from Text B and decide whether the author's purpose is to inform, to persuade, or to entertain.

1. *You've seen them dragging their feet down the street, eyes glued to 5-inch screens, fingers tip-tapping away. To say that young people are in love with their smart phones would be an understatement. It's more like they're obsessed.* (Para.1)

   Purpose:

2. *There are more than 3 million of them, for both Apple and Android devices, and it got me wondering. Many of these apps have graduated to life savers. I know I couldn't exist without many of them. Could you?* (Para. 7)

    Purpose:

3. *Almost 90% of Millennials say their phones never leave their sides. The first thing that 80% of Millennials do every morning is reach for their smart phones, and 78% spend more than two hours a day texting, surfing, talking, tweeting and—more importantly for businesses— shopping, banking and more.* (Para. 2)

    Purpose:

Text B

Waze Forever

1. You've seen them dragging their feet down the street, eyes **glued** to 5-inch screens, fingers tip-tapping away. To say that young people are in love with their smart phones would be an **understatement**. It's more like they're **obsessed**.

2. Almost 90% of Millennials say their phones never leave their sides. The first thing that 80% of Millennials do every morning is to reach for their smart phones, and 78% spend more than two hours a day texting, **surfing**, talking, tweeting and—more importantly for businesses— shopping, banking and more.

3. Companies that don't speak mobile are missing the boat, because young consumers are expecting it, even demanding it. For consumers of all generations what this means is that they can have access to a crop of new, more **complicated** apps on the way. If Millennials had their way, they'd be able to pay bills by **snapping** a photo of them (45%), enroll for everything from credit cards to **gym** memberships using a photo of their driver's license (33%) and take some pain out of tax time by **inputting** W-2's by photo (33%).

4. Companies such as Progressive Insurance, Bank of America and Apple are at the forefront of the trend, but that's only the start. And the mobile trend is being driven by Millennials—perhaps the very **dawdlers** in front of you on the sidewalk with their faces in their smart phones.

5. I'm no Millennial, but I keep mine by me 24/7, too. The farthest the smart phone gets from my body is when I **charge** it overnight.

6. With email, texts, Facebook, calendar, weather, **calculator**, mapping and, yes, even phone calls, our lives are **conducted** on the digital **extension** of our arm, and most of that is happening via apps.

7. There are more than 3 million of them, for both Apple and Android devices, and it got me wondering. Many of these apps have graduated to life savers. I know I couldn't exist without many

of them. Could you?

8. I threw this question to the Facebook community recently, and the **response** was overwhelming. Some of the replies I received were surprising. SoulCycle kept Kelly on track and reminded her to get to her spinning class.

9. As for me, I have a number of **contenders**. There is a bunch I use every day:

I start in the morning with the free 7 Minute Workout app, which gives me some exercises to get going. I continue through the day with Dashlane, my password manager, which remembers all those **pesky** letter, number and symbol **combinations**; Cleartune helps **tune** my guitar; Camera Awesome is for taking photos and prettying up the pictures, and so many news apps: *Google News*, *The Hollywood Reporter*, *NPR One* and *USA TODAY*.

10. Many **respondents** offered Uber as the app that had most changed their lives—and it's a good one. Some people have **ditched** their cars, and saved thousands on **insurance** and **upkeep** with the low-cost taxi choice.

11. But I still drive—hey, I'm an L.A. guy—and so I'm with Liz, Beth, Diane and so many others who chose the app that changed their lives, and mine, forever.

12. Waze.

13. Do you remember what life used to be like? Paper maps in the car? Always getting lost and then being **isolated** from the digital world? There is nothing more **frustrating** to me than getting lost when I am driving.

14. Now, our phones tell us, in amazing detail, how to get around, and we get to see so much more of it, because Waze comes up with those very unique side-street **routes**. It even lets us know, to the minute, what time we will arrive to our destination. Driving has never been this much fun.

15. Remember the GPS units we used to put in our cars? Does anyone **yearn** for the days when you'd start the trip by typing in the address, slowly, key by key, to start your journey?

16. Google quickly made GPS units irrelevant when it **launched** Google Maps, first for **desktop** in 2004 and then it became the default map app for the iPhone. Apple in 2012 kicked Google off the iPhone to launch its own, inferior mapping service, only to meet poor reviews. Google Maps got **principal** position in the App Store for folks to return to the app they loved. Apple Maps, meanwhile, has yet to catch up.

17. Meanwhile, Google snapped up Waze, a company formed in Israel, for $1.1 billion in 2013 and has let both mapping services **coexist**.

18. Google Maps is great—it's even added some of Waze's social tools—**gathering** information from users for real-time updates on accidents. And Waze added Google's **precision** search. But Google always seems more **intent** on showing the dull freeway options while Waze has those crazy backstreet routes.

19. I'm for anything that gets me out of traffic and arrives more quickly.

20. Waze forever!

(819 words)

Notes

Millennial: (also known as Generation Y) the demographic cohort following Generation X. There are no precise dates for when this cohort starts or ends; demographers and researchers typically use starting birth years ranging from the late 1970s to early 1980s and ending birth years ranging from the mid-1990s to early 2000s.

W-2: a United States federal tax form issued by employers, stating how much an employee was paid in a year.

Progressive Insurance: one of the largest providers of car insurance in the United States.

Waze: a GPS-based geographical navigation application program for smart phones with GPS support and display screens, providing turn-by-turn information and user-submitted travel times and route details, downloading location-dependent information over the mobile telephone network. It was developed by the Israeli start-up Waze Mobile, which was acquired by Google in 2013 (although US and UK regulators were considering whether Google's purchase might violate anti-trust laws).

◀ New Words

glue	/gluː/	*vt.*	1. (*infml.*) continually close to sth.; unwilling to leave sth. 紧附于，不愿离开　2. ~ **A (to/onto B); ~ A and B (together)** to stick or join a thing or things with glue 用胶水黏合
		n.	[C, U] thick sticky liquid used for joining things 胶；胶水
understatement	/'ʌndəsteitmənt/	*n.*	1. [C] a statement that makes sth. seem less important, impressive, serious, etc. than it really is 保守的陈述　2. [U] the practice of making things seem less impressive, important, serious, etc. than they really are 轻描淡写
obsessed	/əb'sest/	*a.*	unable to stop thinking about something; too interested in or worried about something 心神不宁的；着迷的；困扰的
surf	/sɜːf/	*v.*	to use the internet（互联网）冲浪，漫游
complicated	/'kɔmplikeitid/	*a.*	difficult to understand or explain because there are many different parts 复杂的；难以理解的
snap	/snæp/	*vt.*	to take a quick photograph of (sb.)（很快地）给（某人）拍照

gym	/dʒim/	*n.*	[C] gymnasium 体育馆；健身房
input	/'input/	*vt.*	~ **sth. (into/to sth.)** (*computing*) to put (data) into a computer 将（数据）输入计算机
dawdler	/'dɔːdlə(r)/	*n.*	[C] someone who takes more time than necessary; someone who lags behind 游手好闲的人；懒人
charge	/tʃɑːdʒ/	*vt.*	1. to put a charge into (sth.) 给……充电 2. ~ **sb. (with sth.)** to accuse sb. of sth., esp. formally in a court of law 指控；控告
calculator	/'kælkjuleitə(r)/	*n.*	[C] a small electronic machine that can add, multiply, etc. 计算器
conduct	/kən'dʌkt/	*vt.*	1. to direct (sth.); to control, to manage 指挥；控制；操纵；管理；主持；经营 2. to lead or guide (sb./sth.) 领导、指导、引导 3. (*fml.*) oneself well, badly, etc. behave in the specified way 表现
extension	/ik'stenʃn/	*n.*	1.[U] (*fml.*) action of stretching out a limb or finger 伸展 2.[U] process or action of extending; state of being extended 伸长；延长；延展；伸展；提供；给予 3. [C] telephone line leading from the main phone or switchboard to another room or office in a (large) building; its number 电话分机；分机号码
response	/ri'spɔns/	*n.*	[C, U] answer 回答；答复
contender	/kən'tendə/	*n.*	[C] a person who takes part in a competition or tries to win sth. 争夺者；竞争者
pesky	/'peski/	*a.*	causing trouble; annoying 引起麻烦的；恼人的
combination	/kɔmbi'neiʃn/	*n.*	[U] joining or mixing together of two or more things or people; state of being joined or mixed together 结合，混合，联合
tune	/tjuːn/	*vt.*	to adjust (a musical instrument or note) to the correct pitch 为（乐器）调音；调（音）
		n.	[C, U] (series of notes with or without harmony forming a) melody, esp. a well-marked one 曲调
respondent	/ri'spɔndənt/	*n.*	1. [C] a person who answers questions, especially in a survey 参与者；受访人 2. [C] (*law*) a person who is accused of sth. 被告
ditch	/ditʃ/	*vt.*	(*infml.*) to abandon (sb./sth.); to get rid of 抛弃；摆脱
		v.	to land (an aircraft) in the sea in an emergency 迫降
insurance	/in'ʃuərəns/	*n.*	[C, U] (contract made by a company or society, or by the state, to provide a) guarantee of compensation for loss, damage, sickness, death, etc. in return for regular payment 保险（契约）
upkeep	/'ʌpkiːp/	*n.*	[U] (cost or means of) keeping sth. in good condition and repair; maintenance 保养；维修；养护；维护费
isolate	/'aisəleit/	*vt.*	to separate one person, group, or thing from other people or things 孤立；隔离

isolated	/'aisəleitid/	*a.*	happening only once or existing only in one place 孤立的
frustrating	/frʌ'streitiŋ/	*a.*	annoying; discouraging 使人心烦的；使人讨厌的；使人灰心的；使人沮丧的
route	/ru:t/	*n.*	[C] way taken or planned to get from one place to another 路；路途；路线
yearn	/jɜ:n/	*vi.*	~ **(for sb./sth.)** to desire strongly or with compassion or tenderness; to be filled with longing 渴望
launch	/lɔ:ntʃ/	*vt.*	to make a product available to the public for the first time（使）上市；发行
desktop	/'desktɒp/	*n.*	[C] a computer with a keyboard, screen and main processing unit, that fits on a desk 电脑桌面
principal	/'prinsəpl/	*a.*	(only before noun) most important 最重要的；首要的；主要的
coexist	/ˌkəuig'zist/	*vi.*	1. ~ **(with sb./sth.)** to exist together at the same time or in the same place 共处；共存　2. (of opposing countries or groups) to exist together without fighting 和平共处
gather	/'gæðə(r)/	*vt.*	~ **sth. (together/up)** bring together (objects) that have been spread about 收集，收拢
		vi.	~ **round (sb./sth.); (~ sb./sth.)**. to round (sb./sth.) come or bring sb./sth. together in one place 聚集；集合；召集
precision	/pri'siʒn/	*n.*	[U] (also preciseness) exactness and clarity; quality of being precise 准确（性）；明确（性）
intent	/in'tent/	*a.*	1. ~ **(on/upon sth./doing sth.)** (a) having the stated firm intention　热衷的；坚决的 (b) occupied in doing sth. with great concentration 专心的；专注的　2. (of looks, attention, etc.) full of eager interest and concentration 专心的，渴望的

☺ New Expressions

be in love with sb./sth.	to fall in love with sb./sth. 爱上；热爱
reach for	to try to get sth. by one's hands 伸手去拿
miss the boat	to lose an opportunity to do something by being slow to act 错过机会，坐失良机
have access to	to have the right to enter a place, use sth., see sb., etc. 拥有进入权；有使用权；拥有接触的机会
at/in/to the forefront	to be in the most noticeable or important position 处于最显要的位置、地位
as for	used to start talking about sb./sth. 至于；关于
get going	to begin or set in motion; start to be active 开始；出发；着手
pretty up	to use special care in dressing, making-up, etc. 美化
come up with	to suggest or think of an idea or plan 想出，提出（主意或计划）

yearn for	have a desire for... 渴望……
kick off	force to go away sb. 赶走某人
snap up	get hold of or seize quickly and easily 抢先弄到手

Reading Comprehension

Understanding the text

I. Choose the best answer to each of the following questions.

1. According to Para. 2, which of the following statements is true?

   A. 90% of Millennials say their phones never leave their sides.

   B. The first thing that 80% of Millennials do every morning is to get their smart phones.

   C. Almost 78% of people spend more than two hours a day texting, surfing, talking and tweeting.

   D. Many people spend more than two hours a day shopping and banking.

2. According to the text, why are companies that don't speak mobile missing the boat?

   A. Because young consumers are expecting it, even demanding it.

   B. Because consumers of all generations are expecting it, even demanding it.

   C. Because young consumers are crazy about it.

   D. Because consumers of all generations will buy mobile products.

3. When is the smart phone farthest from the author's body during the whole day?

   A. When the author is working.　　　　B. When the author charges his smart phone overnight.

   C. When the author is eating.　　　　D. When the author is driving.

4. According to the text, what's the function of Cleartune?

   A. To remember all those pesky letter, number and symbol combinations.

   B. To take photos and prettying up the pictures.

   C. To read news.

   D. To help tune the author's guitar.

5. According to many respondents, which app has most changed their lives?

   A. Camera Awesome.　　　　B. Dashlane.

   C. Uber.　　　　D. 7 Minute Workout.

6. About Waze, which one is NOT true?

   A. Waze comes up with those very unique side-street routes.

   B. It lets us know, to the minute, what time we will arrive to our destination.

C. Driving has never been this much fun without Waze.

D. It has become the default map app for the iPhone.

7. Which one of the following statements is true about Google Maps?

   A. It was launched for desktop in 2002.

   B. It became the default map app for the iPhone.

   C. It cooperated with Baidu.

   D. It is the most popular app in App Store.

8. According to the text, what is added to Google Maps?

   A. Google's precision search.   B. Crazy backstreet routes.

   C. Some of Waze's social tools.   D. Inferior mapping service.

Critical thinking

II. Work in pairs and discuss the following questions.

1. What do you think are the differences between you and the generation of your parents in the aspect of using smart phones?

2. How often do you check your smart phone during a single day?

3. What kind of app do you like most?

4. What has the smart phone brought about to your life?

5. What functions do you expect smart phones will have in the future?

Language Focus

Words in use

III. Fill in the blanks with the words given below. Change the form where necessary. Each word can be used only once.

ditch	combination	launch	precision	obsessed
intent	isolate	pesky	principal	gather

1. You never know how to take care of yourself. I need my hands to help you get rid of the _____ white hair you hate so much when you grow old, to trim your nails and to feed you.

2. On both large and small farms, one of the _____ inhibitions to expansion of production

can be insecurity of tenure.

3. Heads of government from more than 100 countries will _____ in Geneva for the forum which will be held next month.

4. If you are _____ on learning to speak Portuguese, there is no better place than this language-training school.

5. If someone is _____ with a person or thing, they keep thinking about them and find it difficult to think about anything else.

6. Making machine gears requires absolute _____ and considerable expertise.

7. She seemed determined to _____ herself from everyone, even him.

8. I suggested that we not only dump the two companies, but that we also should _____ any other business not involved in computer programming.

9. The architecture in the town center is a successful _____ of old and new.

10. Marks & Spencer recently hired super model Linda to _____ its new range.

Expressions in use

IV. Fill in the blanks with the expressions given below. Change the form where necessary. Each expression can be used only once.

be in love with	miss the boat	have access to	pretty up
reach for	at the forefront of	yearn for	kick off
snap up	come up with		

1. If we don't offer a good price for the house now, we'll probably _____.

2. My dear Eliza, he must _____ you, or he would never have called on us in this familiar way.

3. People all over the world _____ social environment characterized by stability, progress, and peaceful development.

4. Maybe the next challenge should be to _____ the wind turbines to make them more aesthetically pleasing.

5. It's great to see a large technology company like IBM _____ this trend.

6. People in these cultures believe that they are close to power and should _____ that power.

7. Instead, analysts believe that motorists view the situation as an opportunity to _____ bargains.

8. We can't _____ the island where they have lived for several generations.

9. The president was moved to _____ these suggestions after the hearings.

10. A man in the gangway suddenly stood up to _____ something in the overhead locker.

Sentence structure

V. Complete the following sentences by translating the Chinese into English, using "imperatives + and / or + statements" structure. Here the imperative sentence is similar to an "if" clause.

> **Model:** _____ (拜访美国人的家里，你能看到似乎每个房间里都有 iPhone、Mac 和 iPad). You might even spot an Apple TV.
>
> → <u>Visit many American homes and you're apt to see iPhones, Macs and iPads in seemingly every room.</u> You might even spot an Apple TV.

1. It seems you had a bad headache. _____
   (照医生的话去做，要不然你的头疼会更严重).

2. The words on the PPT are too small. _____
   (站到那边去，你会看得更清楚).

3. The ground is so slippery. _____
   (走路小心点，否则你可能会摔倒).

VI. Rewrite the following sentences by using "There is nothing more + a. + than..." to practice the structure of comparison. Make changes where necessary.

> **Model:** To get lost is much more frustrating to me than anything else when I am driving.
>
> → There is nothing more frustrating to me than getting lost when I am driving.

1. To improve your English listening skills, listening practice is much more helpful than anything else.

   _____

2. To achieve your dream, never giving up is much more important than anything else.

   _____

3. To pursue a better life, time is more precious than anything else in the world.

   _____

Unit 6
Social Networking

People need to know one another to be at their honest best.

— *Robbins Staca (British writer)*

The web is like a dominatrix. Everywhere I turn, I see little buttons ordering me to submit.

— *Nytwind (American computer scientist)*

Social networking has changed the way people interact with each other. It has become a universal method of communicating among family members, friends and even strangers. People are spending more and more time on social networking sites. In many ways, social media has led to positive changes in the way people communicate and share information. If you claim that you are a fashion insider, it means you have already used at least one social media platform, but you may still have some questions about social networking. Is social media playing a helping or hindering role in your life? Is it safe? Can it really increase productivity and build brand awareness—or is it simply a place to kill a considerable amount of time? These are good questions for you to consider.

Section

Pre-reading Activities

I. *To figure out what generation you belong to is fairly easy. Just take the quiz by checking (√) the following statements that are true for you. You can judge according to the grading criteria (each question is worth 2 points, totally 20 points).*

(   ) 1. Do you have more than one Social Networking Services?

(   ) 2. Do you have your own web page?

(   ) 3. Do you watch videos on the Internet?

(   ) 4. When you stay at home, do you always spend your time on online activities instead of watching TV or other traditional entertainment?

(   ) 5. Have you paid for and downloaded music or films from the Internet?

(   ) 6. Do you blog for professional reasons?

(   ) 7. Do you always take photos with your cell phone?

(   ) 8. Do you always use your cell phone to do online shopping?

(   ) 9. Do you have a habit of taking photos of the food before you eat it?

(   ) 10. Have you influenced your parents in the aspect of online activities?

4–10 points: Generation X (from the 1960s to the early 1980s)

11–16 points: Generation Y (from the mid-1980s to the early 2000s)

17 or more points: Generation Z (from the mid-1990s or the early 2000s to the present)

II. *Work in pairs and discuss the following questions.*

1. What do you think are the criteria to evaluate a social networking website?

2. Nowadays, what role, in your opinion, does social networking play in people's lives?

How One Mysterious Vlogger Changed the Internet

1. In June 2006, a 16-year-old girl began a video blog on YouTube. Her name was Bree, and she'd been **lurking** in the **burgeoning** community for a while. She was a self-described girl, and she thought her hometown was really **boring**—"Maybe that's why I spend so much time on my computer."

2. She was funny, friendly, and had great eyebrows. Her first few videos were **cute**, introducing her friend Daniel and complaining about being home-schooled and having to do homework in June. It soon became clear she was pretty lonely, which was probably why her username was Lonelygirl15.

3. Bree was one of a slowly-growing community video bloggers on YouTube. They poured their lives into their **webcams**. Their follower bases grew slowly but **steadily**, with regular videos about their day-to-day lives. They were largely ignored by the mainstream media, who at the time **dismissed** YouTube as just a **repository** for cat videos.

4. Lonelygirl15 changed all that. Her followers quickly **ballooned** and she became one of the young site's most popular stars. She was featured in *New York Times*. She had her own **forum**. Hundreds of people wanted to be her friend on MySpace.

5. The truth is, Bree wasn't real. Lonelygirl15 actually had a small team of writers. Bree and her best friend Daniel were played by actors.

6. YouTubers and the media had been **duped**. Yet this was no **mere** flash in the **trick**—this was YouTube's first web series. This was the first time someone proved you could actually make **profits** on YouTube.

7. And that changed everything.

8. Remember Lonely Island's *Lazy Sunday* video? It was the one where Andy Samberg and Chris Parnell rapped about a Sunday getting cupcakes and going to the movies. Miles Beckett does this because that's the video that began his obsession with YouTube.

9. "Someone posted it on MySpace, and I think it was in December 2005." he said. "And that's how I found out about YouTube."

10. Back then, YouTube was just getting started. It wasn't yet a year old, but it was growing

quickly. In the next summer it would be one of the fastest growing sites on the Internet and would go on to be bought by Google for $1.65 billion. Then a doctor, Beckett was among the millions of visitors to the site in its **infancy**, following the community and learning from it.

11. One of the most-viewed videos from the pre-Lonelygirl15 **era** of YouTube was of two guys **lip-syncing** to the *Pokémon* **theme** songs. It was all filmed on their webcam and netted them about 24 million views before it was **removed**.

12. Beckett had been **enlightened**. How could you really tell what was real and what was **fake** on YouTube? Anyone could buy a webcam or camera phone and **upload** what they wanted. So how easy would it be to create an entirely **fictitious** YouTuber?

13. "I thought it would be really cool if there was a video blogger and you told the story just like you made a TV show," he said.

14. He sat on this idea for a while. Then, one evening at a karaoke bar in LA, he met Mesh Flinders. The two hit it off so well; Beckett took a chance. He told Flinders about this new medium and his idea for a new story on it. Within a matter of days, they began writing the **script**. Within two weeks, they had the entire plot points for the first three months of videos.

15. The story revolves around a girl. Our **protagonist**, Bree, is a home-schooled 16-year-old girl who doesn't have a lot in the way of friends. Her days are spent on the Internet, doing homework or hanging out with her friend Daniel. She seems like a happy-go-lucky teenager, curious about science and history… But there is a **exception** that her parents are part of some strange **religion**, possibly a **cult**.

16. For Flinders, who grew up on a commune in Northern California, it was actually a story which was a long time in the making. "I didn't see the outside world until I was 14," he said. "So I knew what a girl who had been home-schooled her whole life would be like—because that's what I was like."

17. When it came to the most important thing, people needed to believe Bree was real. Beckett and Flinders watched all the main YouTubers, studying how they spoke and what kind of background they used. So with Lonelygirl15, they did everything they could to make it feel completely authentic. They had a plan, the webcam and the scripts, which can come in handy. All they needed now, was the right girl for the part.

18. Jessica Lee Rose was not interested in the Internet. Sure, she had a MySpace profile, but it wasn't something she used every single day. She had just moved to Los Angeles after graduating from New York Film Academy in Burbank, working two jobs while pursuing a professional acting career. Though she was 19 at the time, it wasn't a huge stretch for the **casual** viewer to think she could be 16. It also turned out she too, like Bree, had been home-schooled at one point. Best of all? She was fresh off the plane. No casting **agency** in the city had seen her yet. Rose was perfect for the part in so many ways.

19. Now the work could begin.

20. "Hi guys! This is my first video blog. I've been watching for a while and I really like some of you guys on here."

21. "My name is Bree. I'm 16…"

(921 words)

Notes

vlogger: a portmanteau of the words video and blogger. A vlogger is someone who posts embedded videos regularly to their blog, in addition to or in place of text and other content. Some vloggers post videos that feature themselves or have been recorded independently, while others might post videos within a certain genre such as humor, science, or sports.

YouTube: an American video-sharing website headquartered in San Bruno, California, United States. The service was created by three former PayPal employees in February 2005. In November 2006, it was bought by Google for $1.65 billion.

Lonely Island: an American comedy trio, formed by Akiva Schaffer, Andy Samberg, and Jorma Taccone in Berkeley, California in 2001.

Lazy Sunday: a song and short video by American comedy troupe Lonely Island. It was released on December 17, 2005 when it was broadcast on *Saturday Night Live* as their second digital short.

Myspace: a popular social networking website offering an interactive, user-submitted network of friends, personal profiles, blogs, groups, photos, music and videos internationally.

◀ New Words

lurk	/lɜːk/	*vi.*	1. to wait near a place trying not to attract attention 隐藏；隐匿　2. (*fig.*) to linger (esp. in the mind) without being clearly shown 潜藏
burgeoning	/ˈbɜːdʒənɪŋ/	*a.*	(*fml.*) growing rapidly; flourishing 迅速成长的；茂盛的
boring	/ˈbɔːrɪŋ/	*a.*	uninteresting; dull; tedious 无趣的；单调的；乏味的
cute	/kjuːt/	*a.*	attractive; pretty and charming 有吸引力的；漂亮的；逗人喜爱的
webcam	/ˈwebkæm/	*n.*	[C] a camera that records moving pictures and sound and allows these to be broadcast on the internet as they happen 网络摄像机
steadily	/ˈstedili/	*a.*	1. gradually 逐渐地；稳步地　2. calmly and in a controlled way 冷静地，镇定地

dismiss	/dis'mis/	*vt.*	1. ~ **sb./sth. (as sth.)** to decide that sb./sth. is not important and not worth thinking or talking about 不予考虑 2. ~ **sb. (from sth.)** to remove sb. (esp. an employee) from a position 免除职务；开除；解雇 3. ~ **sb. (from sth.)** to send sb. away; to allow sb. to leave 把某人打发走；让某人离开
repository	/ri'pɔzitri/	*n.*	1. [C] place where things are stored or may be found, esp. a warehouse or museum 仓库，博物馆 2. [C] (*fig.*) person or book that receives and stores confidences, secrets, information, etc. 可信任的人；心腹；知己；知识宝库
balloon	/bə'luːn/	*vi.*	to swell out like a balloon 膨胀如气球
		n.	1. [C] brightly-colored rubber bag that is filled with air, used as a child's toy or a decoration 气球 2. [C] large flexible bag filled with hot air or gas to make it rise in the air, often carrying a basket, etc. for passengers 热气气球
forum	/'fɔːrəm/	*n.*	[C] [*usu. sing.*] place where important public issues can be discussed 论坛
dupe	/djuːp/	*vt.*	to deceive or trick sb. (into doing sth.) 欺骗；哄骗
		n.	[C] person who is duped; fool 受骗的人；傻子
mere	/miə(r)/	*a.*	nothing more than; no better or more important than 仅仅；只不过；不超过
trick	/trik/	*n.*	[C] thing done in order to deceive or outwit sb. 诡计；计谋
profit	/'prɔfit/	*n.*	[C, U] money that you gain by selling things or doing business, after your costs have been paid 利益；收益；盈利
		v.	(*fml.*) to give sb. an advantage 使……得到；有利于
infancy	/'infənsi/	*n.*	[U] 1. (*fig.*) early stage of development or growth 初期 2. the state or period of being an infant; early childhood 婴儿期；幼儿期
era	/'iərə/	*n.*	[C] period in history starting from a particular time or event 纪元；年代；时代
lip-sync	/'lipsiŋk/	*v.*	to pretend to be singing songs when in fact they are just moving their lips 假唱, 对口型
theme	/θiːm/	*n.*	[C] 1. subject of a talk, a piece of writing or a person's thoughts; topic 主题；核心；题目 2. [C] (*music*) melody that is repeated, developed, etc. in a composition, or on which variations are compo（乐曲的）主题，主旋律
remove	/ri'muːv/	*vt.*	1. ~ **sth./sb. (from sth.)** to take sth./sb. away from one place to another 移开 2. to dismiss sb. from a post, etc. 免去……的职务 3. to get rid of sth. by cleaning 去掉或清除……
enlighten	/in'laitn/	*vt.*	(*fml.*) to give sb. information about sth. so that they understand more about it 启发；指导；教导
fake	/feik/	*a.*	not genuine 假的；伪造的
upload	/ˌʌp'ləud/	*vt.*	(*computing*) to move data to a larger computer system from a smaller one 上传
fictitious	/fik'tiʃəs/	*a.*	imagined or invented; not real 想象的；虚构的；假的

script	/skrɪpt/	*n.*	1. [C] text of a play, film, broadcast, talk, etc.（戏剧、电影、广播、讲话等的）剧本，脚本，讲稿　2. [U] (a) handwriting 笔迹 (b) printed or typewritten cursive characters resembling this 书写体的字
protagonist	/prə'tægənɪst/	*n.*	1. [C] chief person in a story or chief participant in an actual event, esp. a conflict or dispute 主人公；主要参与者，主要人物　2. [C] (*fml.*) chief character in a drama; hero（戏剧的）主角
exception	/ɪk'sepʃn/	*n.*	[C, U] (an instance of) leaving out or excluding; person or thing that is not included 除外；例外；不包括在内的人或物
religion	/rɪ'lɪdʒən/	*n.*	[C] particular system of faith and worship based on such a belief 宗教
cult	/kʌlt/	*n.*	1. [C] a religious group, often living together, whose beliefs are considered extreme or strange by many people 异教；异端　2. [U] someone or something that has become very popular with a particular group of people 风行；流行；崇拜
casual	/'kæʒuəl/	*a.*	1. made or done without much care or thought; offhand 不经意的；随便的　2. happening by chance 偶然的；碰巧的　3. (of clothes) for informal occasions; not formal（衣物）便服的，非正式的
agency	/'eidʒənsi/	*n.*	1. [C] business or place of business providing a (usu. specified) service 代理；经销处　2. [C] government office providing a specific service 政府的特种机构

✪ New Expressions

complain about (doing) sth.	to say that doing sth.or sth. is dissatisfied, unhappy, etc. 投诉；抱怨；诉苦；发牢骚
be featured in	be included or shown as a special or important part of sth., or be included as an important part 在……中被专题介绍；被特写
sit on	to have received a letter, report, etc. from sb. and then do not reply or take any action concerning it 拖延；积压；搁置
hit it off	to like someone and become friendly immediately 相处得好，合得来
take a chance	to decide to do sth., knowing that it might be the wrong choice 冒险
revolve around	to have sth. as a main subject or purpose 以……为主题（目的）；围绕……
hang out with	to spend a lot of time in a place or with someone 经常出入；厮混
be curious about	to have a strong desire to know about sth 好奇的
when it comes to	when you are dealing with sth. or talking about sth. 在某个方面；说到……
be interested in	to have an interest in sth. or doing sth. 对……有兴趣
come in handy	be useful in particular situation 派上用场

Reading Comprehension

Understanding the text

I. Answer the following questions.

1. Why did Bree think her hometown was really boring?

2. What is the content of Bree's first few videos?

3. Why did Bree choose "Lonelygirl15" as her username?

4. Are Bree and her friend Dianel real?

5. Before the Lonelygirl15 era of YouTube, what were the main contents of most-viewed videos?

6. Where did Miles Beckett get the chance to meet Mesh Flinders?

7. Why did Flinders say that he knew what a girl who had been home-schooled her whole life would be like?

8. What did Beckett and Flinders do to make people believe Bree was real?

Critical thinking

II. Work in pairs and discuss the following questions.

1. Why are people interested in the vlogger like "Lonelygirl15"?

2. What do you think about "online celebrities"?

3. Do you want to be an online celebrity? Why or why not?

4. Have you uploaded some videos to your social networks? If yes, what are those videos mainly about?

Language Focus

Words in use

III. Fill in the blanks with the words given below. Change the form where necessary. Each word can be used only once.

theme	dismiss	profit	infancy	exception
enlighten	casual	steadily	fake	remove

1. He has been _____ from his position because of his incompetence.

2. The father-son relationship is a recurring _____ in her novels, which she has been

exploring for so many years.

3. Can you distinguish between an authentic antique and a(n) _____ one.

4. Nobody seemed to be anxious to _____ me about the events that led up to the dispute.

5. The president could only be _____ from power once free elections were organized.

6. Such _____ dress would not be correct for a formal occasion so go back to change it.

7. The number of people going to the cinema seems to dwindle _____ .

8. On the basis of our sales forecasts, we may begin to make a(n) _____ next year.

9. In virtually every sport, with the possible _____ of women's gymnastics, the players are now bigger and stronger than before.

10. China's e-business is still in its _____ and remains to develop.

Word building

The suffix *-ic* combines with nouns to form adjectives. (For explanation, refer to Word building in Unit 3.)

Examples

Words learned	Add *-ic*	New words formed
class	→	classic
energy	→	energetic
history	→	historic
tragedy	→	tragic

The suffix *-ion* combines with verbs to form nouns. (For explanation, refer to Word building in Unit 3.)

Examples

Words learned	Add *-ion*	New words formed
administer	→	administration
realize	→	realization
add	→	addition

The suffix *-ize* combines with nouns or adjectives that refer to a state or condition in order to form verbs. Verbs formed in this way describe the process by which the state or condition mentioned is brought about.

Examples

Words learned	Add *-ize*	New words formed
special	→	specialize
popular	→	popularize
normal	→	normalize
modern	→	modernize

IV. add -ic, -ion , or -ize to or remove them from the following words to form new words.

Words learned	New words formed
-ic	
academy	
chaos	
-ion	
confirm	
locate	
reflect	
provide	
install	
register	
quotation	
-ize	
summery	
industrial	
memory	

V. Fill in the blanks with the newly-formed words in Activity IV. Change the form where necessary. Each word can be used only once.

1. Different schools teach different types of syllabus, from the highly _____ to the broadly vocational.

2. This section discusses the tools needed for software _____ and overall package management.

3. The _____ of drinking water and sanitation services in health facilities is a top priority.

4. In Greek mythology, Narcissus fell in love with his own _____ in a pool of water.

5. They have found a body but, as yet, they do not have _____ that it is the missing man.

6. With no one to keep order the situation in the classroom was _____.

7. Do not try to _____ any questions, just remember concepts which are more useful.

8. Please write your home address on the _____ form so that we can send you some gifts later.

9. The poem is still under copyright, so you have to pay to _____ it.

10. We also realized the growing need and necessity to _____ certain sectors of the economy.

11. We should _____ from both the subjective and objective aspects to make sure that the result is more reliable.

12. The best thing about the _____ of the house is its proximity to the town center.

Banked cloze

VI. Fill in the blanks by selecting suitable words from the word bank. You may not use any of the words more than once.

A. comes	B. necessary	C. touch	D. authentic	E. connect
F. balloon	G. enlighten	H. upload	I. fictitious	J. smaller
K. quickly	L. rise	M. real	N. conversation	O. inner

Social networking isn't for everyone, but it's now such a 1) _____ part of all our lives. Let's look the positive impact of social networks.

Social networking sites can help you make and keep friends. It has never been easier to make friends than it is right now, mainly thanks to social networking sites. Just a few decades ago it was pretty tough to 2) _____ with people, unless you were the overly outgoing type to make 3) _____ with anyone at a party. The 4) _____ of mobile phones helped change this, connecting people in a new way, but then social networks sprang up and the whole idea of friendship changed once more and forever.

It's entirely possible to have hundreds of friends on Facebook. They may not be friends you know on a personal level and spend time with in the 5) _____ world on a weekly basis. But they're friends nevertheless. There are several people I consider friends who I have never met—indeed, I may never meet them—but that doesn't lessen the connection we have thanks to social networks.

Social networking sites have made the world a smaller place. It isn't just your 6) _____ circle of close friends and even closer family members that social networking sites allow you to communicate with easily and effectively, either. They open the world up to you, making it a 7) _____ place than it has ever been before. When it 8) _____ to social networks everyone is equal, regardless of location.

Family living abroad can be kept abreast of the latest happenings in your world as 9) _____ as those living next door. Friends who you haven't seen since school, and who have since moved away, are able to keep in 10) _____.

Expressions in use

VII. Fill in the blanks with the expressions given below. Change the form where necessary. Each expression can be used only once.

complain about	be featured in	hit it off
revolve around	hang out with	come in handy
curious about	take a chance	when it comes to
be interested in		

1. This restaurant _____ the newspaper because of its good service.

2. We spent the entire evening talking and I thought we really _____.

3. All tasks must _____ the pivot and we must do everything possible to prevent anybody else from interfering with it.

4. I _____ the job you advertised in today's newspaper.

5. While there I remembered the special glue would _____ in fixing my broken shelf stool.

6. Yet the majority of these employees have no voice, especially _____ their own safety.

7. I don't know why she _____ James, after all they've got nothing in common.

8. But many defectors from the North _____ how they are treated in the South.

9. I don't know whether we have enough money to last the whole holiday as we have planned, but I'm prepared to _____ on it.

10. I am very _____ other cultures and different social customs.

Structure Analysis and Writing

Structure Analysis

Focus on a comparison / contrast essay

You already learned how to write a comparison / contrast essay in Unit 5. This unit will show more on this useful writing mode.

First of all, let us review the **point-by-point** format. If you compare two generations, you may organize the details as follows.

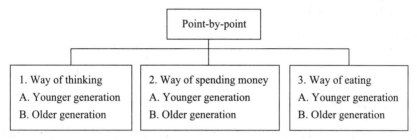

In this unit, you will learn how to organize your points by using the **subject-by-subject** format.

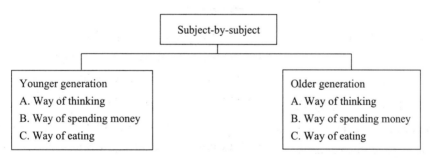

Unlike the **point-by-point format, the subject-by-subject format** needs to talk about everything (details) about the first subject and then talk about the second subject. The same points should be discussed for both subjects in the same order.

Now, take a look at Para. 3 and Para. 4 of Text A. From this part, you can know how comparison and contrast method is used to develop ideas.

They poured their lives into their webcams. Their follower bases grew slowly but steadily, with regular videos about their day-to-day lives. They were largely ignored by the mainstream media, who at the time dismissed YouTube as just a repository for cat videos. (Para. 3)

Her followers quickly ballooned and she became one of the young site's most popular stars. She was featured in New York Times. She had her own forum. Hundreds of people wanted to be her friend on MySpace. (Para. 4)

Subject A: Video bloggers on YouTube

1. their follower bases grew slowly but steadily

2. were largely ignored by the mainstream media

Subject B: Lonelygirl15

1. her followers quickly ballooned

2. was featured in *New York Times*

Structured Writing

Read the sample essay and see how it develops in the pattern of subject-by-subject.

Topic	Sample essay
City life vs. country life	At present, many people leave their hometown for big cities to earn more money and get good jobs. It is really hard to say which is better than the other, city life or rural life, because each has its merits and shortcomings.
Introduction	
Thesis statement: It is really hard to say which is better than the other, city life or rural life, because each has its merits and shortcomings.	On one hand, the life in a city is more colorful and meaningful because you can usually find many interesting places to go to whenever you want to relax yourself. Besides, city dwellers can gain access to better information and educational facilities. There usually are many excellent schools in cities where teachers are of high level and teaching facilities are advanced. On the other hand, there are more environmental problems in cities, such as industrial pollution, automobile exhaust
Body	
Subject A: City life	
1. More colorful and meaningful	
2. Better service and educational facilities	
3. More environmental problems	

Subject B: Country life	and thick haze, which are harmful to people's health.
1. More peace and quietness	As for living in country, firstly, people can enjoy pure nature. The life in country is more peaceful and quiet. Secondly, because things go slowly in country, people there may have slim chances to be admitted to colleges or gain better education. Finally, there is less noise and pollution in countries that you can breathe in fresher air. Therefore, the life there can be more healthy.
2. Slim chances to enjoy the same education which is available in cities	
3. Less noise and pollution	
Conclusion	
Whatever life people choose, they may never feel perfectly satisfied, for conveniences and inconveniences always coexist.	In conclusion, whatever life people choose, they may never feel perfectly satisfied, for conveniences and inconveniences always coexist. In my opinion, the more comfortable, the better.

VIII. Write an essay of no less than 150 words on one of the following topics. One topic has an outline that you can follow.

Topic

Fresh foods vs. canned foods

Introduction

Thesis statement: The purpose of this essay is to compare and contrast the differences between eating fresh foods and eating canned foods.

Body

Subject A: Fresh foods

1. have great flavor and taste

2. more healthy

3. cheaper

Subject B: Canned foods

1. lack a lot of its flavor characteristics

2. become toxic if consumed too often

3. more expensive

Conclusion

Therefore, it is important that you should consider your possibilities and choose the best type of foods for your convenience and lifestyle.

More topics:

- Study abroad or at home

- My two best friends

Translation

IX. Translate the following paragraph into Chinese.

Since civilization came into being, cultural exchanges commenced. Human culture on the whole has resulted from the accumulation and exchanges of each country and nation. In the modern world, there is no innate culture without any foreign influence, and the fact is almost so. The four great ancient Chinese inventions gave an enormous push to the world's ancient cultural development. Similarly, many important modern and contemporary western scientific achievements have been changing the present-day Chinese life. The opening up policy which we will abide long becomes a fundamental policy of our country, which will usher in a brighter future for our international cultural exchanges. We should make use of everything that may benefit us from every foreign country applying it to our material and spiritual civilization. Simultaneously we should introduce to the other countries the things they show interest in. Thus through mutual communication, understanding and friendship will be enhanced and worldwide development of science and culture accelerated.

X. Translate the following paragraph into English.

两千多年前，亚欧大陆上勤劳勇敢的人们探索出多条连接亚欧非几大文明的贸易和人文交流通路，后人将其统称为"丝绸之路"。千百年来，"和平合作、开放包容、互学互鉴、互利共赢"的丝绸之路精神薪火相传，推进了人类文明进步，是促进沿线各国繁荣发展的重要纽带，是东西方交流合作的象征，是世界各国共有的历史文化遗产。

Section

Reading Skills: *Understanding Text Organization*

Authors use different organizations to build their ideas. Identifying text organization can help readers understand the whole text. It also helps readers make a summary of the text.

There are many patterns that can help authors convey their purposes for writing, such as chronological order, spatial order, cause and effect, comparison and contrast and main idea.

Chronological order: It is also known as time order.

Structure words: first, then, after, finally, etc.

Spatial order: It is most frequently used in description.

Structure words: next to, behind, across from, below that, above that, to the right of and so forth.

Cause and effect: It is used when one thing under discussion is a result of another or when one event causes another to happen.

Structure words: cause, effect, as a result, consequently, etc.

Comparison and contrast: A comparison shows how things are similar while a contrast shows how things are different.

Structure words: either... or, some, other, not only... but also..., both... and..., etc.

Main idea: The main idea states the author's purpose for a whole text or a paragraph. Look at the following steps to learn how to find the main idea.

1. Read the title. Some texts or paragraphs will have a heading or title that describes the main idea of the passage.

2. Read the first paragraph of the text or the first sentence of the paragraph.

3. Read the text or the paragraph from beginning to end. If the main idea is not stated in the first paragraph of the text or the first sentence of the paragraph, it may be stated in the last paragraph or the last sentence.

4. Read the full text or paragraph. If the first and the last paragraphs or sentences do not identify the main idea, you need to summarize the main idea by using some highlighted sentences or words like: "The most important aspect is..." or, "It's most interesting that..."

Example:

When it comes to the most important thing, people needed to believe Bree was real. Beckett and Flinders watched all the main YouTubers, studying how they spoke and what kind of set up they used. So with Lonelygirl15, they did everything they could to make it feel completely authentic. They had a plan, the webcam and the scripts, which can come in handy. All they needed now, was the right girl for the part. (Para. 17, Text A)

Question. What is the main idea of this paragraph?

Answer: When it comes to the most important thing, people needed to believe Bree was real.

Now, read the following paragraph and give the main idea of this paragraph.

I'm the definition of what tech companies call a "late adopter". When I first heard about the phenomenon of combining mobile phones with cameras, I thought the idea of giving up my Nokia 6100 and brick-like digital camera for something that did both—surely not as well—was crazy. (Para. 1, Text B)

Main idea:

 Text B

Facebook: Greed in Love

1. I'm the definition of what tech companies call a "late adopter". When I first heard about the **phenomenon** of combining mobile phones with cameras, I thought the idea of giving up my Nokia 6100 and brick-like digital camera for something that did both—surely not as well—was crazy.

2. When a friend **specified** this new thing called Facebook, I was dissatisfied with it and couldn't understand why you wouldn't text a message to your friends, or share your photos over email, rather than posting them for everyone you knew to see. And I laughed at the idea of Twitter: who'd go for a rubbish version of Facebook?

3. **Needless** to say, I've now **enthusiastically** embraced them all. But when I read that Facebook wants us to spend more time on it, the old late-adopter questions went through my mind. Users already spend an average 50 minutes a day on Facebook. Like most people I know, I use it mainly to keep up to date with friends, spy on my exes and show off about my social life. Fun up to a point, but I certainly don't do that for almost an hour a day. How, then, does Facebook want to **eke** more time out of us?

4. I spend far more than 50 minutes a day on social media in total; I just spend much more time on Twitter. The average Briton spends 80 minutes a day managing an average of four social networks. So it's not the total time on social networks that I find it hard to get my head around. I read Twitter when I'm **commuting**, when I'm watching TV, and when I'm on hold waiting

to speak to my bank. It decreases my **productivity** in some ways. But for me, the benefits far outweigh the **downsides**; I read news. thinking if I were limited to reading one daily newspaper.

5. As I suspect most people do, I fit social media around my life rather than vice versa. Because I can use social media while doing other things—traveling, watching, waiting—I'm sure there's scope for the total time I spend on it to increase. But there's got to be a limit, because I have real-world things that require **exclusive** attention: reading to my kids, dinner with friends, and meetings at work.

6. So I read Facebook's desire to **capture** extra time more as a grab on the rest of the time we spend online and on other apps. It wants 30 minutes that we spend on other types of social media; if Facebook had its way, there'd be no Twitter, LinkedIn or Pinterest. Just as Microsoft sought to position itself as the only software **option**, and Apple as the only choice for **interconnected** phones and tablets, Facebook wants to be the only social media site you'll ever use. There are reasons to think that it might achieve it. It has an **inherent** advantage of **ubiquity**; an amazing 85% of online adults have an account on one of Facebook's four services (the others being Instagram, Messenger and WhatsApp). And its striking success comes from the way it has **seamlessly** evolved over time. From its **humble origins** as a university-style online message board, it fast became a way of making public **declarations** of love and stalking people you haven't seen in years. Now it's used to generate support for big political **campaigns** and as a way for **celebrities** to share updates with their followers. But it wants more—to become the only platform we use to share content; once you open it up, there'll be no reason to leave it.

7. Would a world where we all spend more time on Facebook be so bad? Despite my initial **skepticism** I am, on balance, a fan. Of course there are downsides **concerning** Facebook. It **nurtures** the show-off in us all. When on holiday, I find it as hard as the next person to resist posting a photo of a nice palm tree. It has changed my attention span; I rarely watch a big live TV event without scanning Facebook or Twitter to see what people are saying about it—although I think this makes things more fun. I find the enthusiastic virtue-signaling a bit **distasteful**, even as I take part in it. I wonder if changing your profile picture or posting a video of the ice-bucket challenge makes it easier to **assuage** any **guilt** you might feel at not getting involved with real social change.

8. But Facebook **highlights** its **quest** about being "the everything app" that is worrying. We pay for Facebook through the ads we consume. That's why Facebook cares so much about the time we spend with it; the more time we spend, the more advertising we will get. Its reach is already **massive**, so its growth strategy depends on directing us to ever-more **tailored** content, so that we use it for everything.

9. It seems to me this is the **fatal** flaw in Facebook's plan. As lovely as my friend's baby photos are, much of the best content I interact with on social media is free to access, but created by

people paid to produce it. And the only sustainable business model for that free-to-access quality content is the same online advertising revenue that sustains Facebook and Google.

10. As we all know, those platforms are hovering up an increased share. To the extent it gets invested, their ad revenue is spent not on the content itself but on their surfaces. It's hard to see how a declining share of online advertising available for producers of content won't **undermine** the quality of what gets shared. I'm only a lowly late adopter, but I do wonder if Facebook is at risk of destroying itself.

(961 words)

Notes

Facebook: an American for-profit corporation and online social media and social networking service based in Menlo Park, California, United States.

Twitter: an online news and social networking service where users post and read short 140-character messages called "tweets".

LinkedIn: a business and employment-oriented social networking service that operates via websites. Founded on December 14, 2002, and launched on May 5, 2003, it is mainly used for professional networking, including employers posting jobs and job seekers posting their CVs.

Pinterest: a web and mobile application company that operates a photo sharing website. Registration is required for use. The site was founded by Ben Silbermann, Paul Sciarra and Evan Sharp.

Instagram: a mobile photo-sharing application and service that allows users to share pictures and videos either publicly or privately on the service, as well as through a variety of other social networking platforms, such as Facebook, Twitter, Tumblr, and Flickr.

New Words

phenomenon	/fə'nɔminən/	n.	1. [C] fact or occurrence, esp. in nature or society, that can be perceived by the senses 现象 2. [C] remarkable person, thing or event 非凡的人、物或事
specify	/'spesifai/	vt.	to state sth. in an exact and detailed way 具体指明；明确说明；详述
needless	/ni:dlis/	a.	completely unnecessary 不必要的，完全不必的
enthusiastic	/inˌθju:zi'æstik/	a.	showing enthusiasm 热心的；热情的；热衷的
enthusiastically	/inˌθju:zi'æstikli/	a.	with enthusiasm; in an enthusiastic manner 热心地；满腔热情地

eke	/iːk/	*vt.*	1. (~ **sth. out**) to make a small supply of sth. last longer by adding something else to it or by using it sparingly 使……的供应持久；节约使用 2. to manage to make (a living) laboriously by doing this 竭力维持
commute	/kə'mjuːt/	*vi.*	to travel regularly by bus, train or car between one's place of work (usu. in a city) and one's home (usu. at a distance) 通勤
		vt.	1. ~ **sth. (to sth.)** to replace (one punishment) by another that is less severe 减（刑） 2. ~ **sth. (for/into sth.)** to change sth., esp. one form of payment, for or into sth. else 改变
productivity	/ˌprɒdʌk'tivəti/	*n.*	1. [U] ability to produce (eg. goods or crops); state of being productive 生产力；多产性 2. [U] efficiency, esp. in industry, measured by comparing the amount produced with the time taken or the resources used to produce it 生产效率
downside	/'daunsaid/	*n.*	[*sing.*] the disadvantages or less positive aspects of sth. 不利的一面，不利因素
exclusive	/ik'skluːsiv/	*a.*	excluding all but the thing specified 唯一的；排他的
capture	/'kæptʃə(r)/	*vt.*	1. to take or win (sth.) by force or skill 夺取；赢得 2. to take (sb./sth.) as a prisoner 俘获
		n.	1. [U] capturing or being captured 捕捉；被捕捉 2. [C] person or thing captured 被捕获的人或物；俘虏；战利品
option	/'ɒpʃn/	*n.*	1. [C] thing that is or may be chosen; choice 可供选择的事物；选择 2. [U] power or freedom of choosing; choice 选择权；选择自由；选择
interconnect	/ˌintəkə'nekt/	*v.*	(of two or more things) to connect with or be related to each other（使）互相连接，互相联系
inherent	/in'hiərənt/	*a.*	~ **(in sb./sth.)** existing as a natural or permanent feature or quality of sb./sth. 内在的；固有的；本来的
ubiquity	/juː'bikwəti/	*n.*	[U] the fact that something or someone seems to be everywhere 无处不在；普遍存在
seamlessly	/'siːmlisli/	*a.*	(*computing*) with no spaces or pauses between one part and the next 无缝的
humble	/'hʌmbl/	*a.*	1. (of a person, his position in society, etc.) low in rank; unimportant 低下的，卑微的 2. (of a person or his words or actions) having or showing a low or modest opinion of one's own importance; not proud 谦虚的
		vt.	to make (sb./sth./oneself) humble; to lower the rank or self-importance of 使变得卑微；降低……的地位

155

origin	/'ɔridʒin/	*n.*	1. [C, U] starting-point; source 起点；开端　2. [C] [*usu. pl.*] person's parentage, background 血统；背景；出身
declaration	/ˌdeklə'reiʃn/	*n.*	[U] declaring; formally announcing 宣言；宣布；正式声明
campaign	/kæm'pein/	*n.*	1. [C] series of planned activities with a particular social, commercial or political aim　运动　2. [C] series of military operations with a particular aim, usu. in one area 战役
celebrity	/si'lebrəti/	*n.*	1. [C] famous person 名人　2. [U] being famous; fame 名望；名声
skepticism	/'skeptisizəm/	*n.*	[U, *sing.*] an attitude of doubting that claims or statements are true or that sth. will happen 怀疑论，怀疑主义
concerning	/kən'sənin/	*prep.*	about or relating to 关于；有关；涉及
nurture	/'nɜːtʃə(r)/	*vt.*	1. to encourage the growth of (sth.); to nourish 培育，培养；滋养　2. to care for and educate (a child) 养育，教养，教育
		n.	[U] care; encouragement; support 照顾；鼓励；支持
distasteful	/dis'teistfl/	*a.*	unpleasant or offensive 使人不愉快的；不合口味的；讨厌的；味道差的
assuage	/ə'sweidʒ/	*vt.*	(*fml.*) to make (sth.) less severe; to soothe 减轻；缓和；平息
guilt	/gilt/	*n.*	1. [U] anxiety or unhappiness caused by the knowledge of having done wrong 不安；内疚　2. [U] blame or responsibility for wrongdoing 责任；罪责
highlight	/'hailait/	*vt.*	1. to make a problem or subject easy to notice so that people pay attention to it 使……突出；使注意力集中于　2. to mark written words with a special colored pen, or in a different color on a computer（在计算机上用不同颜色）突出显示
quest	/kwest/	*n.*	[C] act of seeking sth.; search or pursuit 寻求；寻找；搜索；追求
		v.	to try to find sth.; to search 试图找到；搜索
massive	/'mæsiv/	*a.*	large, heavy and solid 巨大的
tailored	/'teiləd/	*a.*	1. made for a particular person or purpose 特制的；专门的　2. (of clothes) made to fit well or closely 合身的
fatal	/'feitl/	*a.*	1. ~ **(to sb./sth.)** 1 causing or ending in death 致命的　2. causing disaster 灾难性的　3. (*fml.*) fateful; decisive 命中注定的；决定性的
undermine	/ˌʌndə'main/	*vt.*	to make sth., especially sb.'s confidence or authority, gradually weaker or less effective 逐渐削弱

⊛ New Expressions

combine... with...	to make a combination between... and... 结合……
be dissatisfied with	not feel satisfied with sth. / sb. 对……很沮丧

laugh at	to mock or ridicule sb./sth. 取笑，讥笑
keep up	to maintain a required pace or level 保持；继续
spy on sb./sth.	to watch sb./sth. secretly, often in order to discover information about him, her, or it 暗中监视；窥探
in total	including everything 总共，一共
get one's head around	to come to understand it even though it is difficult to comprehend 理解，明白
on the go	very busy 忙个不停的，特别忙的
vice versa	the other way round, with the terms or conditions reversed 反之亦然；反过来情况也一样
take part in	to join in 参与，参加
interact with	to mutually communicate with or react to 与……相互作用；与……相互影响
at risk	in danger of sth. unpleasant or harmful happening 有危险；冒风险

Reading Comprehension

Understanding the text

I. Choose the best answer to each of the following questions.

1. How do you understand the phrase "late adopter" in Para. 1?

   A. A person or group that is crazy about a new product or technology.

   B. A person or group that is slow to start using a new product or technology.

   C. A person or group that is eager to start using a new product or technology.

   D. A person or group that hates to start using a new product or technology.

2. What does the author think about Twitter?

   A. It's a combination between mobile phones and cameras.

   B. It's a brick-like digital camera.

   C. It's a rubbish version of Facebook.

   D. It's a new product or technology.

3. Which one of the following is NOT mainly done by the author on Facebook?

   A. To keep up to date with friends.

   B. To spy on his exes.

   C. To show off about his social life.

   D. To upload some videos.

4. Which one of the following is not the activity requiring exclusive attention mentioned in Para. 5?

    A. Reading to your kids.   B. Dinner with friends.

    C. Dating with girlfriend.   D. Meetings at work.

5. What does the sentence "once you open it up, there'll be no reason to leave it" in Para. 6 imply?

    A. Facebook wants to become the only platform we use to share content with the others.

    B. People may be obsessed with Facebook.

    C. Facebook has a magic power.

    D. Facebook has a bad effect on people.

6. What is author's attitude towards Facebook's quest for being "the everything app"?

    A. Positive.   B. Worried.

    C. Neutral.   D. Excited.

7. Why does Facebook care so much about the time people spend on it?

    A. Because Facebook wants to be the most popular social platform.

    B. Because the more time people spend on it, the more advertising people will pay to Facebook.

    C. Because people don't like to use Facebook.

    D. Because the more time people spend on it, the more popularity Facebook will get.

8. What is the only sustainable business model for the free-to-access quality content mentioned in Para. 9?

    A. A way of making public declaration of love and stalking people you haven't seen for years.

    B. To capture extra time more as a grab on the rest of the time we spend online and on other apps.

    C. An inherent advantage of ubiquity.

    D. The same online advertising revenue that sustains Facebook and Google.

Critical thinking

II. *Work in pairs and discuss the following questions.*

1. What do you think of social networking? What are the advantages and disadvantages of it?

2. How often do you check your social platforms?

3. Do you think Facebook can be the "only platform we use to share content"? Why or why not?

Language Focus

Words in use

III. Fill in the blanks with the words given below. Change the form where necessary. Each word can be used only once.

nurture	highlight	distasteful	undermine	massive
enthusiastic	specify	capture	inherent	downside

1. The _____ of this approach is a lack of clear leadership.

2. _____ people always love what they are doing, regardless of money or title or power.

3. A succession of scandals and revelations has _____ his position and reputation over the past year.

4. Remember that pointing out your small mistakes is part of her job, and it may be as _____ to her as it is to you.

5. Freakish weather conditions have caused _____ traffic hold-ups in the area.

6. Last year Collins wrote a moving ballad which _____ the plight of the homeless.

7. He was _____ by enemy forces and sent to a prison camp for the rest of the war.

8. My contract _____ that I must give a month's notice in advance if I leave my current job.

9. Mainline feminism was arguing for the _____ beauty of the natural woman.

10. To identify and _____ talent, we have to first understand what students and teachers think and need.

Expressions in use

IV. Fill in the blanks with the expressions given below. Change the form where necessary. Each expression can be used only once.

combine with	be dissatisfied with	spy on	interact with
keep up	take part in	at risk	laugh at
in total	get my head around		

1. These two chemicals will _____ each other at a certain temperature.

2. He has tried to explain the principles behind the technology dozens of time, but I just can't _____ them.

3. The company agreed to _____ high levels of output in order to compensate for the supplies lost.

4. Tourism must _____ the local culture as to build a characteristic industry.

5. Students should do surveys, visit museums, _____ charity work and hand in reports for teachers to decide on their marks.

6. Those in charge of hiring worry an over educated candidate will demand too much pay or _____ what's being offered.

7. I thought you were a new customer and now I know that you only came to _____ me and my menu.

8. However, this fragile system, on which the global economy used to depend, is now _____ of collapsing.

9. He may _____ our discomfiture now, but before long he'll be laughing on the other side of his face.

10. _____, 917 self-made billionaires generated more than $ 3.6 trillion of wealth globally between 1995 and 2014.

Sentence structure

V. Rewrite the following sentences by using "The more... the more..." structure. Make changes where necessary.

> **Model:** If we spend more time on it, we will get more advertising.
>
> → The more time we spend, the more advertising we will get.

1. If you do more exercise, you will become more healthy, and your everyday tasks will seem easier.

   _____

2. If the actor is more handsome, the film will become more attractive to the audience.

   _____

3. If you read more books, you will get more knowledge to enrich yourself.

   _____

VI. Complete the following sentences by translating the Chinese into English, using "When it comes to…".

> **Model:** _____（当说到最重要的一点）, people needed to believe Bree was real.
>
> → <u>When it comes to the most important thing</u>, people needed to believe Bree was real.

1. She is normally a quiet person, _____
   （但当说到音乐的时候，她就变成一个完全不同的人了）.

2. _____（当谈到电脑游戏的时候，学生都变得很
   活跃）, and every one is eager to talk about his favorite game.

3. She is a vulnerable person, _____
   （当谈到她的婚姻的时候，她变得更难过了）.

Unit 7
Women in IT Industry

Because I am a woman, I must make unusual efforts to succeed. If I fail, no one will say, "She doesn't have what it takes." They will say, "Women don't have what it takes."

— *Clare Boothe Luce (American playwright and*

stateswoman)

Being a full-time mother is one of the highest salaried jobs in my field, since the payment is pure love.

— *Mildred B. Vermont (amateur journalist)*

Women make up half of the population, but only around a quarter of female voices are quoted by the media. On Motherboard, this figure appears to be even lower. A study on 2012 US election coverage found women were even massively underrepresented in coverage of "women's issues" such as abortion and women's rights. A 2013 study found that over two months, front-page *New York Times* stories quoted over three times as many male sources as female sources. We need to change this. We all know gender inequality in tech is a tough nut to crack. Women throughout the economy face persistent wage inequality. At the end of the day, no one can easily fix gender inequality, but we can all do our part—by being a little bit mindful and a little bit sensitive to the fact that those around us might have a different set of experiences.

Section
A

Pre-reading Activities

I. Look at the set of pictures regarding some successful women in different domains. Match their names with the pictures and discuss with your classmates about their achievements in different fields.

Names	Picture numbers
Marissa Mayer	4
Hillary Clinton	2
Yang Lan	3
Audrey Hepburn	1

II. Work in pairs and discuss the following questions.

1. Do you think men and women are equal? Why or why not?

2. What do you know about feminism?

3. Do you know some unfairness happened to women in IT industry? If yes, please share it with your classmates.

Do Women Enjoy "It"?

1. The tech industry has **created** a wealth of opportunities but it has also emerged as anything but **uneven** for women.

2. In 2014 companies finally began to **acknowledge** this fact. **Acknowledgment** is the first step, but are the next steps towards a solution clear to us? Intel recently announced a $300 million **fund** to **boost** the **diversity** of the company's work force over the next three years, a **commendable** and forward-thinking initiative. It's certainly a step in the right direction and hopefully other tech **giants** will follow their lead. But is this really a question of resources? Or does a change in attitude need to come first?

3. Reversing gender inequality in tech requires more than money. Our industry needs to be committed to offering the same opportunities to all qualified **candidates**. The numbers don't lie. Women are underrepresented. And the numbers show that tech is still very much a boys' club.

4. In 2013, **surveys** by the US Department of Labor found that women make up 26% of the total tech industry and that only 20% of software developers are female. And it's not just employees. Female **entrepreneurs** also struggle when it comes to finding **investors**. Currently, only 7% of venture capital funding goes to female-led businesses.

5. Recent diversity reports from within the tech industry also show a **gloomy** yet unsurprising picture of women's **participation** in the workplace. Facebook and Instagram reported that only

31% of their employees were female. Google, Apple and Twitter reported 30%.

6. Pinterest, 80% of whose user base is female, reported a **slightly** better **ratio**. Women account for 40% of their total workforce. However, even those numbers are somewhat **misleading**. Looking more closely, we find that women hold only 19% of leadership positions at Pinterest.

7. Unfortunately, this is the rule in tech, rather than the exception. Even when women make it in the door, they often don't make it to the top.

8. In tech industry, Fiverr's taking its journey towards gender equality. At Fiverr, 41% of total employees are female, and, while this isn't ideal, it's a good start. Perhaps more importantly, 50% of top management at Fiverr is female. It's a jaw-dropping ratio for anyone familiar with the tech industry and the **composition** of its leadership. In addition to the position taken by female as chief operating officer, Fiverr's female vice presidents are in charge of human resources, corporate marketing, product and finance.

9. As the vice president said, "We didn't achieve this number by offering egg-freezing benefits to women. We didn't achieve it due to positive **discrimination** towards women. And we didn't achieve it through an initiative to push for gender equality at the company. To **accomplish** gender **parity** at Fiverr, we would rather provide all candidates with equal opportunities." They evaluate **applicants** based on their skills and experience, as well as their potential and their passion for the role. They also **disregard** factors that they feel are irrelevant such as a person's connections in the industry, family situation, and race. They also found that when hiring is determined by merit, female applicants have the same chances of being selected as their male **counterparts**.

10. Research also tells us that companies that have **adopted** more **inclusive** hiring policies are **reaping** concrete benefits. In 2012, Dow Jones released a study of venture-backed companies from 1997 to 2011. In those companies that were **classified** as "successful", the percentage of female executives was 7.1%, compared with 3.1% at unsuccessful firms.

11. Additionally, a recent study by Thompson Reuters found that companies with mixed gender boards performed **marginally** better, on average, compared to a **benchmark index**, such as the MSCI World. These companies not only had lower tracking errors but, in many cases, also had better returns.

12. Some female activists call for policies that require companies to hire women with the aim of boosting gender equality. It is believed **affirmative** action can be an appropriate measure, but only in certain sectors. Women have the right to be heard, and to influence the political, social and economic agenda. They have the ability to positively affect global trends. However, affirmative action policies shouldn't be applied when **recruiting** employees, because it's not necessary. When choosing objectively, that person should be a woman, at least 50% of the time, because there are so many talented women out there. They deserve to be chosen because they are bright, creative, hard

working and committed, not **solely** because they are women.

13. According to the World Economic Forum's recently released Global Gender Gap Report, it's going to take 80 years to reach gender parity in the workplace. But can we afford to wait so long to close the gap? If we don't act now, our daughters and granddaughters will face the same career challenges that women of our generation have struggled to overcome.

14. Tech companies should adopt a moral commitment to equality and make a conscious effort to hire the best and brightest, regardless of gender. Of course, there is no easy fix when inequality has been rooted in workplace culture for generations. But we're innovators, and we solve difficult problems every day. We shouldn't require 80 years or hundreds of millions of dollars to address the issue of gender inequality in our own field.

(862 words)

Notes

Fiverr: a global online marketplace offering tasks and services, beginning at a cost of $5 per job performed, from which it gets its name. The site is primarily used by freelancers who use Fiverr to offer services to customers worldwide.

Thompson Reuters: a multinational mass media and information firm with operational headquarters at Times Square in Manhattan, New York City.

MSCI World: a stock market index of 1,643 "world" stocks. It is maintained by MSCI Inc., formerly Morgan Stanley Capital International, and is used as a common benchmark for "world" or "global" stock funds.

Venture capital: the money invested in a new enterprise, esp. a risky one.

World Economic Forum: a Swiss nonprofit foundation, based in Cologny, Geneva.

❸ New Words

create	/kriːˈeit/	*vt.*	to cause (sth.) to exist; make (sth. new or original) 创造；创建；创作
uneven	/ʌnˈiːvn/	*a.*	not uniform or equal; varying 不一致的；不相等的；有差异的
acknowledge	/əkˈnɔlidʒ/	*vt.*	1. to accept that sth. is true 承认（属实） 2. to accept that sb./sth. has a particular authority or status 承认（权威、地位） 3. to tell sb. that you have received sth. that they sent to you 告知，收悉 4. to publicly express thanks for help you have been given（公开）感谢

acknowledgment	/ək'nɔlidʒmənt/	*n.*	1. [U] an act of accepting that sth. exists or is true, or that sth. is there 承认 2. [U] an act or a statement expressing thanks to sb.; something that is given to sb. as thanks 感谢；谢礼 3. [C] a letter saying that sth. has been received 收件复函 4. [U] a statement, especially at the beginning of a book, in which the writer expresses thanks to the people who have helped 致谢，鸣谢
fund	/fʌnd/	*n.*	[C] sum of money saved or made available for a particular purpose 专款；基金
boost	/buːst/	*vt.*	to increase the strength or value of (sth.); to help or encourage (sb./sth.) 增强；提高；帮助；鼓励
		n.	[C] increase; help; encouragement 增加；帮助；鼓励
diversity	/dai'vəsəti/	*n.*	1. [C, U] the quality or fact of including a range of many people or things 多样性；多样化 2. [C, U] a range of many people or things that are very different from each other 差异（性）；不同（点）
commendable	/kə'mendəbl/	*a.*	deserving praise and approval 值得赞扬的
giant	/'dʒaiənt/	*n.*	1. [C] a very large and powerful organization 大公司；强大的组织 2. [C] a person who is very good at sth. 伟人；卓越人物
candidate	/'kændideit/	*n.*	[C] ~ **(for sth.)** a person who is trying to be elected or is applying for a job 候选人，申请人
survey	/sə'vei/	*n.*	[C] investigation（对部分人的行为、意见等的）调查
entrepreneur	/ˌɔntrəprə'nɜː/	*n.*	[C] a person who sets up businesses and business deals 企业家；承包人；主办者
investor	/in'vestə/	*n*	[C] person who invests money 投资者
gloomy	/gluːmi/	*a.*	1. without much hope of success or happiness in the future 前景黯淡的；悲观的 2. sad and without hope 忧郁的；沮丧的；无望的 3. nearly dark, or badly lit in a way that makes you feel sad 黑暗的；阴暗的；幽暗的
participation	/paːtisi'peiʃn/	*n.*	[U] (action of) participating in sth. 参加
slightly	/slaitli/	*a.*	to a slight degree 轻微地；稍稍
ratio	/'reiʃiəu/	*n.*	[C] relation between two amounts determined by the number of times one contains the other 比；比率

misleading	/ˌmisˈliːdiŋ/	*a.*	giving the wrong idea or impression and making you believe sth. that is not true 误导的；引入歧途的
composition	/ˌkɔmpəˈziʃn/	*n.*	1. [U] the parts of which sth is made; make-up 成分；组成部分 2. [C] short piece of non-fictional writing done as a school or college exercise; essay 作文；散文
discrimination	/diˌskrimiˈneiʃn/	*n.*	[U] the practice of treating sb. or a particular group in society less fairly than others 区别对待；歧视；偏袒
accomplish	/əˈkʌmpliʃ/	*vt.*	to succeed in doing or completing sth 完成
parity	/ˈpærəti /	*n.*	[U] ~ **(with sb./sth.)** / ~ **(between A and B)** the state of being equal, especially the state of having equal pay or status 平等，相同，对等
applicant	/ˈæplikənt/	*n.*	[C] a person who makes a formal request for sth. especially for a job, a place at a college or university, etc. 申请人
disregard	/ˌdisriˈgɑːd/	*vt.*	not to consider sth.; to treat sth. as unimportant 不理会；不顾；漠视
counterpart	/ˈkauntəpɑːt/	*n.*	[C] a person or thing that has the same position or function as sb./sth. else in a different place or situation 职位（或作用）相当的人；对应的事物
adopt	/əˈdɔpt/	*vt.*	to formally accept a suggestion or policy by voting 正式通过，表决采纳
		v.	to take sb. else's child into your family and become its legal parent(s) 收养；领养
inclusive	/inˈkluːsiv/	*a.*	including a wide range of people, things, ideas, etc. 包容广阔的；范围广泛的
reap	/riːp/	*vt.*	1. to obtain sth., especially sth. good, as a direct result of sth. that you have done 取得（成果）；收获 2. to cut and collect a crop, especially wheat, from a field 收割（庄稼）
classify	/ˈklæsifai/	*vt.*	1. to arrange sth. in groups according to features that they have in common 分类；归类 2. **(~ sb./sth. as sth.)** to decide which type or group sb./sth. belongs to 划分；界定
marginally	/ˈmɑːdʒinəli/	*a.*	very slightly; not very much 轻微地；很少地；微不足道地
benchmark	/bentʃmɑːk/	*n.*	[C] something that can be measured and used as a standard that other things can be compared with 基准

index	/'indeks/	*n.*	1. [C] a system that shows the level of prices and wages, etc. so that they can be compared with those of a previous date 指数　2. [C] a list of names or topics that are referred to in a book, etc., usually arranged at the end of a book in alphabetical order or listed in a separate file or book 索引
affirmative	/ə'fɜːmətiv/	*a.*	an affirmative word or reply means yes or expresses agreement 肯定的；同意的
recruit	/ri'kruːt/	*vt.*	(~ **sb. to sth./~ sb. to do sth.**) to find new people to join a company, an organization, the armed forces, etc. 吸收（新成员）；征募（新兵）
		n.	[C] a person who joins an organization, a company, etc. 新成员
solely	/'səuli/	*a.*	only; not involving sb./sth. else 仅；只；单独地

✿ New Expressions

a wealth of	numerous; plenty 很多的
committed to	to devote oneself to 致力于；委身于；以……为己任
make up	to form, compose or constitute sth. 形成；构成
in addition to	besides; over and above 除……之外
in charge of	be responsible for 负责；主管
account for	If a particular thing accounts for a part or proportion of something, that part or proportion consists of that thing, or is used or produced by it. (数量、比例上) 占
on average	in general; overall 平均；普通；通常
call for	to say publicly that something must happen 呼吁；主张
at least	not less than 至少
regardless of	paying no attention to sth./sb.; treating sth./sb. as not being important 不管；不顾；不理会

【Reading Comprehension】

Understanding the text

I. Answer the following questions.

1. What did Intel recently announce?

2. What does our industry need to do in order to reverse gender inequality?

3. What are Fiverr's female vice presidents in charge of?

4. How was gender parity accomplished at Fiverr?

5. How did Fiverr evaluate the applicants?

6. Why do female interviewers deserve the chance of being chosen as male ones do?

7. Why can't we wait for another 80 years to reach gender parity in the workplace?

8. What should tech companies do in hiring new employees?

Critical thinking

II. Work in pairs and discuss the following questions.

1. Do you agree women's role is getting more and more important at work? Why or why not?

2. To your best knowledge, what are the differences between men and women when it comes to their respective working styles?

3. If you were a male employee, how would you accommodate your working style to your female boss'?

4. If you were a female boss, what would you do to get along with your employees?

5. How do you perceive women's role at the management level in the future?

Language Focus

Words in use

III. Fill in the blanks with the words given below. Change the form where necessary. Each word can be used only once.

acknowledge	commendable	candidate	discrimination	parity
disregard	affirmative	recruit	boost	uneven

1. Lower interest rates can _____ the economy by reducing borrowing costs for consumers and businesses.

2. _____ by employers on the grounds of race and nationality was illegal, while in some countries it's very prevalent.

3. China's efforts to eliminate local transmission of measles are both necessary and highly _____.

4. He was desperately eager for a(n) _____ answer.

5. Women have yet to achieve wage or occupational _____ in many fields.

6. Whoever planted the bomb showed a total _____ for the safety of the public.

7. The lawyer was being groomed as a(n) _____ for the next mayor.

8. Some of the victims are complaining loudly about the _____ distribution of emergency aid.

9. The leaders of this country _____ the scope of the problem, and I believe they are trying to do the right things.

10. In particular, they have identified the need to _____ competent professionals.

Word building

The suffix *-al / -ial* combines with nouns to form adjectives. It can also combine with verbs to form nouns. (For explanation, refer to Word building in Unit 1)

Examples

Words learned	Add *-al / -ial*	New words formed
fate	→	fatal
horizon	→	horizontal
mechanic	→	mechanical
occasion	→	occasional
logic	→	logical
deny	→	denial

The suffix *-ity* combines with adjectives or sometimes verbs to form nouns. Nouns formed in this way refer to the state or condition described by the adjectives or indicated in the verbs.

Examples

Words learned	Add *-ity*	New words formed
relative	→	relativity
continue	→	continuity
actual	→	actuality

IV. Add -al / -ial or -ity to or remove them from the following words to form new words.

Words learned	New words formed
-al / -ial	
margin	
tradition	
influence	
manager	
coast	
survive	
editor	
memory	
-ity	
secure	
flexible	
original	
prior	

V. Fill in the blanks with the newly-formed words in Activity IV. Change the form where necessary. Each word can be used only once.

1. These public areas offer a subtle blend of _____ charm with modern amenities.

2. With the changes in the world's climate, dinosaurs died, but many smaller animals lived on. It was the _____ of the fittest.

3. All the _____ personnel at the factory are hired on contract.

4. Women are more likely to give _____ to child care and education policies.

5. Local radio stations serving _____ areas often broadcast weather forecasts for yachtsmen.

6. This simplicity provides programmers with freedom and _____ because of which they can mold software into any form to do almost anything.

7. She capitalized on her knowledge and experience in fashion and landed a(n) _____ job in fashion magazine.

8. I am sure that this meeting will contribute to the reinforcement of peace and _____ all over the world.

9. Innovation is not simply about increasing investment, but also about transforming the learning environment to foster creativity, _____ and critical thinking in education.

10. The museum will serve as a(n) _____ to those who struggled for the liberation of the island.

11. Chaplin was not just a genius, he was among the most _____ figures in film history.

12. The tribunals were established for the well-integrated members of society and not for _____ individuals.

Banked cloze

VI. Fill in the blanks by selecting suitable words from the word bank. You may not use any of the words more than once.

A. dominated	B. fulfilling	C. ratios	D. roughly	E. certainly
F. surface	G. limited	H. served	I. backgrounds	J. engaging
K. balanced	L. disappointed	M. satisfied	N. applying	O. used

Every time we advertise for software developers I'm consistently 1) _____ by the lack of women 2) _____. Looking back over the last 8 years, 3) _____ 1 out of every 20 applicants for a software development role at Aventa Systems has been female. When I first started in the computing industry 25 years ago, it was a very male 4) _____ industry. I had hoped that by the 21st century we'd have a much more 5) _____ work force but sadly that does not look to be the case. At the present moment in time we have no female software developers and that's terrible. We do have women 6) _____ senior roles within our technical teams and on our management team but these are project managers and business analysts, not developers. When we advertise for project managers and business analysts the 7) _____ are much more balanced. The last time we advertised for a project manager 75% of the candidates were women.

So maybe it's not a general IT industry issue but a job role issue. It may look like that on the 8) _____ but project managers and business analysts tend to come from a wider variety of 9) _____. One of our project managers 10) _____ her time in the police force and ended up in a PM/BA role before leaving to join Aventa. Another of our business analysts was in the RAF before a career change into IT and business analysis roles. So is the issue that we're not attracting enough women into software development at a young age?

Expressions in use

VII. Fill in the blanks with the expressions given below. Change the form where necessary. Each expression can be used only once.

a wealth of	at least	on average	account for
committed to	in addition to	call for	make up
in charge of	regardless of		

1. _____ his pay, the boss said he would leave him ten days' holiday with salary every year.

2. View your current job as paid practice for your future dream job. Even in a miserable job, you have _____ opportunities to polish your skills.

3. They earn less than men, _____, and bear more responsibility for looking after children and the elderly.

4. The fields give high and stable yields _____ climatic circumstances.

5. If you want to get ahead in life, you must _____ achieving your dreams.

6. They have received _____ twenty thousand pounds each but had gone to court to demand more.

7. Computers _____ 5% of the country's commercial electricity consumption.

8. Those who care about it most will be among the first to _____ its renewal and reform.

9. One of the most important tasks I am _____ is communicating with worldwide subsidiaries.

10. North Africans _____ the largest and poorest immigrant group in this country.

Structure Analysis and Writing

Structure Analysis

Focus on an example essay

In this unit, you will learn how to write an example essay. An example essay is one of the most basic essays in academic writing. To make your thesis statement convincing and valid, you need to support it with specific examples.

Here are some essential points about how to organize and develop examples around the thesis statement.

1. **Number of examples**

   - How many examples you should use in an example essay depends on the topic itself.

   - Some topics require numerous examples, whereas others simply need three or four. For example, if the thesis statement is "My country is increasingly prosperous", you should provide numerous examples for adequate support since the topic is broad. But if your topic is "San Francisco has some of the most unusual sights in California", you just need present three or four examples to develop and support the topic.

2. **Choice of examples**

   - Examples should be chosen from a range of areas relevant to the topic.

   - Examples should be representative of a class or category.

3. **Principle of organization**

   - Basically examples are arranged according to time, degree of familiarity, or level of importance or interest. You may organize the examples according to the time order, or start with the most familiar point and end with the least familiar, or start with the least important (interesting) point to the most important (interesting) point.

4. **Transition to introduce examples**

   - Transitions for the first developmental paragraph:

     Take… for example/instance

     One example of… is…

     First, consider the case of…

     One of the cases is…

     To begin with…

   - Transitions for the second developmental paragraph:

     Another example of… is…

     An additional example is…

     Another case is…

     Here is another example.

     Second (Next), consider…

   - Transitions for the third developmental paragraph:

     Still another example of… is…

     Third, consider…

     There is still another case concerning…

     Finally, there is the example of…

Usually the structure of an example essay is as follows.

Paragraph 1: Introduction

- Explain, in your own words, what the issue is. Include a thesis statement, which is a clear statement of your point of view.

Paragraph 2: Point one in support of your thesis

- Explain the point you are making with the aid of a specific example.

Paragraph 3: Point two in support of your thesis

- Explain the point you are making with the aid of a specific example

Paragraph 4: Qualification

- Explain that, under certain circumstances, the opposite point of view might be correct. (This is to show that you are aware of all aspects of the issue, even though you are 80% ~ 90% convinced of your thesis.) Sometimes this paragraph is replaced by another point and / or further discussion or reasoning.

Paragraph 5: Reinforcement of thesis

- Show how your viewpoint, despite the qualification you have just made, is more persuasive under the present circumstances.

Structured Writing

Read the sample essay and see how it develops with details.

Topic	Sample essay
Learning from failure **Introduction** Thesis statement: The principle of rising after each fall to try again applies to all struggles. **Body** Example 1: Winston Churchill did not exhibit signs of greatness as a child.	When failure knocks you down, will you have the guts to get up and get going? Or will you give up? Achieving success can be difficult. At times, distractions, delays and defeats discourage everyone. Giving up seems better than going on. But the principle of rising after each fall to try again applies to all struggles. History informs us that stories of success are also stories of great failures. Take the young Winston Churchill as an example. He did not exhibit signs of greatness as a child. He hated mathematics and, at Ascot School, he had to be frequently caned by the principal. When he changed his school to Brighton, his reputation as a dunce followed him. The story goes that the ladies running the school were so relieved when Churchill left that they declared a half-holiday.

Example 2: Albert Einstein was "mentally slow" when he was at school. **Example 3: Charles Darwin was voted the "dullest boy of the year".** **Conclusion** Learn from your failure and keep going. Some things take a lot of time. Staying on course can keep you focused on what you need to do.	At Harrow, he failed the entrance examination. He also failed the entrance test to Sandhurst Military College twice and scraped through on the third attempt. He was undeterred by these failures and went on to become the greatest Prime Minister England ever had. At school, Albert Einstein was so dull that he was called "Dull Albert". His teacher described him as "mentally slow, unsociable and adrift forever in his foolish dreams". He did not even pass the entrance examination to get into Zurich Polytechnic School. Only in the fourth attempt did he make the grade. Today Einstein is regarded as the architect of the Nuclear Age. Charles Darwin, father of the Theory of Evolution, was voted the "dullest boy of the year". He had to give up a medical career and his father told him, "You care for nothing but shooting, dogs and rat catching." In his autobiography, Darwin wrote, "I was considered by all my masters and by my father, a very ordinary boy, rather below the common standard in intellect." And yet every student knows about Darwin today. These men were like any other students. The only difference was that every time they failed, they bounced back. This is called failing forward, rather than backward. You learn and move forward. Ask yourself after every failure: what did I learn from this experience? Learn from your failure and keep going. Some things take a lot of time. Staying on course can keep you focused on what you need to do. Like Winston Churchill, Albert Einstein and Charles Darwin you may have to persevere in the face of almost inevitable defeat. You must remember that your goals should be moral and reasonable. But if your goals are both, then stay on course. Don't quit. A second effort or a third or a fourth pays off.

VIII. Write an essay of no less than 150 words on one of the following topics. One topic has an outline that you can follow.

Topic God helps those who help themselves

Introduction

Thesis statement: Only when standing on our own feet could we survive hardships for a life-long time.

Body

Example 1: Hawking suffers from severe disease; he has never abandoned himself and refuses to be dependent on others.

Example 2: Disabled athletes rely on themselves to win other's respect and admiration.

Conclusion

It is self-dependence that helps us withstand storms.

More topics:

● Female leaders in my eyes

● On volunteering

Translation

IX. Translate the following paragraph into Chinese.

The number of people studying abroad is on the gradual rise in China, but it might not be a good investment. Job applicants with a foreign diploma have no edge over their domestically trained peers. But for those already studying abroad and those planning to pursue foreign education, the opportunity to expand their horizons outweighs any financial concerns. Students now value studying abroad as their personal development more than an "investment" to improve their competitive power in the job market.

X. Translate the following paragraph into English.

乒乓球是中国的国球，也是世界流行的体育项目。20 世纪 60 年代以来，中国选手赢得了世界乒乓球比赛的大部分冠军，因此中国在该项运动中占有统治性的地位。乒乓球的起源有许多不同的说法，最流行、最被广泛认可的一种说法就是乒乓球在 1900 年起源于英国。在英语中，它也被称为 "Ping Pong"，因为在击打时会发出 "Ping Pong" 的声音。在 1988 年的奥运会上，乒乓球被列为正式的比赛项目。

Section B

Reading Skills: *Critical Thinking and Reading*

Critical reading refers to a careful, active, reflective, analytic reading. Critical thinking involves reflecting on the validity of what you have read in light of your prior knowledge and understanding of the world.

For example, consider the following (somewhat humorous) sentence from a student essay.

Parents are buying expensive cars for their kids to destroy them.

As the terms are used here, critical reading is concerned with figuring out whether, within the context of the text as a whole, "them" refers to the parents, the kids, or the cars, and whether the text supports that practice. Critical thinking would come into play when deciding whether the chosen meaning was indeed true, and whether or not you, as the reader, should support that practice.

We can distinguish between critical reading and critical thinking in the following ways:

● Critical reading is a technique for discovering information and ideas within a text.

● Critical thinking is a technique for evaluating information and ideas, for deciding what to accept and believe.

With these definitions, critical reading would appear to come before critical thinking. Only once we have fully understood a text (critical reading) can we truly evaluate its assertions (critical thinking).

Here are two examples from Text A.

Example 1:

The numbers don't lie. Women are underrepresented. And the numbers show that tech is still very much a boys' club. (Para. 3)

Example 2:

Even when women make it in the door, they often don't make it to the top. (Para. 7)

The two examples show that we have to recognize not only what the text says, but also how that text portrays the subject matter. We have to read critically the expressions of "boy's club" and "make it to the top" and thus we can figure out what the writer wants to express. The writer wants us to understand thoroughly women's position in tech industry.

Read the following sentences from Text B and think critically about the writer's meaning.

1. *When did requiring potential employees to get half naked and drunk in a hot tub become okay? Would this have been a requirement if I were a man?* (Para. 6)

   The writer's meaning through critical thinking: _____

2. *If more people share their stories, we can shine a brighter light on this problem.* (Para. 12)

   The writer's meaning through critical thinking: _____

You Don't Look Like a Programmer!

1. I went to a software developer conference in San Francisco about a month ago. All the conversations started with: "Have you played this video game?" or "Did you watch that game last night?" I don't play video games or watch any sports, so I sat quietly. No one tried to talk to me or asked me what I do or what I'm doing at that particular talk. I felt **alienated**. I looked around to find other female developers. There were only four women in a room of about 20 people. It made me **wonder**: Why do I feel so alone? Why are there so few female developers?

2. I hate being asked what I do **professionally**. I love what I do, but I get a small panic attack every time someone asks. Sometimes this happens.

   Me: "I'm a software engineer!"

   Stranger: "That's awesome! What's your stack?"

3. But much more often than not, this happens.

   Me: "I'm a software engineer!"

   Stranger: "Really? You don't look like a software engineer!"

4. Why don't I look like a software engineer? Is it my **gender**? Is it my age? Other things I commonly hear are: "Oh, are you an **intern**?" and "Oh, are you a student?" No, I am not an intern, and no, I am not a student. Like I said before, I am a software engineer. I know that I do not fit the common **stereotype** of a programmer, but that stereotype needs to change. These **subtle** and not-so-subtle **sexist comments** are not okay.

5. I moved to San Francisco about a year and a half ago. I didn't have a job **offer**, but I had a degree in computer science and a year of experience as a front end engineer and a whole lot of **enthusiasm**. That enthusiasm soon wore down.

6. This is a culture that focuses heavily on drinking and partying, and in order to fit in I was required to join. I **interviewed** with two guys who were starting a new company. The interviews went well, and it seemed like there was a good cultural fit at first. I even got an offer. Then I got a

phone call. I had to spend the weekend with them in Tahoe so we could ski and drink (in hot **tubs**) and get to know each other. When did requiring potential employees to get half **naked** and drunk in a hot tub become okay? Would this have been a requirement if I were a man?

7. This behavior has become accepted in our society. People make excuses for these **inexcusable** comments and actions. "Because you should be used to it by now. Because there are so few women in computer science." I will never accept those excuses. I will never get used to it.

8. In the US, women receive almost 50% of the **bachelors**' degrees in STEM (science, tech, engineering, math) fields. But women receive less than 20% of the bachelors' degrees in computer science.

9. I started the CS program at UT Dallas at age 16. I got my bachelor's degree in CS at age 19 in the spring of 2012. In my graduating class, less than 10% of the students were women. It didn't start this way. About a third of the students in my first year classes were female. In my second year that number dropped **significantly**, and in my third and final year, I was either the only girl or one of two girls in the class. This didn't come as a shock. I was constantly put down by my male peers (even though I consistently made the top test scores). No one took me seriously. Everyone just assumed that I would change majors. "Do you even like computers, Kelly?" That just made me want it more because anything you can do I can do better.

10. The programmers **portrayed** in **media** are all **overwhelmingly** male. The recent films about hacking feature male hackers and are geared towards men. And the films that do have female hackers in **minor** roles **objectify** the women and paint them as **helpless**. **Spoiler alert:** there is a female hacker in *Furious 7*, but she's nothing like the male hacker in *Blackhat*. She can code like hell and kick ass. She doesn't fight; she can't defend herself and has to be saved multiple times. The male characters **ogle** at her and **remark** that "with a body like that, she shouldn't spend all her time behind a computer".

11. I love being a software engineer. I love that my work is being used by all of you. But it's difficult being female and a software engineer. I have been **marginalized**, made to feel like I am **inferior** and **incapable**. I have been alienated because I do not fit the programming culture. But I refuse to let it get to me!

12. I don't expect things to change overnight, but things must change soon. I've shared my story in hopes that more people realize that the gender gap in computer science is a problem that is only growing. If more people share their stories, we can shine a brighter light on this problem.

13. A year ago, I did not have the **confidence** to speak up, and it made me feel bad about myself. Now if anyone makes an **inappropriate** comment, I will call them out on it. To the men reading this: we need your help here. Stand up for women when you see them treated badly. Stand up for women when you hear them talked about disrespectfully.

(915 words)

Notes

Furious 7: a 2015 American action film directed by James Wan and written by Chris Morgan. It is the seventh installment in the *Fast and the Furious* franchise.

Blackhat: a 2015 American action thriller mystery film co-written, co-produced and directed by Michael Mann.

◉ New Words

alienate	/'eiliəneit/	*vt.*	1. ~ **sb. (from sth./sb.)** to make sb. feel that they do not belong to a particular group 使格格不入；使疏远　2. to make sb. less friendly or sympathetic towards you 使疏远；使不友好；离间
wonder	/'wʌndə(r)/	*v.*	to feel great surprise, admiration, etc.; to marvel 感到惊奇；惊叹；惊讶
professionally	/prə'feʃənəli/	*a.*	1. in a way that is connected with a person's job or training 在工作上地；在职业上地　2. in a way that shows skill and experience 娴熟地；老练地；内行地
gender	/'dʒendə(r)/	*n.*	1. [C, U] sexual classification; sex（生理上的）性别分类, 性　2. [C, U] (in certain languages) classification of a noun or pronoun as masculine or feminine（某些语言的）性
intern	/in'tɜːn/	*n.*	[C] an advanced student or a recent graduate, especially in medicine, who is being given practical training under supervision 实习生；实习医生
stereotype	/'steriətaip/	*n.*	[C] a fixed idea or image that many people have of a particular type of person or thing, but which is often not true in reality 模式化观念；老一套；刻板印象
		vt.	[often passive] to form a fixed idea about a person or thing which may not really be true 对……形成模式化的看法
subtle	/'sʌtl/	*a.*	1. not very noticeable or obvious 不易察觉的；不明显的；微妙的　2. behaving in a clever way, and using indirect methods, in order to achieve sth. 机智的；机巧的；狡猾的　3. good at noticing and understanding things 敏锐的；头脑灵活的
sexist	/'seksist/	*n.*	[C] a person who treats other people, especially women, unfairly because of their sex or who makes offensive remarks about them 性别歧视者
comment	/'kɔment/	*n.*	1. [C, U] ~ **(about/on sth.)** something that you say or write which gives an opinion on or explains sb./sth. 议论；评论；解释　2. [C, U] criticism that shows the faults of sth. 批评；指责
offer	/'ɔfə(r)/	*n.*	[C] statement offering to do or give sth. to sb. 提议，建议
		vt.	to put forward sth. (to sb.) to be considered and accepted or refused; to present 提出；提供

enthusiasm	/in'θjuːziæzəm/	*n.*	[U] strong feeling of admiration or interest; great eagerness 热爱；热心；热情
interview	/'intəvjuː/	*vt.*	1. to conduct an interview with sb. (eg. a job applicant) 面试　2. (of a reporter, etc.) to ask sb. questions in an interview 采访，访问
		n.	1. [C, U] meeting at which sb. (eg. sb. applying for a job) is asked questions to find out if he is suitable 面试；面谈　2. [C] meeting at which a reporter, etc. asks sb. questions in order to find out his views 采访，交谈
tub	/tʌb/	*n.*	[C] bath 洗澡
naked	/'neikid/	*a.*	without clothes on 裸体的
inexcusable	/ˌinik'skjuːzəbl/	*a.*	too bad to accept or forgive 不可宽恕的；无法原谅的
bachelor	/'bætʃələ(r)/	*n.*	1. [C] a first university degree 学士　2. [C] a man who has never been married 未婚男子；单身汉
significantly	/sig'nifikəntli/	*a.*	1. to an important or considerable degree 重要地；重大地　2. in a way that conveys a special meaning 意味深长地；意义深远地
portray	/pɔː'trei/	*vt.*	1. (~ **sb./sth.**) to act a particular role in a film/movie or play 扮演　2. ~ **sb./sth.** (as sb./sth.) to describe or show sb./sth. in a particular way, especially when this does not give a complete or accurate impression of what they are like 将……描写成；表现　3. (~ **sb./sth.**) to show sb./sth. in a picture; to describe sb./sth. in a piece of writing 描绘；描画；描写
media	/'miːdiə/	*n.*	(the media) [*pl.*] means of mass communication, eg. TV, radio, newspapers 大众传播工具，大众传播媒介
overwhelming	/ˌəuvə'welmiŋ/	*a.*	very great or very strong; so powerful that you cannot resist it or decide how to react 巨大的；压倒性的；无法抗拒的
overwhelmingly	/ˌəuvə'welmiŋli/	*a.*	压倒性地；不可抵抗地
minor	/'mainə(r)/	*a.*	smaller, less serious, less important, etc. 较小的；程度轻的；次要的
objectify	/əb'dʒektifai/	*vt.*	to represent concretely; present as an object 使客观化
helpless	/'helplis/	*a.*	unable to function; without help 无助的；无能的
ogle	/'əugl/	*v.*	to look hard at sb. in an offensive way, usually showing sexual interest 盯着看，痴痴地看
remark	/ri'maːk/	*v.*	to say or write (sth.) by way of comment; to observe 谈论或评论（某事物）；评述
		n.	[C] thing said or written as a comment; observation 评论；评述；注意；察觉

marginalize	/'mɑːdʒinəlaiz/	*vt.*	to make sb. feel as if they are not important and cannot influence decisions or events; to put sb. in a position in which they have no power 使显得微不足道；使处于边缘；使无实权
inferior	/in'fiəriə(r)/	*a.*	of lower rank; lower 级别低的；较低的
		n.	[C] a person who is not as good as sb. else; a person who is lower in rank or status 不如别人的人；级别（或地位）低的人
incapable	/in'keipəbl/	*a.*	not able to do sth. 不能做某事
confidence	/'kɔnfidəns/	*n.*	1. [U] a belief in your own ability to do things and be successful 自信心；把握 2. [U] ~ **(in sb./sth.)** the feeling that you can trust, believe in and be sure about the abilities or good qualities of sb./sth. 信心；信任；信赖
inappropriate	/inə'prəupriət/	*a.*	not suitable or appropriate (for sb./sth.) 不恰当的，不适合的

☺ New Expressions

more often than not	usually 经常地
wear down	to make sb. gradually weaker or less determined until they eventually do what you want 消磨……斗志
focus on	to direct one's attention on something 集中注意力于，把……集中于……上
fit in	to conform harmoniously to other members of a group or other things in a setting 与……相处融洽；适应环境
make excuses for	to find a reason or justification to do something 找借口
be used to	to get adapt to; to be accustomed to 习惯于；适应
put down	to treat sb. in an unpleasant way by criticizing sb. in front of other people or making sb. appear foolish 当众批评；捉弄
take seriously	to attach importance to 重视；认真对待
speak up	to speak one's opinion without fear or hesitation 无所顾忌地说话
stand up for	to defend or support sb. and make your feelings or opinions very clear 捍卫，支持

[Reading Comprehension]

Understanding the text

I. Choose the best answer to each of the following questions.

1. Where was the software developer conference held?

   A. New York.   B. Washington D.C.

   C. San Francisco.   D. Los Angeles.

2. Why did the author feel alienated in the conference?

   A. Because she didn't play video games or watch any sports, and she didn't know what to talk with the others.

   B. Because there were more male software developer there.

   C. Because men there had prejudice against women.

   D. Because she didn't know anyone else there.

3. Why did the author hate being asked what she did professionally?

   A. Because she was impatient to answer this kind of questions.

   B. Because she got a small panic attack every time someone asked the relevant question.

   C. Because she didn't love being a soft engineer at all.

   D. Because she thought it's a kind of violation of her privacy.

4. What changes happened during the four years of the author's college life?

   A. Male students began to respect female students gradually.

   B. The number of male students who studied CS program became bigger and bigger.

   C. The number of female students who studied CS program became bigger and bigger.

   D. The number of female students who studied CS program was declining all the time.

5. What is the image of the female hacker in *Furious 7*?

   A. She doesn't fight.

   B. She can't defend herself.

   C. She has to be saved multiple times by others.

   D. All of the above.

6. What's the reason that the author had been alienated?

   A. Her personality was not so easygoing.

   B. She didn't have the urge to make friends.

   C. She didn't fit the programming culture.

   D. She didn't have a good reputation in programming circle.

7. What's the author's intention to share her story?

   A. She wanted more people to realize that the gender gap in computer science was a problem that was only growing.

   B. She wanted to gain more sympathy from other people.

   C. She just wanted to give vent to her anger towards male.

   D. She wanted to get people's attention to provide more opportunities for female.

8. What did the author suggest people do in order to change the difficult situation for female software engineers?

   A. To call people out if anyone made an inappropriate comment.

   B. To stand up for women when you saw them treated badly.

   C. To stand up for women when you heard them commented disrespectfully.

   D. All of the above.

Critical thinking

II. Work in pairs and discuss the following questions.

1. What is the stereotype of a programmer in your opinion?

2. Do you want to be a software programmer if you were a female in current society? Why or why not?

3. If you have to choose either to work outside or stay home to be a housewife / househusband, which one would you choose? Why?

4. Can you give some suggestions to those who are going to choose a career in the circle of computer science?

Language Focus

Words in use

III. Fill in the blanks with the words given below. Change the form where necessary. Each word can be used only once.

professionally	subtle	stereotype	ogle	overwhelmingly
assume	alienate	inexcusable	marginalize	inferior

1. No one can avoid making mistakes, but it is _____ to make the same mistake again and again.

2. Many men feel their body shape doesn't live up to the _____ of the ideal man.

3. I like to look at the guys in the mirrors as I walk away and watch them _____ at me.

4. The company has a(n) _____ trained workforce, to provide users with the service of improved quality.

5. Those poor men have always been _____, exploited, and constantly threatened.

6. But after learning that he was suffering from AIDS, they start to deliberately _____ him.

7. What he said was so _____ that we could hardly make out his true intention.

8. The government officials hope that trade will pick up when the two countries _____ to hard currency.

9. In this country, a woman who did not marry was thought to be _____ and abnormal.

10. The House of Commons has _____ rejected demands to bring back the death penalty for murder.

Expressions in use

IV. Fill in the blanks with the expressions given below. Change the form where necessary. Each expression can be used only once.

put down	be used to	take sb. seriously	stand up for
focus on	fit in	wear down	speak up
make excuses for		more often than not	

1. People say you shouldn't _____ holes in your experience or apologize for your shortcomings.

2. Together, let us listen to people and _____ their hopes and aspirations.

3. Learn how wonderful you are, and remove the need to hurt others. Others do not have to be _____ for you to feel great.

4. I think some of the players have yet to _____ the change in color and design.

5. He finds it's hard to _____ his thoughts _____ one thing for longer than five minutes.

6. Uncle Herbert never argued, never _____ himself.

7. She joined a painting club but didn't seem to _____, so she left eventually.

8. None can match your sheer will-power and persistence in _____ the opposition.

9. Scientists and doctors have begun to _____ the risk of depression in Children.

10. Behind many successful men there is, _____, a woman who makes this success possible.

Sentence structure

V. Rewrite the following sentences in each group by using "would rather +v.". Make changes where necessary.

> **Model:** We accomplish gender parity at Fiverr.
>
> We provide all the candidates with equal opportunities.
>
> → To accomplish gender parity at Fiverr, we would rather provide all candidates with equal opportunities.

1. I have no idea about the price of their products.

   I give up the attempt to guess how much they will ask.

   _____

2. I try to save money.

   I prefer to be home alone and don't want to go shopping.

   _____

3. The young lady prefers to be living in the foreign countries.

   Things are much more different in the foreign countries.

   _____

VI. Complete the following sentences by translating the Chinese into English, using "anything but…" to emphasize someone or something doesn't have a particular quality.

> **Model:** The tech industry has created a wealth of opportunity but _____
> （它也显示了对于女性来说一点儿都不公平）.
>
> → The tech industry has created a wealth of opportunity but <u>it has also emerged as anything but even for women.</u>

1. _____（我不能忍受肮脏的氛围，并且觉得我的离开根本不是不礼貌之举）, so I got the next bus back home.

2. The appearance of the product looks very nice and magnificent, _____（但在质量方面，它一点儿都不好）.

3. When she was 18 years old, _____（很多人都参加了她的生日聚会，可是她一点儿都不兴奋）.

Unit 8
Memories in Our Life

The danger of the past was that men became slaves. The danger of the future is that men may become robots.

— *Erich Seligmann Fromm (German social psychologist, humanistic philosopher)*

Today is not yesterday. We ourselves change. How then can our works and thoughts, if they are always to be fittest, continue always the same?

—*Thomas Carlyle (Scottish philosopher)*

Some things turned around for a lifetime.

Create good memories today, so that you can have a good past.

Don't give up the things that belong to you and keep those lost things in memory.

Distance could make you forget about them, but the memories would always be there.

Define your life with the actions you take, the love you give and the memories you make.

I always knew looking back on the tears would make me laugh, but I never knew looking back on the laughs would make me cry.

Why should a lifetime to forget someone, because you do not try to forget, but always remember, in looking forward, in the dream.

Dreaming in the memory is not as good as waiting for the paradise in the hell.

Some memories, are doomed to be unable to cancel, is just like some people, is doomed to be unable to substitute.

People say that bad memories cause the most pain, but actually it's the good ones that you know won't happen for the second time.

Recapturing the past is a tricky business. While most memories are simply souvenirs of a happier time, others can be quite deadly.

Section

A

Pre-reading Activities

I. *Look at the following pictures about memories, and discuss the meanings hidden behind the pictures with your classmates. Try to dig out the hidden meanings as much as possible.*

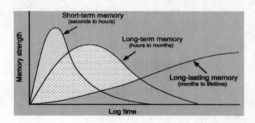

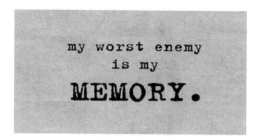

II. Work in pairs and discuss the following questions.

1. What's your attitude toward preserving memory?

2. Do you want to preserve your memory? If yes, what ways will you choose to preserve it?

3. Share one of your memories with your classmates. Does this memory influence you in a positive way or a negative way? And how?

Memories Last Forever!

1. A few months before she died, my grandmother made a decision. Bobby, as her friends called her, was a farmer's wife who not only **survived** the World War II but also found in it **justification** for her natural **hoarding talent**. So she kept old envelopes and bits of cardboard **cereal** boxes for note taking and lists. She kept frayed blankets and **musty** blouses in case she needed material to **mend**. She was also a **meticulous chronicler**. She kept **albums** of photographs of her family members, as is the case with the love letters my late grandfather sent her while she traveled the world with the Merchant Navy.

2. Yet in the months leading up to her death, the emphasis shifted from hoarding to sharing. Every time I visited, my car would be filled with **stuff** as old as I expected, such as unopened **cartons** of orange juice, balls of fraying wool, **damp antique** books. The memories, too, began to move out. She sent **faded** photos to her family and friends, as well as letters detailing some of her experiences.

3. On the afternoon of April 9, she posted a letter to one of her late husband's friends. In the envelope, she **enclosed** snapshots of my grandfather and his friend playing as children. "You must have them," she wrote. It was a demand but also a plea, perhaps, that these things not be forgotten when, a few hours later, she slipped away in her favorite armchair.

4. The hope that we will be remembered after we are gone is both **elemental** and **universal**. Poet Carl Sandburg captured this feeling in his 1916 poem *Troths*.

Yellow dust on a bumblebee's wing;

Grey lights in a woman's asking eyes;

Red ruins in the changing sunset;

embers.

I take you and pile high the memories;

Death will break her claws on some;

I keep.

5. Since the first paintings were scratched on cave walls, humans have sought to **confound** the final vanishing of memory. Oral history, diary, **memoir**, photography, film, and poetry, they're all tools in our arsenal in the war against time's whitewash. Today, we bank our memories onto Internet servers. There's the Facebook time line that records our life events, the Instagram account on which we store our likeness, the Gmail inbox that documents our conversations, and the YouTube channel that broadcasts how we move, talk, or sing. We collect and **curate** our memories more thoroughly than ever before.

6. We save what we believe to be important, but what if some essential **context** to our words or photographs is lost? How much better it would be to save everything? Everything we know and all that we remember, the love affairs and heartbreaks, the moments of victory and of shame, the lies we told and the truths we learned. If you could save your mind like a computer's hard drive, would you?

7. San Franciscan Aaron Sunshine's grandmother passed away. "One thing that struck me is how little of her is left," the 30-year-old man told me. "It's just a few **possessions**. I have an old shirt of hers that I wear around the house. There's her property, but that's just faceless money. It has no more **personality** than any other dollar bill."

8. Her death inspired Sunshine to sign up with Eternime, a web service that strives to preserve a person's memories after death. It works like this: while you're alive, you grant the service access to your Facebook, Twitter, and email accounts, uploaded photos, geographic location history, and even Google Glass recordings of things that you have seen. The data are collected and **analyzed** before being transferred to an artificial-intelligence avatar that tries to **emulate** your looks and personality. The avatar learns more as you interact with it, with the aim of better reflecting you after you're gone.

9. "It's about creating an interactive **legacy**," says Marius Ursache, one of Eternime's co-creators. "Your great-grandchildren will use it instead of a search engine or time line to access information about you—from photos of family events to your thoughts on certain topics to songs you wrote but never published."

10. Research in this area is **ongoing**. Beyond all the discussions about how we could save our

minds, is that something any of us truly wants? Humans long to **preserve** their memories because they remind us of who we are. If our memories are lost, we **cease** to know who we were and what it all meant. But at the same time, we change and alter our memories to create the **narrative** of our lives. To record them with equal weight might not be useful, either to us or to those who follow us.

11. Through our **descendants**, we reach for a way to live on beyond our passing. All parents take part in a grand relay race through time, passing the **gene baton** on and on through the centuries. Our physical traits—those eyes, this **temperament**—endure in some **diluted** or altered form. So, too, perhaps, do our metaphysical **attributes**.

12. I asked Sunshine why he wanted his life to be recorded. "To be honest, I'm not sure," he said. "The truly beautiful things in my life are too **ephemeral** to be preserved in any meaningful way. A part of me wants to build monuments to myself. But another part of me wants to disappear completely." That might be true of us all. We desire to be remembered, but only the parts of us that we want to be remembered.

13. Despite my grandmother's careful **distribution**, many photographs remained in her house. These unknown faces meant a great deal to her in life, but in a curious way, they have become a burden to those of us left behind.

14. My father asked my grandmother's **vicar** what he should do with the pictures; to just throw them away seemed **disrespectful**. His advice was simple. Take each photograph. Look at it carefully. In that moment, you honor the person in it. Then you may **discard** it and be free.

(991 words)

Notes

Merchant Navy: the title bestowed by King George V on the British merchant shipping fleets following their service in the First World War.

Carl Sandburg: (January 6, 1878—July 22, 1967) an American poet, writer, and editor who won three Pulitzer Prizes: two for his poetry and one for his biography of Abraham Lincoln. During his lifetime, Sandburg was widely regarded as "a major figure in contemporary literature", especially for volumes of his collected verse, including *Chicago Poems* (1916), *Cornhuskers* (1918), and *Smoke and Steel* (1920). At his death in 1967, President Lyndon B. Johnson observed that "Carl Sandburg was more than the voice of America, more than the poet of its strength and genius. He was America."

◁ New Words

survive	/sə'vaiv/	v.	to continue to live or exist in spite of nearly being killed or destroyed by (sth.) 幸存
justification	/ˌdʒʌstifi'keiʃn/	n.	[C, U] **(for sth./doing sth.)** a good reason why sth. exists or is done 正当理由
hoard	/hɔːd/	vt.	to collect and keep large amounts of food, money, etc., especially secretly 贮藏；囤积
		n.	[C] (of sth.) a collection of money, food, valuable objects, etc., especially one that sb. keeps in a secret place so that other people will not find or steal it 贮存，聚藏；秘藏
talent	/'tælənt/	n.	1. [U] people who have this 有才能的人；天才；人才 2. [C, U] ~ **(for sth.)** (instance of) special or very great ability 特殊的能力；才能；才干
cereal	/'siəriəl/	n.	[C, U] (any of various types of) food made from the grain of cereals 谷类食物；麦片粥
musty	/'mʌsti/	a.	smelling damp and unpleasant because of a lack of fresh air 有霉味的；发霉的
mend	/mend/	vt.	to return (sth. broken, worn out or torn) to good condition or working order; to repair 修理，修补
meticulous	/mi'tikjuləs/	a.	paying careful attention to every detail 细心的；小心翼翼
chronicler	/'krɔniklə/	n.	[C] a writer of history, especially in the past 记录者
album	/'ælbəm/	n.	[C] book in which a collection of photographs, autographs, postage stamps, etc. can be kept（收存照片、签名手迹、邮票等的）册子
stuff	/stʌf/	n.	[U] unnamed things, belongings, activities, subject-matter, etc. 东西、财物、活动、题材等
carton	/'kɑːtn/	n.	[C] light cardboard or plastic box for holding goods 纸板箱；纸板盒
damp	/dæmp/	a.	not completely dry; slightly wet 不完全干燥的；潮湿的
antique	/æn'tiːk/	a.	old and often valuable 古老的；古董的
		n.	[C] an object such as a piece of furniture that is old and often valuable 古董
fade	/feid/	v.	(cause sth.) to lose color, freshness or vigor（使）褪色，凋落，衰弱
enclose	/in'kləuz/	vt.	to put sth. in an envelope, letter, parcel, etc. 将……放入封套、信件、包裹中
elemental	/ˌeli'mentl/	a.	basic 基本的
universal	/ˌjuːni'vɜːsl/	a.	of, belonging to, affecting or done by all people or things in the world or in a particular group 全体的；影响全体的；全体做的；共同的

confound	/kən'faʊnd/	*vt.*	1. to defeat an enemy 击败，战胜（敌人） 2. to prove sb./sth. wrong 证明……有错 3. to confuse and surprise sb. 使困惑惊讶；使惊疑
memoir	/'memwɑː(r)/	*n.*	[C] written record of (esp. important) events, usu. based on personal knowledge 记录
curate	/'kjʊərət/	*vt.*	to select, organize and look after the objects or works of art in a museum or art gallery, etc. 管理
context	/'kɒntekst/	*n.*	[C, U] circumstances in which sth. happens or in which sth. is to be considered（某事物产生的或应考虑到的）环境，背景
possession	/pə'zeʃn/	*n.*	[C] [*pl.*] something that you own or have with you at a particular time 个人财产；私人物品
personality	/pɜːsə'næləti/	*n.*	[C] characteristics and qualities of a person seen as a whole 人格；个性
analyze	/'ænəlaɪz/	*vt.*	to examine and explain (sth.) 分析；研究
emulate	/'emjuleɪt/	*vt.*	1. to work in the same way as another computer, etc. and perform the same tasks 模仿 2. to try to do sth. as well as somebody else because you admire them 努力赶上
legacy	/'legəsi/	*n.*	1. [C] money or property that is given to you by sb. when they die 遗产；遗赠财物 2. [C] a situation that exists now because of events, actions, etc. that took place in the past 遗留问题；后遗症
ongoing	/'ɒngəʊɪŋ/	*a.*	continuing to exist or progress 继续存在的；进行中的
preserve	/prɪ'zɜːv/	*vt.*	1. to keep a particular quality, feature, etc.; to make sure that sth. is kept 保护；维护；保留 2. [*often passive*] to keep sth. in its original state in good condition 维持……的原状；保存；保养 3. to prevent sth., especially food, from decaying by treating it in a particular way 贮存；保鲜
cease	/siːs/	*v.*	to stop happening or existing; to stop sth. from happening or existing 终止，结束
narrative	/'nærətɪv/	*n.*	[C] spoken or written account of events; story 叙事；故事
		a.	of, or in the form of, story-telling 叙述的；叙事体的
descendant	/dɪ'sendənt/	*n.*	1. [C] a person's descendants are their children, their children's children, and all the people who live after them who are related to them 后裔；后代；子孙 2. [C] something that has developed from sth. similar in the past 派生物
gene	/dʒiːn/	*n.*	[C] unit in a chromosome which controls heredity 基因
baton	/'bætn/	*n.*	[C] short stick carried and handed on in a relay race（接力赛跑用的）接力棒
temperament	/'temprəmənt/	*n.*	1. [C, U] a person's or an animal's nature as shown in the way they behave or react to situations or people 气质，性情，性格 2. [U] the tendency to get emotional and excited very easily and behave in an unreasonable way 暴躁；喜怒无常

dilute	/daɪˈljuːt/	*vt.*	1. to make sth. weaker or less effective 削弱；降低；使降低效果　2. to make a liquid weaker by adding water or another liquid to it 稀释；冲淡
attribute	/ˈætrɪbjuːt/	*n.*	[C] quality regarded as a natural or typical part of sb./sth. 属性；特质；性质
~	/əˈtrɪbjuːt/	*vt.*	~ (sth. to sb./sth.) to regard sth. as belonging to, caused by or produced by sb./sth. 认为……属于……；认为……由……引起或产生
ephemeral	/ɪˈfemərəl/	*a.*	lasting or used for only a short period of time 短暂的；瞬息的
distribution	/ˌdɪstrɪˈbjuːʃn/	*n.*	1. [U] the act of giving or delivering sth. to a number of people 分发；分送　2. [C, U] the way that sth. is shared or exists over a particular area or among a particular group of people 分配；分布
vicar	/ˈvɪkə/	*n.*	[C] (in the Church of England) clergyman in charge of a parish where tithes formerly belonged to another person or an institution（英国国教的）牧区牧师
disrespectful	/dɪsrɪˈspektfl/	*a.*	showing disrespect 无礼的；不尊敬的
discard	/dɪˈskaːd/	*vt.*	to get rid of sth. that you no longer want or need 丢弃；抛弃

⊛ New Expressions

bits of	a handful of; a small number of 少量的
lead up to	to prepare, introduce or go before sth. 于……之前发生；为……做准备；引起
fill with	to be swarming with 装满；充满
slip away	to leave furtively and stealthily 悄悄溜走
pass away	(*euphemism*) die 去世；死亡
sign up	to agree to participate in sth. or get sb. to agree to participate in something, especially by way of a signature 注册；报名；签约
strive to	to make a great effort to achieve sth. 努力，奋斗
long to	to have a desire to do sth. 渴望做……
remind... of	to cause sb. to remember or be newly aware of sb./sth. 提醒
race through	to do sth. in a hurry 匆匆忙忙地做；快速做完某事
throw away	to get rid of sth. that you do not want or need 扔掉，抛弃

⟮Reading Comprehension⟯

Understanding the text

I. Answer the following questions.

1. What decision did my grandmother make a few months before she died?

2. What stuff would my car be filled with every time after I visited my grandmother?

3. According to the text, how do we bank our memories today?

4. What did Sunshine decide to do after he was inspired?

5. What is the main business of the company of Eternime?

6. How does Eternime work?

7. Why did Sunshine want his life to be recorded?

8. What advice did my grandmother's vicar give to me?

Critical thinking

II. Work in pairs and discuss the following questions.

1. Would you like to bank your memories? Why or why not?

2. How do you understand the poem *Troth* in the text?

3. What kind of memories do you think deserve your preservation?

4. Can you brainstorm some other ways to preserve memories?

Words in use

III. Fill in the blanks with the words given below. Change the form where necessary. Each word can be used only once.

hoard	meticulous	distribution	dilute	possession
descendant	preserve	legacy	ephemeral	discard

1. Because people expected prices to rise rapidly, they started to _____ goods.

2. On her father's death, she came into _____ of a vast fortune.

3. These paintings are in some ways a reminder that earthly pleasure is _____.

4. With three years' experience on quality control, I have developed my _____ working attitude and I also emphasize teamwork.

5. Go through your medicine and bathroom cabinets and _____ any medicines and toiletries that are past their prime.

6. The Qin Dynasty left a(n) _____ of a centralized and bureaucratic state that would be

carried onto successive dynasties.

7. Mrs. Stuart is a mixed-raced _____ of both an African slave and an English slave owner.

8. Conservation is an issue which gets a lot of attention these days—whether it means _____ old buildings, or protecting the environment.

9. Inflation is considered to be undesirable because of its adverse effects on income _____.

10. He thought Rear Admiral Henry's presence might _____ the tension of the dinner.

Word building

The suffix *-ence* combines with verbs to form nouns. Nouns formed in this way refer to the action, process, or state described by the original verbs.

Examples

Words learned	Add *-ence*	New words formed
infer	→	inference
occur	→	occurrence

The suffix *-er* combines with verbs to form nouns. (For explanation, refer to Word building in Unit 5.)

Examples

Words learned	Add *-er*	New words formed
thrill	→	thriller
boil	→	boiler

The suffix *-ly* combines with adjectives to form adverbs. Adverbs formed in this way express the idea that something is done in the way described by the adjective. Sometimes *-ly* combines with nouns to form adjectives.

Examples

Words learned	Add *-ly*	New words formed
scarce	→	scarcely
specific	→	specifically
cost	→	costly

The suffix *-ion* combines with verbs to form nouns. (For explanation, refer to Word building in Unit 3.)

Examples

Words learned	Add *-ion*	New words formed
consume	→	consumption
deceive	→	deception
invade	→	invasion
proceed	→	procession

IV. Add -ence, -er, -ly or -ion to or remove them from the following words to form new words.

Words learned	New words formed
-ence	
correspond	
refer	
-er	
carry	
browse	
-ly	
normal	
obvious	
approximate	
-ion	
evolve	
explode	
perceive	
assume	
persuade	

V. Fill in the blanks with the newly-formed words in Activity IV. Change the form where necessary. Each word can be used only once.

1. In some African local languages there is a close _____ between sounds and letters.

2. Even administrative regulations must be accompanied by _____ and education.

3. China is the world's most populous country with a population of 1.3 billion, which makes up _____ a quarter of the world population.

4. In the course of _____, some birds have lost the power of flight.

5. Chinese enterprises are mostly in a development stage, and they need a good _____ for their message to the world.

6. He is interested in how our _____ of death affect the way we live.

7. _____ speaking, the transportation system in Paris carries 950,000 passengers a day.

8. The presence of his immediate family is _____ having a calming effect on him.

9. The above views may or may not be correct, they are only for your _____.

10. After the second _____, all of London's main train and subway stations were shut down.

11. You can select secure communication between your server and a web _____.

12. You would be making a(n) _____ that's not based on any fact.

Banked cloze

VI. Fill in the blanks by selecting suitable words from the word bank. You may not use any of the words more than once.

A. randomly	B. intelligent	C. mistakes	D. paving	E. professional
F. crucial	G. regularly	H. aware	I. stimulate	J. improving
K. useful	L. optimistic	M. pessimistic	N. hindrances	O. saving

    A good memory is 1) _____ to a successful life. You can increase your chances of success at school as well as in your career by 2) _____ the ability of retaining and reviving relevant information. Why does much of your success depend on the power of memory, and how can mental capacity be bettered?

    It may be said that a good memory is your link to success in academic and 3) _____ life. According to researchers, there is an inevitable connection between working memory and school success because memory is the process of reproducing what has been learned and retained especially through associative mechanism which can 4) _____ your brain activities. Thus, lack of good memory may pose 5) _____ in your way to academic success. Apparently, memory plays a vital role in every aspect of your working life. When you have a good memory, you are likely to be more confident and 6) _____, have better jobs and social relationships than your peers with poor memories. By using the capacity of recognizing previous knowledge and experiences, you are empowered with ideas to prepare yourself in achieving your goal, and at the same time you can avoid many problems and 7) _____ in the future.

Apart from the above said, memory can be bettered by avoiding stress, drugs and alcohol, and by getting plenty of exercise and enjoying a good night's sleep. Being 8) _____ of the importance of a good memory to your success is 9) _____ your road to success. As a conclusion, you need to keep stimulating your brain and make it function 10) _____ because the brain is something you "either use it or lose it".

Expressions in use

VII. Fill in the blanks with the expressions given below. Change the form where necessary. Each expression can be used only once.

strive to	pass away	sign up	remind of
race through	throw away	lead up to	slip away
pretend to	fill with		

1. So she simply welcomed him and _____ him _____ the last time they had met.

2. If you _____ know what you don't know, you'll only make a fool of yourself.

3. Millions of us are in danger of "meltdown" because we _____ life at break-neck speed that psychologists have warned.

4. This graph shows the percentage of people, across different European countries, who are willing to donate their organs after they _____.

5. Failing to tackle the deficit would be _____ an opportunity we haven't had for a generations.

6. If anger management is difficult for you, _____ for a course to help you deal with it.

7. Alan Tomlinson has reconstructed the events that _____ the turmoil.

8. May your hopes and dreams come true and may the years ahead _____ happiness.

9. We will _____ provide you with quality products and satisfactory service!

10. If you want to _____, now's a good time; everyone is dancing.

Structure Analysis and Writing

Structure Analysis

Focus on an argumentative essay

In this unit, we will learn how to write an argumentative essay. For this kind of essay, we not only give information but also present an argument with the PROS (supporting ideas) and CONS (opposing ideas) of an argumentative issue. We should clearly take our stand and write as if we are trying to persuade an opposing audience to adopt new beliefs or behavior. The primary objective is to persuade readers to change beliefs that many of them do not want to change. For an argumentative essay to be effective, it must contain certain elements that will persuade the audience to see things from your perspective.

● Find a good topic

To find a good topic for an argumentative essay you should consider several issues at first, and choose a few that spark two solid, conflicting points of the view or very different conclusions. As you look over a list of topics you should find one that really piques your interest.

Though strong interest in a topic is important, it's not enough to make it good material for an argument. You have to consider what position you can back up with reasoning and evidence. It's necessary to have a strong belief, but when shaping an argument you'll have to explain why your belief is reasonable and logical.

● Consider both sides of your topic and take a position

Once you have selected a topic you feel strongly about, you should make a list of points for both sides of the argument and pick a side. One of your first objectives in your essay will be to present both sides of your issue with an assessment of each. Of course, you will conclude that one side (your side) is the best conclusion.

Writing stages

Once you've given yourself a solid foundation to work with, you can begin to craft your essay. An argumentative essay should contain three parts: the introduction, the body, and the conclusion. The length of these parts (number of paragraphs) will vary, depending on the length of your essay assignment.

1. Introduce your topic and assert your opinion

As in any essay, the first paragraph of your argumentative essay should contain a brief explanation of your topic, some background information, and a thesis statement. In this case, your thesis will be a statement of your position on a particular controversial topic.

Example of an introductory paragraph with thesis statement.

Since the turn of the new century, a theory has emerged concerning the end of the world, or at least the end of life as we know it. This new theory centers around the year 2012, a date that many claim, has mysterious origins in ancient manuscripts from many different cultures. The most noted characteristic of this date is that it appears to mark the end of the Mayan calendar. But there is no evidence to suggest that the Maya saw any great relevance to this date. In fact, none of the claims surrounding a 2012 doomsday event holds up to scientific inquiry. The year 2012 will pass without a major, life-altering catastrophe.

2. Present both sides of the controversy

The body of your essay should contain main contents of your argument. You should go into more details about the two sides of your controversy and state the strongest points concerning the counter-side on your issue.

After describing the "other" side, you should present your own viewpoint and then provide evidence to show why your position is the more reasonable one.

Select your strongest evidence and present your points one by one. Use a mix of evidence types, from statistics, to other studies and anecdotal stories. This part of your paper could be of any length, from two paragraphs to two hundred pages.

Re-state your position as the most sensible one in your summary paragraph.

Tips for your essay:

- Avoid emotional language. Overly emotional arguments sound irrational.
- Make sense of the difference between a logical conclusion and an emotional point of view.
- Don't make up evidence, and don't use bad sources for evidence.
- Cite your sources.
- Make an outline.

Structured Writing

Read the sample essay and see how the story develops with details.

Topic	Sample essay
Children limit in China	Children are the keys to paradise. Therefore, everyone wants many keys to paradise. However, China already has a large population. If there is no limit for everyone to have children, it will cause a lot of problems, such as crowded environment, excessive pollution and drastic competition. Therefore, there should be a limit on the number of children people can have, which means every family has one or two children. This policy can improve family life, improve the life of women and develop Chinese society.
Introduction	
Thesis statement: There should be a limit on the number of children people can have, which means every family has one or two children. This policy can improve	

family life, improve the life of women and develop Chinese society.

Body

Reason 1: Initially, improving family life is an important reason that there should be a limit on the number of children in China.

Reason 2: There should be a limit on the number of children in China because it can also improve the life of women.

Reason 3: A limit on the number of children in China can develop Chinese society.

Opponents believe there should not be a limit on the number of children people can have because it is a privacy situation, and no one even the government should decide how many children people can have.

Conclusion

In conclusion, there should be a limit on the number of children people.

Initially, improving family life is an important reason that there should be a limit on the number of children in China. Because parents need to spend a lot of money to raise a child; the life quality of the family will decrease. If Chinese parents have a limit on the number of children, their life would be less stressful and more relax because they have more time to do what they want. In addition, they have more attention for each child. For example. Parents can use more time to teach each child how to live in the society and help each child to solve problems because it is very important for their children's life. Therefore, the quality of the family will be improved.

Secondly, there should be a limit on the number of children in China because it can also improve the life of women. Traditionally, the gender role in China, women need to take care of children. For example, if a family has six children, and parents have jobs, absolutely women should take care of the six children. Therefore, women don't have to work at all. They must stay at home and take care of her children. In contrast, women's role has changed. If a family has two children, women have time to find all kind of jobs that they like, and they also earn money for their family so that it can improve the quality of their life. The important thing that it is very balanced for women's work and life.

Finally, a limit on the number of children in China can develop Chinese society. China already has a large population. If we limit the number of children in China, it will reduce competition. For instant, because of the large population in China, many Chinese people can't find jobs; however, if we limit the number of children in China, the population of China will decrease. Some days in their generation, they will have more opportunity to find jobs. In addition, a limit on the number of children also improves the education. For example, in China, many schools have 40 students for each class. It is very crowded and noisy for students to study. Teachers can't pay all of attention to teaching them. However, if we limit the number of children, the education environment will be very well for the students.

Opponents believe there should not be a limit on the number of children people can have because it is a privacy situation, and no one even the government should decide how many children people can have. This point may be true. However, if every has no limit to have children in China, the population will quickly increase. In addition, life quality of everyone will decrease because people should spend more time to accompany their children, even though women have no time to work at all.

In conclusion, there should be a limit on the number of children people can have because it can improve the quality of the family, change women's role in China and develop Chinese society. Nowadays, the Chinese government carries out a policy that every family has a maximum of two children. Because of this policy, everyone has enough time to do what they want rather than raise many children. Women can also find their favorite jobs and earn money for their family. The important factor that the policy will make Chinese people have more job opportunity in the future. I think that a limit on the number of children is beneficial for China.

VIII. Write an essay of no less than 150 words on one of the following topics. One topic has an outline that you can follow.

Topic

Should college students hire cleaners?

Introduction

Thesis statement: As a university student myself, I firmly believe that university students shouldn't hire cleaners to do cleaning.

Body

Reason 1: For a start, away from our parents, it is in university that we learn to be independent adults.

Reason 2: The spirit of bearing hardships is supposed to be hold tightly.

Reason 3: To do clean-up willingly is a good personal habit that should be kept.

Conclusion

College students should not hire cleaners for any reason.

More topics:

● Should animals be used for research?

● Should cigarette smoking be banned?

Translation

IX. Translate the following paragraph into Chinese.

Mid-Autumn Festival, one of Chinese traditional festivals, is celebrated on the 15th day of the 8th month of the lunar calendar. For thousands of years, Chinese people have associated joy and sorrow, parting and reunion with the waxes and wanes of the moon. Since a full moon is round, which symbolizes wholeness, the Mid-Autumn Festival is also known as the festival of reunion. All family members go to great lengths to get together on this special day, whereas those who cannot return home watch the bright moon to express their longing for their beloved ones.

X. Translate the following paragraph into English.

农历（unar calendar）七月初七是七夕节（Qixi Festival），它起源于汉代，是一个传统节日。在中国古代传说中，牛郎和织女（cowherd and weaver girl）会在每年的这一天相会。七夕节是中国传统节日中最具浪漫色彩的一个，现在一般被称为"中国情人节"。对于年轻的姑娘们，七夕节是个重要的日子，她们会在这一天晚上向聪明美丽的织女祈求智慧、女红技巧和美满姻缘。

Section

Reading Skills: *Purpose*

You have already learned how to employ certain methods to identify the author's purpose in order to improve your reading in Unit 5. This unit will elaborate more on this useful reading skill. In order to effectively evaluate a passage, it is essential to determine the author's purpose. There are three main purposes for an author to write a passage:

- To inform;
- To entertain;
- To persuade.

An author always has an overall reason or purpose to write a passage. If an author is writing about a tornado, the writer could have many different purposes. Here are some examples.

- To inform the reader about a tornado;
- To compare the current tornado with the past tornado in the region;
- To identify factors that caused the tornado;
- To analyze a state's response to the tornado;
- To persuade readers to donate money to a tornado relief fund;
- To describe one resident's effort to save lives during the tornado.

Some authors explicitly state their purposes. Others leave it for the reader to infer the purpose. Understanding the author's purpose helps the reader better understand the main idea of the passage and follow the author's ideas as they progress. Likewise, an author has a purpose for the various decisions made in crafting the sentences in the passage. In particular, word choice, word placement, and emphasis all work intentionally toward promoting a specific purpose that the author has in mind. The insightful reader will recognize these intentions and follow the author's logic and conclusions by means of these clues. Here are two examples from Text A.

Example 1:

These unknown faces meant a great deal to her in life, but in a curious way, they have become a burden to those of us left behind. (Para. 13)

Example 2:

His advice was simple. Take each photograph. Look at it carefully. In that moment, you honor the person in it. Then you may discard it and be free. (Para. 14)

The two examples show that the author wants to persuade the readers to accept his points of view that the memory about the others may be a burden to us and we can spare ourselves the efforts to keep them.

Answer the following questions about Text B with the help of the clues mentioned in Reading Skills to identify the author's writing purposes.

1. *"What then happens to the hundreds of millions of people who will have no employment (not everyone can become "designers, engineers, IT specialists, logistics experts", after all), and who, incidentally, will not have the income to purchase the wonderful products created by digital manufacturing?"* (Para. 8)

    What hidden messages can you get from the above sentence?

2. *"Yes, 3D printing may indeed be indistinguishable from magic, but it could turn out to be of the blacker variety."* (Para. 9)

    What hidden messages can you get from the above sentence?

Is 3D Printing the Key to Utopia?

1. You know the problem: the dishwasher that has cleaned your dishes **faithfully** for 15 years suddenly stops working. You call out a repairman who identifies the problem: the **filter** unit has finally given up the ghost. "Ah," you say, much **relieved**, "can you fit a new one?" The chap shakes his head **sorrowfully**. No one can do, he explains. The company that made the machine was taken over years ago by another **outfit** and they no longer supply **spares** for your **ancient** machine.

2. Up until now, this story would have had a **predictable** ending in which you sorrowfully **junked** your trusty dishwasher and bought a new one. But there's an emerging technology that could change that. It's called three-dimensional printing.

3. Eh? Surely printing is **intrinsically** a two-dimensional process, involving the **squirting** of colored dyes onto flat sheets of paper? And indeed it is, so perhaps the use of the word "printing" in 3D printing is a bit **naughty**—which is why men in suits tends to call it "additive manufacturing". But there is still a strong **metaphorical correspondence** between the 2D and 3D processes. In the former, we take an electronic representation of a document on a computer screen

and output a **replica** of that on to paper; in the latter, we take a three-dimensional computer model of something and use printing-like technology to create a three-dimensional **version** of it in plastic or other materials.

4. It works like this: a designer uses computer-assisted design software to create a three-dimensional model of an object. Another program then "slices" the model into thin sections and instructs the "printer" to lay down an exact replica of the section in plastic (or other types of) **granules** which are then **fused** to become a solid layer. The process is repeated, slice by slice, until the entire object has been made.

5. What comes **irresistibly** to mind the first time one sees a 3D printer in action is Arthur C Clarke's famous **observation** that "any sufficiently advanced technology is **indistinguishable** from magic". You're sitting there watching the machine busily going about its business and then, suddenly, there's a complex, fully functional object with moving parts—for example the roller-bearings that are essential components in everything that runs on wheels. And then you realize that this is not a technology for making toys and garden gnomes, but something that could transform manufacturing.

6. Why? Because up until now, manufacturing has been ruled by economies of scale. The upfront costs of "tooling up" to manufacture anything—whether it's roller bearings or automobiles—using **conventional** materials and **assembly** methods are huge, so you have to stamp out many thousands of similar products in order to get the price of each one down to a reasonable level. But with 3D printing, the tooling-up costs are much less—essentially consisting of the costs of building the computer model of the product. And since it's easy to tweak a computer model—it's just software, after all—small production runs suddenly become economic. So the technology could enable a shift from the mass production **bequeathed** to us by Henry Ford to what some people call "mass customization".

7. The **disruptive** significance of this has yet to dawn on many governments and corporations. But some observers—for example writers for that great cheerleader of **capitalism**, *the Economist*—are trying to attract their attention by **dubbing** digital-driven manufacturing the "third Industrial Revolution". "Digital technology has already rocked the media and retailing industries," says *the Economist*. Just as cotton mills crushed hand looms and the Model T put **farriers** out of work. Many people will look at the factories of the future and shudder. They will not be full of **grimy** machines manned by men in oily overalls. Many will be **squeaky** clean—and almost deserted. Most jobs will not be on the factory floor but in the offices nearby, which will be full of designers, engineers, IT specialists, marketing staff and other professionals. The manufacturing jobs of the future will require more skills. Many dull, repetitive tasks will become **obsolete**; you no longer need riveters when a product has no **rivets**.

8. Quite so. There's just one fly in this techno-Utopian **ointment**. Just suppose *the Economist*

is right—that digital manufacturing really does wipe out the low-level manufacturing jobs currently provided, here and overseas, by older technology. What then happens to the hundreds of millions of people who will have no employment (not everyone can become "designers, engineers, IT specialists, logistics experts", after all), and who, **incidentally**, will not have the income to **purchase** the wonderful products created by digital manufacturing? The world had lost millions of jobs before—on the land or in the old horse-powered economy—but they were soon replaced by jobs in the car industry or the new service industries. What worries many economists and computer scientists is that today's technologies are going to remove people from economic activity completely. Some argue that a dystopian world is emerging in which good jobs and full-time employment will become the preserve of an educated, computer-literate master. For example Apple, Facebook, Amazon and Google are plainly riding the new wave, but they are not mass employers like Tesco, Ford or General Motors.

9. Yes, 3D printing may indeed be indistinguishable from magic, but it could turn out to be of the blacker variety.

(887 words)

Notes

Arthur C Clarke: Sir Arthur Charles Clarke (December 16, 1917—March 19, 2008), a British science fiction writer, science writer and futurist, inventor, undersea explorer, and television series host.

Henry Ford: (July 30, 1863—April 7, 1947), an American industrialist, the founder of the Ford Motor Company, and the sponsor of the development of the assembly line technique of mass production.

Mass customization: the use of flexible computer-aided manufacturing systems to produce custom output. Those systems combine the low unit costs of mass production processes with the flexibility of individual customization.

***The Economist*:** an English-language weekly news magazine owned by the Economist Group and edited in offices in London.

Tesco: a British multinational grocery and general merchandise retailer with headquarters in Welwyn Garden City, Hertfordshire, England, United Kingdom.

General Motors: an American multinational corporation headquartered in Detroit, Michigan, that designs, manufactures, markets, and distributes vehicles and vehicle parts, and sells financial services.

▶ New Words

faithfully	/'feiθfəli/	*a.*	able to be trusted; conscientious 可信赖地；认真地
filter	/'filtə(r)/	*n.*	[C] device containing paper, sand, cloth, etc. used to hold back any solid material or impurities in a liquid or gas passed through it 过滤器
relieve	/ri'li:v/	*vt.*	to remove or reduce an unpleasant feeling or pain 解除，减轻，缓和
sorrowfully	/'sɔrəufəli/	*a.*	feeling, showing or causing sorrow 感到、显得或引起悲哀或懊悔地
outfit	/'autfit/	*n.*	[C] group of people working together; organization 集体，组织
spare	/speə/	*n.*	[C] spare part (for a machine, car, etc.), esp. an extra wheel for a car（机器、汽车等的）备件
ancient	/'einʃənt/	*a.*	1. very old; having existed for a very long time 古老的；很老的 2. belonging to a period of history that is thousands of years in the past 古代的
predictable	/pri'diktəbl/	*a.*	happening or turning out in the way that might have been expected or predicted 可预见的；可预料的
junk	/dʒʌŋk/	*vt.*	to dispose of (something useless or old) 丢掉
		n.	things that are considered useless or of little value 无用的或无价值的东西
intrinsically	/in'trinsikli/	*a.*	essentially, basically 内在地；本质地；固有地
squirt	/skwɜːt/	*v.*	to force liquid, gas, etc. in a thin fast stream through a narrow opening; to be forced out of a narrow opening in this way（使）喷射；喷
naughty	/'nɔːti/	*a.*	disobedient; bad; causing trouble 不听话的
metaphorical	/ˌmetə'fɔrikl/	*a.*	connected with or containing metaphors 隐喻的；比喻性的
correspondence	/ˌkɔri'spɔndəns/	*n.*	1. [C] ~ **(between A and B)** a connection between two things; the fact of two things being similar 相关；相似 2. [U] ~ **(with sb.)** the activity of writing letters 通信；通信联系
replica	/'replikə/	*n.*	[C] a very good or exact copy of sth. 复制品；仿制品
version	/'vɜːʃn/	*n.*	1. [C] special or variant form of sth. made 种，类 2. [C] account of an event, etc. from the point of view of one person 说法
granule	/'grænjuːl/	*n.*	[C] a small, hard piece of sth.; a small grain 颗粒状物；微粒；细粒

fuse	/fjuːz/	*v.*	(cause sth.) to become liquid by means of heat（加热使某物）变成液体；熔化；熔融
irresistible	/ˌiri'zistəbl/	*a.*	1. so strong that it cannot be stopped or resisted 不可遏止的；无法抵制的　2. so attractive that you feel you must have it 极诱人的；忍不住想要的
irresistibly	/ˌiri'zistəbli/	*a.*	无法抵抗地；不能压制地；极为诱惑人地
observation	/ˌɔbzə'veiʃn/	*n.*	1. [C] remark or comment 言语；评论　2. [U] action of observing; (state of) being observed 观察
indistinguishable	/indi'stiŋgwiʃəbl/	*a.*	1. ~ **(from sth.)** impossible to tell apart from sb. or sth. else 无法分辨的；无法区分的　2. not clear; not able to be clearly identified 不清楚的；无法识别的
conventional	/kən'venʃnl/	*a.*	1. following what is traditional or the way sth. has been done for a long time 传统的；习惯的　2. tending to follow what is done or considered acceptable by society in general; normal and ordinary, and perhaps not very interesting 依照惯例的；遵循习俗的；墨守成规的
assembly	/ə'sembli/	*n.*	1. [U] the process of putting together the parts of sth. such as a vehicle or piece of furniture 装配；组装；总成　2. [C, U] the meeting together of a group of people for a particular purpose; a group of people who meet together for a particular purpose 集会；集会者
bequeath	/bi'kwiːð/	*vt.*	~ **sth. (to sb.)** to leave the results of your work, knowledge, etc. for other people to use or deal with 将……留下
disruptive	/dis'rʌptiv/	*a.*	causing problems, noise, etc. so that sth cannot continue normally 引起混乱的；扰乱性的；破坏性的
capitalism	/'kæpitəlizəm/	*n.*	[U] an economic system in which a country's businesses and industry are controlled and run for profit by private owners rather than by the government 资本主义
dub	/dʌb/	*vt.*	1. ~ **(sb. + n.)** to give sb./sth. a particular name, often in a humorous or critical way 把……戏称为；给……起绰号　2. ~ **sth. (into sth.)** to replace the original speech in a film/ movie or television program with words in another language 配音；译制
farrier	/'færiə(r)/	*n.*	[C] blacksmith who makes and fits horseshoes 蹄铁匠
grimy	/'graimi/	*a.*	covered with dirt 沾满污垢的；满是灰尘的
squeaky	/skwiːki/	*a.*	making a short, high sound; squeaking 吱吱叫的；嘎吱作响的
obsolete	/'ɔbsəliːt/	*a.*	no longer used because sth. new has been invented out of date 淘汰的；废弃的；过时的

rivet	/'rivit/	*n.*	[C] a metal pin that is used to fasten two pieces of leather, metal, etc. together 铆钉
ointment	/'ɔintmənt/	*n.*	smooth greasy paste rubbed on the skin to heal injuries or roughness, or as a cosmetic 软膏；油膏
incidentally	/insi'dentli/	*a.*	in an incidental way 偶然地；不经意地
purchase	/'pɜːtʃəs/	*vt.*	to buy sth. 购买某物
		n.	[U] (action of) buying sth. 购买

✪ New Expressions

call out	to order or ask (sb./sth.) to come by shouting, telephoning, writing, etc.; summon 命令或要求……来；召唤
give up the ghost	fail to work or to make an effort 失效；不能使用；不再努力
take over	to acquire or gain control of (a business company), esp. by obtaining the support of a majority of its shareholders 接收，接管
lay down	to put sth. down, usually because you have finished using it（使用后）放下
go about	to start working on sth. 着手做；开始做
stamp out	to put an end to 杜绝；灭绝
consist of	be composed or made up of sth. 由……组成
dawn on	to begin to realize sth. 开始理解；渐渐明白
a/the fly in the ointment	person or thing that spoils an otherwise satisfactory situation or occasion 令人扫兴的人或事物
wipe out	an event (or the result of an event) that completely destroys sth. 消灭，彻底摧毁
remove from	to take sth./sb. away from a place 除掉；移动
turn out to be	to prove to be 结果是；原来是

Reading Comprehension

Understanding the text

I. Choose the best answer to each of the following questions.

1. Why can't the repairman fit a new dishwasher?

   A. Because he is not professional.

   B. Because he doesn't have appropriate tools to use.

   C. Because he has no confidence to repair it by himself.

D. Because the company that made the machine was taken over years ago by another outfit and they no longer supply spares for the machine.

2. How could we solve the problem mentioned in Para. 1?

   A. To use the emerging technology called three-dimensional printing.

   B. To change the components and parts of the old machine.

   C. To call the service center.

   D. To find a new repairman.

3. What is the characteristics of the printing process of the new printing technology mentioned in the text?

   A. It is naturally an easy process.

   B. It is naturally a difficult process.

   C. It is intrinsically a two-dimensional process.

   D. It is intrinsically a three-dimensional process.

4. Why are the tooling-up costs much less with 3D printing?

   A. Because the technology of 3D printing has been used for many years.

   B. Because it's easy to tweak a computer mode through the technology of 3D printing.

   C. Because almost everyone can master the technology of 3D printing.

   D. Because the technology of 3D doesn't require human labor.

5. Who has paid attention to the disruptive significance of 3D printing technology?

   A. Fortune 500 companies.   B. Schools.

   C. Governments and corporations.   D. Military forces

6. What will many dull and repetitive tasks become?

   A. Unpopular.   B. Useless.

   C. Unwelcome.   D. Obsolete.

7. What worries many economists and computer scientists according to Para. 9?

   A. Today's technologies are going to remove people from economic activity completely.

   B. The hundreds of millions of people will have no jobs.

   C. Everyone is motivated to become designers, engineers, IT specialists and logistics experts.

   D. All of the above.

8. What's the author's attitude towards 3D printing?

   A. Supportive.   B. Opposed.

   C. Indifferent.   D. Controversial.

Critical thinking

II. Work in pairs and discuss the following questions.

1. Have you heard the term of "additive manufacturing"? If yes, what does it refer to?

2. What is the strong metaphorical correspondence between 2D and 3D printings?

3. How does 3D printing work?

4. In your opinion, what positive and negative changes have modern technologies brought about to our life?

Words in use

III. Fill in the blanks with the words given below. Change the form where necessary. Each word can be used only once.

| ancient | indistinguishable | correspondence | irresistibly | conventional |
| disruptive | dub | | observation | obsolete | bequeath |

1. Though caused by different viruses, the two diseases are clinically almost _____.

2. From _____ times our forefathers have labored, lived and multiplied on this land.

3. He spent two years in the wilderness, which his friends _____ "the dark period", then returned back to the civilized world and got a job in a bank.

4. Alcohol can produce violent, _____ behavior, which may ruin your life.

5. Nuclear weapons and the rise of the developing countries have made war among great powers _____.

6. In the early months of the economic crisis, the _____ view was that the world would slide into a downturn.

7. And yet my love of country comes over me like a strong wind and bears me _____, with all these chains, to the battlefield.

8. The diaries are a mixture of confession, work in progress and _____ which has hit the nail on the head.

9. Most people _____ their property to their spouses and children.

10. Another flight would be arranged on Saturday if _____ demand arose.

Expressions in use

IV. Fill in the blanks with the expressions given below. Change the form where necessary. Each expression can be used only once.

call out	lay down	stamp out	turn out to be
dawn on	wipe out	remove... from	go about
take over	a fly in the ointment		

1. You may be wondering why Ms. Barr felt the need to _____ Mr. Black, perhaps he had done something to deserve it.

2. For half a year, she tried to _____ the memory of that terrible summer.

3. If we teach them about life lesson even from beginning, they will _____ adults with confidence and self-motivation.

4. It gradually _____ me that I still had talent and ought to try again.

5. A senior Pakistani government official said the US had been told to _____ infrastructure _____ the air base.

6. Dr. Muffett stressed that he was opposed to bullying in schools and that action would be taken to _____ it _____.

7. Man can have no greater love than to _____ his life for his friends.

8. We were having a picnic, when suddenly there came a downpour, which was rather _____.

9. Keep within the light and you can _____ your tasks without fear or interruption.

10. The widow has _____ the running of her husband's empire, including six London theaters.

Sentence structure

V. Combine the two sentences in each group by using the structure "as is the case with...". Make changes where necessary.

> **Model:** She kept albums of photographs of her family members.
>
> She kept the love letters my late grandfather sent her while she traveled the world with the Merchant Navy.
>
> → She kept albums of photographs of her family members as is the case with the love letters my late grandfather sent her while she traveled the world with the Merchant Navy.

1. People with small stomach can't eat much.

   People usually eat less when they are ill.

   _____

2. The new textbooks would require students to grasp comprehensive skills.

   Other study materials require them to do the same thing.

   _____

3. We have seen encouraging signs of improvement in their daily performance.

   The overall performance has been found to improve according to their administrator.

   _____

VI. Complete the following sentences by translating the Chinese into English, using the structure "as... as...".

> **Model:** Every time I visited, _____ （我的车都会装满
> 和我预期一样的旧东西）, such as: unopened cartons of orange juice, balls of
> fraying wool, damp antique books.
>
> → Every time I visited, <u>my car would fill with stuff as old as I expected</u>, such as:
> unopened cartons of orange juice, balls of fraying wool, damp antique books.

1. Lily is good at swimming, and she is still _____
   （对游泳的热情和认真同一个初学者一样）.

2. He seemed to assume that she was _____
   （跟他知道这个结果时一样失望）.

3. She realized that the pie was not _____
   （像他第一次做的那样美味）.

Glossary

A	
abbreviated	Unit 1A
absorbed	Unit 1A
accessibility	Unit 1B
accomplish	Unit 7A
accord	Unit 2B
account	Unit 3A
acknowledge	Unit 7A
acknowledgment	Unit 7A
adequate	Unit 1A
administrative	Unit 3B
adopt	Unit 7A
affidavit	Unit 4B
affirmative	Unit 7A
agency	Unit 6A
aggregate	Unit 2A
album	Unit 8A
alienate	Unit 7B
allude	Unit 3B
aluminum	Unit 4B
analysis	Unit 2A
analyze	Unit 8A

ancestor	Unit 5A
ancient	Unit 8B
anomalous	Unit 3B
antique	Unit 8A
apparent	Unit 2B
apparently	Unit 4A
applicant	Unit 7A
arsenal	Unit 2A
assembly	Unit 8B
assignment	Unit 1A
assuage	Unit 6B
asynchronous	Unit 2B
attribute	Unit 8A
automatically	Unit 2A
awesome	Unit 2B
awning	Unit 4A

B	
bachelor	Unit 7B
balloon	Unit 6A
barrier	Unit 2A
baton	Unit 8A
benchmark	Unit 7A

beneficial	Unit 1A	columnist	Unit 5A
bequeath	Unit 8B	combination	Unit 5B
bet	Unit 2A	commence	Unit 4A
boost	Unit 7A	commendable	Unit 7A
boring	Unit 6A	comment	Unit 7B
bound	Unit 2A	commercial	Unit 3B
breach	Unit 3B	commute	Unit 6B
brilliant	Unit 2A	companion	Unit 4A
burgeoning	Unit 6A	competent	Unit 1A
C		competition	Unit 3A
calculator	Unit 5B	complaint	Unit 3A
campaign	Unit 6B	complicated	Unit 5B
cancel	Unit 4A	composition	Unit 7A
candidate	Unit 7A	compost	Unit 2B
capitalism	Unit 8B	compound	Unit 3B
capture	Unit 6B	comprehensive	Unit 3B
carton	Unit 8A	conceal	Unit 4B
casual	Unit 6A	concerning	Unit 6B
cathedral	Unit 2B	concur	Unit 1A
cautious	Unit 4A	condense	Unit 1A
cease	Unit 8A	conduct	Unit 5B
celebrity	Unit 6B	confess	Unit 1A
cereal	Unit 8A	confidence	Unit 7B
charge	Unit 5B	confound	Unit 8A
chill	Unit 4B	confront	Unit 4B
chore	Unit 2B	confused	Unit 1B
chronicle	Unit 3B	consult	Unit 5A
chronicler	Unit 8A	contender	Unit 5B
civilization	Unit 2B	context	Unit 8A
claim	Unit 3A	contribution	Unit 2B
classify	Unit 7A	convenience	Unit 3A
coexist	Unit 5B	conventional	Unit 8B
collaboration	Unit 2B	conversant	Unit 2A

convey	Unit 4B		discard	Unit 8A
convince	Unit 4A		discrimination	Unit 7A
correspondence	Unit 8B		dismiss	Unit 6A
counterpart	Unit 7A		disregard	Unit 7A
create	Unit 7A		disrespectful	Unit 8A
credential	Unit 3B		disruptive	Unit 8B
criminal	Unit 4A		distasteful	Unit 6B
critical	Unit 1B		distracted	Unit 4A
crouch	Unit 4B		distribute	Unit 3A
cult	Unit 6A		distribution	Unit 8A
curate	Unit 8A		ditch	Unit 5B
curve	Unit 2A		diversity	Unit 7A
cute	Unit 6A		downside	Unit 6B
D			doze	Unit 5A
damp	Unit 8A		drain	Unit 4A
dawdler	Unit 5B		dramatically	Unit 3B
debit	Unit 4A		dub	Unit 8B
declaration	Unit 6B		dupe	Unit 6A
deduct	Unit 4A		dynamic	Unit 2B
defect	Unit 2A		**E**	
deficit	Unit 1A		edge	Unit 2A
demonstrate	Unit 3B		eke	Unit 6B
depict	Unit 1B		elemental	Unit 8A
derail	Unit 3B		embedded	Unit 2A
derivation	Unit 2A		emergency	Unit 4B
descendant	Unit 8A		empower	Unit 1B
deserve	Unit 4A		emulate	Unit 8A
desktop	Unit 5B		enclose	Unit 8A
devise	Unit 1B		encryption	Unit 3B
differentiation	Unit 1B		endless	Unit 5A
digest	Unit 1A		enlighten	Unit 6A
digital	Unit 3A		ensure	Unit 3A
dilute	Unit 8A		enthusiasm	Unit 7B

hedge	Unit 4A		instantly	Unit 1B
helpless	Unit 7B		insurance	Unit 5B
hesitate	Unit 3A		intent	Unit 5B
hesitation	Unit 3B		intently	Unit 5A
highlight	Unit 6B		interconnect	Unit 6B
hoard	Unit 8A		intern	Unit 7B
hollow	Unit 3B		intersect	Unit 5A
horizon	Unit 1B		intersection	Unit 4B
hub	Unit 5A		intersperse	Unit 1A
humanity	Unit 2B		interview	Unit 7B
humble	Unit 6B		intrinsically	Unit 8B
I			intrusion	Unit 3B
ignore	Unit 1B		investor	Unit 7A
imagination	Unit 2A		invulnerable	Unit 3B
immaturity	Unit 3A		irresistible	Unit 8B
immortal	Unit 5A		irresistibly	Unit 8B
imperatively	Unit 2A		isolate	Unit 5B
implore	Unit 4B		isolated	Unit 5B
inappropriate	Unit 7B		**J**	
incapable	Unit 7B		jab	Unit 2B
incidentally	Unit 8B		junk	Unit 8B
inclusive	Unit 7A		jurisdiction	Unit 4B
index	Unit 7A		justification	Unit 8A
indication	Unit 2A		**L**	
indifferent	Unit 4B		launch	Unit 5B
indistinguishable	Unit 8B		legacy	Unit 8A
inexcusable	Unit 7B		liable	Unit 2A
infancy	Unit 6A		liberty	Unit 4A
inferior	Unit 7B		lip-sync	Unit 6A
influence	Unit 2A		lodge	Unit 4A
inherent	Unit 6B		lurk	Unit 6A
input	Unit 5B		**M**	
insight	Unit 2A		magical	Unit 2A

perform	Unit 3A
perimeter	Unit 3B
persist	Unit 2A
personality	Unit 8A
perspective	Unit 5A
pesky	Unit 5B
pessimistic	Unit 4A
phenomenon	Unit 6D
philosophy	Unit 2B
phishing	Unit 3B
phony	Unit 4B
pique	Unit 1A
plea	Unit 4B
plot	Unit 1B
plunder	Unit 3B
portray	Unit 7B
possession	Unit 8A
precious	Unit 3B
precisely	Unit 1A
precision	Unit 5B
predecessor	Unit 5A
predictable	Unit 8B
preserve	Unit 8A
preventive	Unit 3B
primarily	Unit 1A
prime	Unit 2B
principal	Unit 5B
probation	Unit 4B
proceed	Unit 4A
proclaim	Unit 1A
productivity	Unit 6B
professionally	Unit 7B
profit	Unit 6A

prohibited	Unit 5A
prolong	Unit 4B
promising	Unit 1B
promote	Unit 3A
proper	Unit 3A
property	Unit 3B
proposal	Unit 1B
propose	Unit 2B
prosecutor	Unit 4B
prospect	Unit 2A
protagonist	Unit 6A
purchase	Unit 8B

Q	
quest	Unit 6B
quip	Unit 2B

R	
radically	Unit 1B
range	Unit 1B
rationale	Unit 1A
ratio	Unit 7A
reap	Unit 7A
recall	Unit 1B
recommend	Unit 2A
recruit	Unit 7A
reflection	Unit 5A
reinforce	Unit 1A
release	Unit 3A
relieve	Unit 8B
religious	Unit 2B
remark	Unit 7B
remove	Unit 6A
rent	Unit 3A
repertoire	Unit 2A

repetitive	Unit 2B	slightly	Unit 7A
replaceable	Unit 2B	snap	Unit 5B
replica	Unit 8B	solely	Unit 7A
repository	Unit 6A	solid	Unit 2A
representative	Unit 4A	sorrowfully	Unit 8B
represent	Unit 2A	span	Unit 1A
respondent	Unit 5B	spare	Unit 8B
response	Unit 5B	specifically	Unit 1B
reunion	Unit 4A	specified	Unit 3A
rhythm	Unit 2B	specify	Unit 6B
rivet	Unit 8B	squeaky	Unit 8B
robust	Unit 2B	squirt	Unit 8B
roughly	Unit 1A	stable	Unit 2B
route	Unit 5B	staple	Unit 1A
S		startle	Unit 5A
savvy	Unit 5A	stately	Unit 4B
scam	Unit 4A	status	Unit 5A
scenery	Unit 3A	steadily	Unit 6A
skepticism	Unit 6B	steep	Unit 5A
scope	Unit 1A	stereotype	Unit 7B
screenwriter	Unit 5A	sterling	Unit 5A
script	Unit 6A	stir	Unit 2B
scruffy	Unit 4A	store	Unit 3A
seamlessly	Unit 6B	stride	Unit 1B
secondary	Unit 5A	strive	Unit 2B
seemingly	Unit 5A	stroll	Unit 4B
sentence	Unit 4B	stuff	Unit 8A
series	Unit 3B	submit	Unit 1B
serpent	Unit 5A	substantially	Unit 2A
sexist	Unit 7B	subtle	Unit 7B
siege	Unit 3B	sufficient	Unit 2B
sign	Unit 4B	surf	Unit 5B
significantly	Unit 7B	surrender	Unit 3B

survey	Unit 7A	understatement	Unit 5B
survive	Unit 8A	uneven	Unit 7A
suspicion	Unit 4A	universal	Unit 8A
T		unkempt	Unit 4A
tailored	Unit 6B	upkeep	Unit 5B
talent	Unit 8A	upload	Unit 6A
tedious	Unit 1A	urgent	Unit 3A
temperament	Unit 8A	usurp	Unit 2B
tempt	Unit 5A	**V**	
theme	Unit 6A	vaguely	Unit 4A
thoroughfare	Unit 4B	venture	Unit 3B
thoughtfully	Unit 2B	version	Unit 8B
thrilled	Unit 4B	veteran	Unit 1A
thwart	Unit 4B	via	Unit 1B
tingle	Unit 4A	vicar	Unit 8A
toss	Unit 4B	vigorously	Unit 2B
tote	Unit 4B	**W**	
trait	Unit 2A	wave	Unit 1B
transfer	Unit 3A	webcam	Unit 6A
transmission	Unit 3A	weird	Unit 4A
trick	Unit 6A	whiz	Unit 4B
tub	Unit 7B	withdrawal	Unit 4A
tune	Unit 5B	witness	Unit 3A
U		wonder	Unit 7B
ubiquitous	Unit 5A	**Y**	
ubiquity	Unit 6B	yearn	Unit 5B
unconsciously	Unit 3A	**Z**	
undermine	Unit 6B	zeitgeist	Unit 5A
underscore	Unit 5A		